Leaving Dirty Jersey

Leaving Dirty Jersey

A CRYSTAL METH MEMOIR

JAMES SALANT

EBURY
PRESS

1 3 5 7 9 10 8 6 4 2

Published in 2007 by Ebury Press, an imprint of Ebury Publishing
First published in the USA by Simon Spotlight Entertainment, an imprint of
Simon & Schuster in 2007

Ebury Publishing is a division of the Random House Group

The Random House Group Limited Reg. No. 954009

Addresses for companies within The Random House Group Limited can be found at:
www.randomhouse.co.uk

A CIP catalogue record for this book is available from the British Library

The Random House Group Limited makes every effort to ensure that the papers used
in its books are made from trees that have been legally sourced from well-managed
and credibly certified forests. Our paper procurement policy can be found at:
www.randomhouse.co.uk/paper.htm.

Printed and bound in Great Britain by
Mackays of Chatham Plc, Chatham, Kent

ISBN 9780091920333

For my parents

AUTHOR'S NOTE

This book is a memoir and derives primarily from my memory. I've changed some names, locations, and physical details. Also, I've altered some conversations to make them coherent, and in a very few cases I've changed the chronology. All of that notwithstanding, I've done my best to portray my experiences honestly. *Leaving Dirty Jersey* is not about redemption or recovery, but I would like to think that the last three years of my life have been just that, and nothing has been more crucial to turning my life around than revisiting my past with ruthless honesty.

CONTENTS

I wanted distinction, and the respectable forms of it seemed to be eluding me. If I couldn't have it as a citizen, I would have it as an outlaw.

—Tobias Wolff, *This Boy's Life*

INTRODUCTION: AN ACID-FRIENDLY ATMOSPHERE

The line of evergreens in front of the Princeton Shopping Center was bristling and swaying in the wind, morphing and swirling and streaking the sky neon green, and even tripping on acid I was trying to walk like a tough guy. Swinging my feet slightly to the side in a kind of waddle, I led each step with a shoulder as if wading through water. For once, though, I wasn't scowling. I was happy and smiling, having cut school with two friends. We'd dropped the acid and sniffed some heroin and watched the end of *Casino*. Now we were on our way to the shopping center for pizza, and one of the trees was whispering to me. The words sounded familiar. When I realized that the tree was quoting *Casino*, I laughed, and then sunlight flickered across the grass—dancing flames of iridescence—and I began to burst with a this-is-special feeling. It was a gorgeous day, and nature was putting on a light show for me. Then the cops pulled up.

As soon as they told us to stop and stand over there, the sun seemed too bright: My eyes began to water and I couldn't stop blinking. In my pocket were a bag of pot and eight paper hits of acid. I fidgeted while

1

one of the cops—a short, clean-shaven officer with a nasal voice—explained that he'd just received a call about three guys trying car-door handles in the parking lot we'd just passed through.

My friends, who were black, screamed racial profiling: "You know ain't nobody call. You just wanna harass a bitch." I needed a different strategy, but I couldn't come up with anything better than shaking my head in disbelief, looking nervous and high. Another squad car pulled up.

Afterward, my friends and I would complain about how unfair the whole thing was: We actually hadn't been trying car-door handles, so in our minds it was all bigotry and harassment. It never occurred to us that we looked exactly like the type of people who do try car-door handles and that, in fact, on any drug but acid we were those people.

"Come on over here," said a gray-haired, mustachioed detective in a dark suit, standing by his car. He was talking to me. Trudging over, I stared at the ground and hoped that I was walking normally. "Why don't you empty your pockets for me," he said, "and put everything on the hood, over here."

"You don't have the right to search my pockets," I said.

"Yes, I do." He laughed. And that was that. I placed cash, keys, little scraps of paper—everything that wasn't illegal—on the hood of his car. Then he told me to turn my pockets inside out.

"No," I mumbled.

"No?" he said, raising his eyebrows.

The local paper said that a seventeen-year-old high school senior darted (or maybe it was dashed) down the street in an attempt to escape, but I'm less sure of what I was trying to do. I didn't even know that I was going to run until I'd started, and then, once the boots were thudding and the cops were shouting, it just naturally popped into my head, as if I'd undergone some junkie training program, that I should eat the acid—destroy the evidence.

It is impossible, though, to open a sealed baggy while running from the cops on a head full of acid. It also didn't help that my boots, which were fashionably untied, began to come off. When I tried to kick them off altogether so I could run in my socks, my fashionably baggy jeans fell to my knees. Stumbling, then running like a demented penguin, I shoved the closed baggy into my mouth and started to chew. I had no chance of swallowing—my mouth was parched—but I hoped that the baggy would open in my mouth so I could eat the remaining tabs. It didn't.

The mustachioed detective soon caught up and struck me on the back of the neck, sending me flying through the air. I landed hard, tumbling on the grass, and in another second they were on me, flipping me on my stomach, putting a knee on my back, cuffing me, turning out my pockets, and finding the pot. Finally they pulled me up to my knees.

"Oh, what's this?" said one of the cops, holding the bag of acid, which had fallen out of my mouth. "A little of the LSD, huh?"

"That was about the stupidest damn thing you could have done!" yelled the detective who'd run me down.

"Now, Jim," said another cop. We already knew each other— Officer Summers. He took off his glasses and stooped in front of me with his hands on his thighs. "What did you swallow? I am not fucking around, Jim! What did you swallow?"

"Nothing," I mumbled. "You already got it."

Later, the story to my friends was that I told him to go fuck himself.

Officer Summers shook his head and walked away, leaving me kneeling in my boxers, dirt and grass clinging to my legs. In a few minutes two of the cops hoisted me to my feet and yanked my jeans up roughly. The jeans became tangled with my boxers and didn't quite make it over my hips.

"What's happening now?" I asked another detective, a woman who was standing at the edge of a huddle watching me as the other cops gave each other orders and talked into their radios.

"We're waiting for the ambulance," she said.

"For what?" I said. "I don't want an ambulance. I'm fine."

I was standing in my damp socks, cuffed, a cool breeze blowing across the top of my butt.

"I wish I could believe you."

"But I really didn't eat anything," I said. "I mean, if that's what you think. You saw me try to swallow something, but that fell out of my mouth. You got that."

"You mean the LSD," she said.

"Yeah," I said. "That was everything."

I wanted to ask one of the cops to fix my pants.

"And the pot," said the mustachioed detective.

"Yeah, sure, fine," I said. "But that's it. I didn't eat any stash."

"How do we know that?" the detective snapped. "Look at the size of your pupils."

I wondered if I should tell them that I was on acid. *Tell THEM*

4

that I'm on LSD, that I'm on SDL . . . that I'm nearing hell? Tell them a fucking thing . . .

The ambulance arrived.

"Take any drugs today, son?" an EMT asked me once I was cuffed inside.

"Nope."

"Nothing at all?"

"Well, I smoked a little marijuana earlier."

"That's it?" he said, shining a flashlight in my eyes. "You're sure?"

"Yup."

At the ER, a place I'd never been, the detective walked me from the ambulance to a plain room, empty except for a chair in the center, to which he cuffed me. Then he left me, and a young doctor in a white smock came in with a clipboard and smiled at me good-naturedly.

"So how are *you* doing?" he said.

"I've been better." I laughed.

"I can imagine," he said. "Hell, I hope you've been better than this."

"Like an hour ago I was much better than this."

He read his clipboard and shined a flashlight in my eyes.

"They just came in and messed your day up, huh."

"Yeah, pretty much."

"I hate it when that happens."

"You have no idea." I laughed again. "So what's happening now?"

"Well, we have to take some blood. Between you and them I have no idea what's happening—I just know I have to take some blood and make sure you're okay. Now, what's wrong? You don't look too happy about that."

At seventeen I hadn't started shooting drugs yet, and I was terrified of needles.

"Why do you have to take my blood?"

"To make sure you don't . . . well, die. They're saying you might have eaten something. Now, you're saying you didn't, but we still have to make sure. Are you scared of needles?"

"Very," I said. "But look, I did eat something—four hits of acid around noon. That's why my eyes are dilated. I really didn't eat anything when I ran."

"So you're high on LSD right now? Wow. What a day. Look, I'm sorry, but we have to run the tests either way now that you've been admitted. It's procedure. You'll be okay—the nurses are very good."

I nodded, and on his way out the doctor looked back and smiled and pointed at me and said, "You're gonna be all right." The detective popped in and asked me for my parents' phone number, which at that point I was happy to give. He disappeared for a few minutes, then returned, unlocked the cuffs, and told me to follow him to the bathroom to take a urine test.

"Instead of the blood test?" I asked hopefully.

"Nope. Gotta do 'em both. And Mom and Dad are on their way."

In the past whenever I took acid, I always made sure to be in an acid-friendly atmosphere: a friend's house, or the woods, or any safe place where I could philosophize and giggle, silly with what I considered a deeper appreciation for nature and beauty. Standing in that hospital bathroom, dick-in-cup, with a detective behind me demanding my urine, I was in the least acid-friendly atmosphere I've ever tripped in. Even worse, I'd sniffed some heroin a few hours earlier, so I couldn't piss: I pushed and groaned and looked helplessly over my shoulder at the detective. In response he described the procedure that would be used to force me to urinate if I couldn't do it myself. When he said "urethra," I managed to squeeze out a few drops.

At some point in between the piss and blood my parents arrived at the hospital, looking solemn and distressed as their faces generated tiny bubbles of reflected fluorescent light. They moved slowly toward me, shifting and taking on a radioactive glow—just for a second, and then their oversized earlobes began to vibrate.

"Are you still . . . *high?*" asked my dad, peering at me as if I were the one whose head was melting.

"Yes."

"Having a good time?" asked my mom.

Five foot five and slender with bluish-gray eyes and platinum hair, she stared at me with her lips pressed tightly together, fuming. But she quickly softened. I was near tears, terrified about giving blood. Even the detective began to feel sorry for me, and when the nurse came in wheeling a cart with tubes for my blood, he tried to distract me from the IV. He came over and stood next to me with this huge, creepy smile, while the nurse tied my arm and searched for a vein.

"Hey," he said jovially, snapping his fingers in front of my face. The snap rang and echoed in my ears, and when I looked up he was telling me a joke, his mustache bristling faster and faster as his mouth opened and closed. Occasionally his hand drifted in front of my face, signaling me to look at him rather than at the seemingly endless stream of glowing blood that was being sucked into one, two, three, four tubes—the detective snapped again.

7

"See, it's over," he said.

The nurse was wheeling the cart out of the room. I think—I hope—I thanked him. He didn't even take me to the police station. He decided I'd been through enough for one day and let my parents take me home, where I'm sure he assumed they would punish me themselves.

This, however, was not the first time I'd been in trouble with drugs. Upon returning home from my latest rehab, about three months earlier, I had taken the position with my parents that I was willing to stay away from heroin but that I could and would continue smoking pot and occasionally tripping on acid, because, unlike heroin, pot and acid were "normal," "experimental" drugs. They had not quite agreed, but neither had they smacked me across the face, grabbed me by the shirt collar, and screamed, *Are you out of your fucking mind? No! You've been doing drugs for two years now; there's nothing experimental about it. And besides—no!* Instead, they had done what they always did—talked it over with me, debated, tried to understand where I was coming from—and after a few days the argument had become so complicated and murky that, being a teenager and a junkie, I assumed I'd won.

And so, after the silent car ride from the hospital, when we got home and were all sitting around the kitchen table, my position was: "You agreed that I could smoke weed and occasionally trip. The fact that I've gotten caught doesn't change what our agreement was, so how can you be mad now?" Their position was that I was an asshole, and that at the very least I had to stop using all drugs now. Sensing the futility, if not the absurdity, of arguing further, I lied and agreed to stay clean.

• • •

I was born in New York City, a fact I used to state proudly when I was using drugs, as if it had something to do with the person I'd become. Actually, my only memory of growing up in the city is from my preschool on West 68th Street, a few blocks from Central Park and directly across the street from the apartment where I lived with my parents and my older brother, Joe. The school had a playground on the roof, and every day at recess my mom would wait by the window for me to come outside so she could wave to me, and then all the kids would wave back and laugh. This is the kind of memory that screws with your head when you're trying to convince people that you're a tough thug, when people ask you, "So where you from?" and you say, "New York, yo," and then you remember your mom smiling in the window, all those happy kids waving to Mrs. Salant.

I was two when my family moved out of the city to East Hampton, New York; my parents decided that they didn't want my brother and me growing up in the city, even on the Upper West Side. Three years later we moved again, to Princeton, New Jersey, this time for the public school system, which my parents had heard was excellent. I grew up there in a largish house on a street where fathers rode their mowers every Sunday.

So it wasn't the school of hard knocks for me but a nearly idyllic upper-middle-class childhood. My mom and I were very close. When my brother was born, she gave up her career teaching Russian literature in favor of starting a small private therapy practice, so she was always home to cook dinner and limit my Nintendo time and encourage me to read. Even when I was young, we had an almost uncanny intuitive connection, finishing each other's sentences, picking up on each other's emotions. My dad was home less often. A psychoanalyst, he lived most of the week in Manhattan, sleeping nights in the back of his office so he could see patients in the early morning. But when he did come home—same time every Thursday—my brother and I ran to meet him at the train and the whole family hugged. He and my mom fought very rarely; there was never a hint of trouble with their marriage.

Perhaps the only reason my childhood wasn't wholly idyllic was my brother, Joe. Over the years my parents have come up with many theories to explain why Joe was so troubled. My mom believes that he was psychologically and emotionally scarred by his complicated forceps birth and resulting tunnel vision. Although she took him to visual therapy three times a week, he didn't have full range of vision until he was eight, when he finally learned how to catch a ball. Other theories have ranged from left temporal lobe damage to a sort of mild autism to frustration at growing up with introverted, intellectually oriented parents while being more athletically oriented himself (eventually, after overcoming his tunnel vision, he would become a star basketball player). Whatever the reason, Joe was by all accounts exceptionally difficult. Until he was about four (the year I was born) there were certain words you couldn't say around him or he would throw a fit. Tissue. Awning. Hello. Two years old, in a stroller, he would be riding in the elevator with my mother on their way home, and an old woman would get on, smile at him, and open her mouth to form a word, and he would scream, "No hello!" Or a taxi driver would ask my parents which building they wanted to be dropped off in front of, and they would point, stammering, "That one, over there, the one with the green . . . with the green thing." "Awning?" the driver would say, at which point my parents would cringe and my brother would scream, "No awning!" All of which is funny, unless of course you're inside the elevator or the taxi—unless you're the kid's parents, cringing and apologizing and wondering what the hell is wrong with your child.

As a baby I was Joe's temperamental opposite. I did not have a difficult birth, nor did I have tunnel vision. According to my mom I hardly even cried at night. I liked to be held. I could fall asleep anywhere. I was an easy baby, *much* easier than Joe, easier to care for, easier to love.

So Joe was intensely jealous of me, absurdly competitive. When he was ten and I was six, we both played the same Nintendo hockey game. I was better than he was, though I quickly learned to let him win whenever we played each other. Once he came into my room while I was winning against the computer, and he asked which level of difficulty I was playing. When I said "hard," Joe explained that earlier in the day he had opened the Nintendo box and adjusted the setting so that hard was actually easy, and easy actually hard. It didn't make any sense, but I knew better than to ask questions. "Oh," I said. "So that's why it's been so easy." He sat next to me and didn't say anything until I scored. "See, they never would have let you do that on hard." The next goal: "You know, I think they made the easy one easier." "Yeah," I said, "I think so too." Watching me win, Joe brooded until the final period, when he turned to me imploringly. "Listen, Jim," he said. "You gotta let them score here." "Why?" "Just trust me: You gotta let them tie it up and go to overtime, or else in the final seconds they'll just score point after point. They'll be real cheap and beat you in the last five seconds. You gotta let them tie it up right now; just trust me." I nodded and let the computer tie the score. When overtime started, Joe left the room.

One of the reasons I was so quick to play along with his nonsense was that I knew that if we did argue—if he started pinching and pushing me, shouting "fat boy" in my face—and I had to call my mom, she wouldn't be able to control him. Likely he would shout at her for taking my side, shout about her being unfair and my being fat, until eventually she would lose control and shout back. Then she would walk away, as angry with herself as she was with him, and Joe would push me one last time before following her into the kitchen, where the shouting would escalate to screaming, while I hid in my room eating Hostess Twinkies.

My dad was better, but not much: He didn't join in the screaming, but he didn't exactly take control, either. When I was twelve, Joe and I played a game of football in the backyard against two of his friends, and whenever I dropped the ball, he yelled at me. The score was close and I dropped a few pivotal passes, and Joe carried on about it for so long that his friends told him to leave me alone. They left soon afterward, and I walked up the back porch and into the kitchen, where I sat next to my dad at the table. Joe followed, yelling after me. Pussy. Faggot. He pulled open the sliding glass door and stood in front of us, his head just below the hanging pots and pans, calling me names as he muddied the white tile floor.

"They didn't leave because of me," I said.

"What? You think I care that they left?" Joe said. "They can go; I don't give a shit. I care that my little brother can't catch a fucking ball. How can *my* little brother not catch a ball?"

I started to say that I hadn't wanted to play in the first place, but I stopped. That's what I would have said when I was ten, and I wasn't ten anymore. Joe's friends were older, I'd tried, fuck him.

My dad was watching us thoughtfully, brow furrowed, hands cupped over his mouth, a forefinger on either side of his nose, thumbs propping his chin. I knew that he wanted me to stand up to Joe.

"Whatever," I said. "It's not like I played that badly. I dropped like two passes. I got Tom's tall ass covering me, and the passes weren't exactly perfect."

"Weren't perfect! You can't get better passes than that. Perfect spiral. And Tom wasn't covering you—they were both on me. Look, Dad, I'm quarterbacking, Dan's at the line of scrimmage, I act like I'm gonna run, and then I draw Tom to me 'cause he knows Dan can't catch me. Then I throw a perfect pass, and fat boy over here drops the fucking ball."

My dad started to object at "fat boy," but I yelled over him: "Hey, fuck you! I played. What the fuck more do you want from me? And that's not how it happened—maybe once—but I caught some too, and I broke up that pass."

We were getting louder, but the tone was shifting. Joe seemed more excited than angry, more like a competitive brother than an enemy.

"Broke up a pass," he said incredulously, stooping and putting his hands on his knees.

"Yeah, when Tom broke away from you and you told me to cover him."

My dad chuckled. Joe snuck a look at him and half smiled, unsure of how to react. He was on the fence: He could soften and laugh about the game. Or he could ride his sibling jealousy for all it was worth, letting his hatred for me boil over because we were ganging up on him.

"What? You didn't break up any pass," he said, still stooping. Then he appeared to remember which pass I was talking about—one that, though I did get a hand on it, was definitely more of a drop than a breakup. Tom, trying to be nice, had said that I'd deflected it.

"That pass!" Joe shouted, and to express his disbelief he began to spring up from his stoop, throwing his arms in the air.

He was still directly below the hanging pots and pans. There was no time to say anything, but my dad and I both saw it coming. And that of course made it even funnier when Joe banged his head against my mom's favorite cast-iron pan.

"Fuck!" he shouted, grabbing his head.

He stared menacingly at the pan, as if he were about to hit it. Then he turned to us, and for an instant it seemed he recognized how silly the whole thing was, how ridiculous it was to threaten a pan; it seemed he was about to laugh. But then he saw how hard *we* were laughing, and he became furious. He opened the drawer and snatched up a butcher knife, stepped toward me, and screamed, "Fat faggot!" He came right up to me and stopped, hovering with the knife. I didn't think he would cut me, but I made sure to look scared so he didn't feel I was daring him.

"Stop it! Stop it!" said my dad, standing and grabbing for Joe's wrist. Joe pulled away and stepped back against the counter.

"Put it down!" my dad said.

Joe hesitated before putting the knife on the counter. My dad picked it up, held it for a second, then placed it carefully on the table in front of him.

"You never, *never* use a knife!" he said, voice quivering.

Joe stormed out of the room.

With his analyst's beard and shrewd squint, my dad speaks on almost any subject with aggressive and often convincing authority, an authority that had always made me feel safe, believing Dad was in control. But on that day, when I was twelve, I saw clearly that he wasn't at all in control. He hadn't known what Joe was going to do with the knife any more than Joe had. He said, "You never use a knife"—said it with all the desperate authority he could muster—and yet I didn't feel the least bit safer. In fact I almost wanted to laugh at him for saying something ridiculous. *"You never use a knife?" That's what, Dad, a family rule? Bats and guns are okay, though, right? Just never a knife?*

That happened in 1996. Joe had already started drinking and smoking pot, and he'd thrown a few parties at the house while my parents were away. Girls came to these parties, drunk high-school girls who flirted with my brother and the rest of the guys while I watched movies with a friend in the basement. Sometimes I would come upstairs for food or soda, and the crowd would be drinking in the kitchen and smoking on the back porch. My brother, high, talking to a girl, and happy in a way that he was on only these nights, would turn to me and ask me if I was okay, did I need anything? Concern from Joe was a rare thing, but it felt so natural, so right. "Is this your brother?" the girl would say. "He's got the same eyes as you. He's cute." I was the cute twelve-year-old brother who smiled shyly and then jerked off at night.

"You're not gonna tell Mom and Dad, are you?" Joe would say.

"Hell, no."

The following year, 1997, Joe, a sophomore in high school, officially made the shift from troubled kid to criminal. This was the first year of lawyers and pending charges, of lies followed by confessions followed by more lies, of "specialists" and rehabs and money pissed away. It all began on January seventeenth, when the police came to our house at four thirty a.m. and arrested Joe for selling pot to an undercover officer. I awoke to men's voices. I walked out of my room, looked into Joe's. He was handcuffed and facing the wall in an undershirt and a pair of warm-up pants. There were two detectives in bulletproof vests and heavy boots, yellow jackets and striped pants, POLICE on their backs. One was searching the room; the other was standing behind Joe with a hand on his shoulder. They hulked and towered. Joe looked so skinny.

It was midweek: My dad wasn't home.

My mom was standing in the doorway in her nightgown, arms crossed, speaking with the detective who had his hand on Joe's shoulder. She spoke slowly, in a low but clear voice, a disaster voice, a one-step-at-a-time-this-is-too-much voice. "What exactly did he do?" There was police talk, edgy for all its courteousness, lots of *ma'am*s. She nodded as they explained the charges. "Where are you taking him?" I stepped closer. She was trembling. "How long will you hold him?" One of the detectives opened a pine cigar box that my dad had given Joe, opened it and showed the other detective. Empty, but there may have been some marijuana residue—that's what they told my mom, with guns on their hips. "When will I be able to see him?"

In the months and years before, whenever my mom had cried in her room about Joe, I would come and sit next to her, and put a hand on her back, and feel her anguish, and breathe with her. It would always be hard, but she'd always thank me. She'd say, "What would I do without you?" As a child, knowing that I was needed gave me more than enough strength to sit with my mom's pain. But at four thirty a.m., with Joe handcuffed against the wall, there was nothing I could do for her. She saw me and put her hands on my shoulders. She asked if I was okay and said I could go back to bed.

Immediately after closing the door to my room, I stopped thinking about Joe or my mom. For years I'd hidden in this room whenever my mom and brother were screaming, and I'd always worried, always felt *something*. Not now, though: I was numb. Joe handcuffed, my mom shaking, the cops with their guns—it was all too much for me. So I stopped caring. I stood for a while and stared out my window. A deer was standing perfectly still in front of the line of evergreens that bounded our backyard. I watched it with a misty appreciation of nature and beauty, but then I became bored. I got into bed and went back to sleep.

After spending a weekend in a juvenile detention center, Joe came home and started bragging. It turned out he was one of thirty of what the *Princeton Packet* called "street-level dealers" who had been arrested in a "predawn raid." It was "the largest drug bust in Princeton history," and Joe talked about it at our dinner table with an insider's authority, told us who had snitched on whom and how the cops were so stupid, how the raid could have been more effective and whom they should have arrested, why they really wanted to get so-and-so and could you please pass the A.1. sauce?

Even more pathetic was how my parents listened and asked questions. They were desperate to understand what had just happened to all of us, and Joe was at least acting as if he knew something. So they let him hold forth, trying to distill whatever truth they could from his bragging. They gave him their best attention, better than they possibly could have given if he'd been talking about schoolwork. They did exactly what the police and the papers had done and what the kids at Princeton High School would do for another six months until he would leave for his first out-of-state rehab: They validated and solidified his adolescent identity as a criminal.

Over the next couple of months I felt smaller and younger and less important than I ever had. Occasionally at dinner, while discussing Joe's situation, my parents would turn to me and ask what I thought or how I felt, but I knew they did it only because they'd just remembered me. I knew that what I thought didn't matter.

Even Joe paid less attention to me. He stopped bullying. He didn't need to anymore. All eyes were already on him, and after his house arrest ended, he began staying out all night, drinking and smoking pot and experimenting with other drugs. He began fighting with my mom more often and more viciously than ever before. They would scream so loudly that the couple from the house across the street would call or stop by to make sure we were okay. I continued hiding in my room, staring out the window, not feeling a thing.

A few years later I started smoking pot. It was certainly ironic, given our family history, but it wasn't a hugely rebellious act. I was fifteen and my friends from grade school had started smoking, experimentally, as kids do at that age. I was actually one of the last in our group to try it. I was still a good boy who cared about his mommy. But soon after my first joint something happened to me—some sea change washed over me—and from that point onward all I cared about was getting fucked up.

Maybe, still numb from the trauma of the raid, I was more susceptible to bad influences; maybe it was all just pent-up teenage rebellion. Or maybe I'd seen all the concern and attention my parents had lavished on Joe for his screaming and bullying and doing drugs and being arrested, and I figured, *What the hell? That seems to work.* Or maybe I wanted to prove that I wasn't the sweet kid anymore—maybe, entering adulthood, I wanted to prove that I could outdo Joe in any and every way, as a criminal, as a junkie, even as a source of pain to my parents, because wasn't I furious with them, too? With my dad for being away so often, for not taking control? With my mom for crying and screaming all the time, for making me, her teenage son, comfort her? With both of them for letting Joe ruin our lives? Probably it was a bit of all that and more.

My parents sent Joe around the country, from program to program. At nineteen Joe joined the Navy, only to be kicked out immediately after boot camp for failing a drug test. My parents let him come home for a time while they decided where to send him next. When I told Joe that I was smoking pot, he was thrilled. We got high together and he introduced me to a few of his friends, twenty-some-year-old tough guys in backward baseball caps living with single parents in the affordable-housing sections of Princeton—tough guys whom I came to idolize and tried to emulate. They became my friends and then suppliers once my parents sent Joe away again, this time to an apartment in Raleigh, North

Carolina, where he was supposed to go to DeVry University but smoked crack instead. About a year later the Raleigh arrangement fell apart: My parents spent thousands of dollars in repairs for the apartment, which had been taken over by junkies, and then brought Joe home again, now sniffing heroin.

By then, at seventeen, I'd been arrested once for pot; my parents had sent me to a month-long wilderness rehab in Montana; I'd made a few of my own drug connections; and I was using and selling coke, Ecstasy, and LSD. Joe introduced me to heroin, and within a few months my parents sent me to another rehab, this time in West Virginia. It was about six months after that, in the fall of 2001, that I ran from the cops while tripping on acid. And though I'd been about to cry in that emergency room, grateful to the detective for telling me a joke, that's not how I told the story after the fact, nor was the story that the papers printed about a confused, pathetic kid addicted to drugs. No, by all accounts I was a crazy, drug-dealing junkie on acid who'd tried to escape and eat his stash (for which the courts gave me a slap on the wrist: conditional discharge).

And as I reveled in my new image, I became more addicted to heroin, so within a year I needed to sniff more bags than I could afford just to keep from getting sick. One day I was out of money and a friend with a needle started raving about how much more efficient shooting was than sniffing: not only would I not be sick, but also I would be as high as I was the first time. He was right. Soon I was like a kid at an amusement park who's just discovered he's courageous enough to go on the scary rides. Over the following months, as I gave myself my first track marks, I ratcheted up my drug dealing too, taking weekly trips to New York with my thug friends, buying coke and Ecstasy for us to sell, until eventually I had a reputation in Princeton as a more serious criminal than Joe had ever been.

In the spring of 2002, when he was twenty-one, Joe admitted to my parents that he was addicted to heroin, and they sent him to the New Standard Young Adult Haven in Banning, California.

In the fall of 2002, when I was eighteen, I was arrested during a raid on a house in Princeton. I actually walked right into it. High, I didn't see the unmarked police cars in front of the house. The cops searched my car and found ten Ecstasy pills, but when they searched me, they did not find the coke and heroin in the fifth pocket of my jeans. So, after waiting about fifteen minutes while they searched the house, I asked to use the bathroom—said I couldn't hold it: I needed to shit. They uncuffed me, and one of the officers stood outside the bathroom with the door open while I pretended to strain. I reached into my pocket, took out the coke, and palmed it. Next I went for the heroin, but in order to keep the wax paper bags dry, I had put them in cigarette cellophane, which crinkles, crinkles, crinkles. The cop heard it. He said, "Whad'ya got there?" I stood and dropped the drugs in the toilet. He rushed me and yelled for backup. Bare-assed, I hip-checked him, boxed him out. Hit the lever. The toilet, however, had economical water pressure, and I watched my drugs swirl and bob while boots came stomping down the hall. The cops threw me in the bathtub and cuffed me, then scrambled to fish the drugs out of the toilet. There was shouting and heavy breathing, adrenaline pumping. I was bleeding. So was a cop. But when it was all over and they sat me in a chair, I became strangely calm. I knew I'd be going to the police station—I knew I'd

21

spend the night kicking heroin and my parents would be devastated—but the calm was overwhelming. I recognized it immediately. I had felt it while staring out the window of my room. I was being toughened, and I wanted more.

The next day my parents put up my bail and picked me up at the police station. This time there would be no slap on the wrist, no conditional discharge. My parents' lawyer said my best bet to avoid jail time would be to enter a long-term program out of state. That way I would be out of New Jersey, away from all my friends, and he could advise the judge that I was already receiving treatment. So a month after my last arrest my parents sent me to the same program they'd sent my brother, New Standard Young Adult Haven. New Standard, however, is not a rehab, but a boarding school for semidelinquent adults ages eighteen to twenty-eight; before I could enroll, I had to graduate from a ninety-day rehab program called Get Straight for Life, in Grand Terrace, a small town a few miles west of Riverside, California.

I spent just one year in California, and the day I returned to New Jersey I was clean, and I have been since, for two and half years now. But I didn't clean up in New Standard. I spent only a couple of weeks there before moving to Riverside, where I shot crystal meth and lived as a petty criminal among other criminals, some not so petty. For one year I traded my comfortable home in upper-middle-class Princeton, New Jersey, for motels and convict squatter pads in Riverside, California. This story is about that year.

PART 1: SKETCHING RIVERSIDE

CHAPTER 1. GET STRAIGHT FOR LIFE

In the fall of 2002 my parents bought three tickets from New Jersey to California: two round-trips for them and a one-way ticket for me. At the airport in Newark I tried to do my last shot in the bathroom, but just as I was mixing the heroin and water my dad walked in and asked me, through the stall, what I was doing.

"What do you think? Going to the bathroom," I said.

"The flight's leaving soon."

I tried to wait him out, holding a needle in my left hand and balancing a Sprite bottle cap full of dope on my thigh. But he didn't move. His feet remained planted under the stall door, and I ended up drinking the heroin and flushing the paraphernalia. I didn't start to kick on the flight, but I wasn't high, and I could feel the withdrawal coming.

If you've ever woken fifteen minutes before your alarm is set to go off and wished that that fifteen minutes would last forever, then you know what being high on heroin feels like. You're warm, relaxed; stretching triggers dull tremors of pleasure. A heroin high is everything that makes sleeping feel good, but intensified and with that little *It's really time to get up now* voice switched off.

Heroin withdrawal feels exactly the opposite. The second and third days are probably the worst, when you're likely to cramp up and start dry-heaving, but even after that passes it's impossible to get comfortable for about a week. Whichever side you're lying on starts to hurt, your joints and muscles all ache, and you're never the right temperature. You're shaking, teeth chattering, until you put on one blanket too many, and then you feel as if you're about to suffocate. You're not hungry, and if you force yourself to eat, the food tastes terrible—your mouth tastes terrible.

So basically, when I did start to kick, a few hours after arriving in California, I felt as if I had the flu. One big difference, though, was that I was also overwhelmingly depressed. In becoming addicted to heroin, I'd essentially traded all my little problems for one big problem (scoring) and all my little pleasures for one big pleasure (being high). But now the heroin was gone and I couldn't remember what it was like to feel good without it, so there wasn't even anything to look forward to once the sickness ended. I felt as if there was nothing to live for.

My parents and I stayed one night in a hotel, and the next day they drove me to New Standard, which was located in a business park: white brick buildings with plate-glass window facades that were opaque and usually blank except for a slickly designed graphic sticker on the door saying something like LOGITECH or INFONEX. At the time Joe was also enrolled at New Standard, having graduated Get Straight for Life (GSL) several weeks earlier. My parents would visit Joe at a separate location (the New Standard staff didn't want us seeing each other) once I was fully enrolled and on my way to GSL.

When you're a kid, your parents bring *home* with them wherever they go, so it wasn't until after they'd left, when two New Standard counselors were driving me to GSL in Grand Terrace, that I realized just how far from home I was: three thousand miles away, kicking heroin among strangers. Scared, I tried to act tough. I sat in the backseat of the van, frowning and responding curtly to the counselors' polite questions, each of which I managed to construe as a sort of veiled threat, criticism, or accusation. "So, you're a long way from home, huh?" "Man, you look pretty sick—what were you *doin'* out there in Jersey?" "You wanna stop and get a drink?" Eventually they gave up on me and talked baseball with each other.

Listening to them argue stats and make playoff predictions, I couldn't help recognizing that the counselors truly didn't care if I wanted to sulk in the backseat. They were indifferent but not malevolent. They weren't my enemies. Slowly I realized that there was nobody to be angry with—nobody to blame for my situation but me—and though I'd resisted having this realization, afterward I felt better. I stared out the window, and even though I was sniffling and the withdrawal was getting worse, I began to like the California landscape.

We were driving down a busy four-lane street, and outside my window citrus trees were flashing by, blurring into each other, lush and dense, when suddenly there was a break in the groves and I caught a glimpse of a pickup truck shooting across a barren field, kicking up dust in the middle of nowhere. In Grand Terrace we turned off the main street onto a bumpy dirt road lined with navel orange trees, which we stayed on for miles before pulling into a gravel driveway with a sign that read GET STRAIGHT FOR LIFE. GSL was a rectangular two-story building with a flat roof. A few patches of wood chips with leafy plants and flowers in wide terra-cotta pots flanked the front door, and a concrete sidewalk wound around the entire building to the weight room in the back, branching off to each of the dorm rooms along the way.

We took my bags from the backseat and went inside. The New Standard counselors then handed me off to a GSL counselor, who led me into a lounge and asked me to sit on a couch while he searched my bags. Then, after the counselor had gone through all my clothes and toiletries, a cheery woman in her late thirties with curly red hair called me into the staff office, a narrow room lined with filing cabinets. It was called the fishbowl, the woman said, because three of the walls were mostly glass and faced the two lounges and the cafeteria. The woman gave me forms to fill out, telling me that the nurse would be here soon, and that once I was done with the forms the nurse would give me pills for my detox and then I could go to bed. As I filled them out, I saw other recovering junkies ("clients" was the official euphemism) coming out of their rooms and walking through the cafeteria and the lounges, looking over with mild interest, pointing, hey, there's the new guy.

The nurse didn't arrive for a few hours, and in the meantime the staff rotated and I threw a temper tantrum. I shouted at the counselor who was now watching me—a short, trim man in his forties with spiky hair and a neat goatee—shouted about how sick I was, and how the woman with the red hair had said that the nurse would be there hours ago. When he said that I might have misunderstood, I shouted that I knew what the woman had told me. She'd said "soon" hours ago. So either she hadn't known when the nurse was going to arrive, in which case she was incompetent, or she'd deliberately manipulated me, lied to me, *disrespected* me. *Either way, I wasn't stayin' in no fuckin' place where people are incompetent, where people lie to you, where they have you sittin' in an office for hours, shivering, while motherfuckers walk by, lookin' at you all hard and shit, like you won't fuck them up.* When the counselor told me that I was welcome to leave, but that maybe I should call my parents first, since he knew it was important to them that I be there, I told him that now *he* was disrespecting me, talking about my parents as if he knew them. I stared at him threateningly, with my jaw clenched and my hands clutching the arms of my chair as if I needed to hold myself back. He stared back at me, a little bored, and asked if I wanted to use the phone or not.

I did. I called my parents and told them I was leaving. My parents took me much more seriously than the counselor did. They begged me to stay, reminding me of my charges in New Jersey, of the bail money they would lose, of everything they'd done for me and all the shit I'd put them through—couldn't I please stay, for them if not for me? They'd been visiting Joe when I called, and they even put him on the phone to talk some sense into me. Joe pleaded with me too, promising that GSL wasn't that bad, and that in three months we would be together—couldn't I hold on for him?

I had never planned on leaving, of course. I was just scared, hysterical, paranoid—needing somebody to *listen to me.* Even so, I wouldn't have let the scene drag on for nearly as long as it did if part of me didn't find it gratifying—gratifying that Joe and my parents seemed to believe that I really was about to leave, that I was tough and crazy enough to walk back down that dirt road, kicking, with no money.

Eventually I promised my parents I would stay. I would stay for them. I hung up the phone and apologized to the counselor, and then the nurse arrived and gave me a handful of pills. I was shown to my room, where I passed out almost immediately.

For the first week at GSL I was officially on detox, sleeping and watching movies, heavily medicated with muscle relaxants, benzodiazepines, sleeping pills, and an antibiotic for the plum-colored abscess in the crook of my arm. Some nights the meds knocked me out; others I spent huddled on the toilet, blowing hot air on my feet, legs, and chest with a hair dryer borrowed from the nurse. There were six beds to a room, six clients, and we each had our own chest of drawers and a pinup board for pictures. The rooms were large enough so we weren't cramped, but the beds were small. My mattress was plastic, my fitted sheet too loose: By the end of each night I was lying on sticky plastic.

Other clients were assigned to watch me throughout the day in case I went into seizure. They took two-hour shifts, bringing me food and water and operating the TV and VCR. Most of the clients at GSL wanted to be on "detox watch," since it got them out of group, and they rushed for the sign-up sheet that was posted outside my door every morning. Also, I slept most of the time, so watching me really meant watching movies on my TV. I remember waking groggily from a medicated sleep to find a dark-skinned Mexican, covered in tattoos of women's faces, sitting in a chair next to me and watching *As Good as It Gets*. When he saw me he said, "Yeah, man, I put this on for you. I thought you'd wanna watch it." Everyone seemed to know which movies I wanted to watch, before they'd even met me.

Another reason everybody wanted to be on detox watch was that only I could smoke whenever I wanted, and of course my guardian had to accompany me. So everybody knew when I wanted to smoke too. Not that I minded: Once the nurse started tapering my meds and I became well enough to tell one person from another, I began to use my detox privileges to show the other clients that I was cool (one of the very few things that mattered to me while kicking and depressed). "Do you think you wanna smoke sometime soon?" one of them would ask. "Of course *I* want to smoke." Wink, wink. "Let's go."

Outside there was a patio facing a large field, at the end of which was a basketball court and two cabins. The cabins were where senior clients slept, clients who'd been in GSL for a while and, the thinking was, could be trusted away from the main building. Beyond the field was a dry stretch of shrubs, brambles, and eucalyptus trees.

Around my third or fourth day at GSL I came out to the patio with my guard to smoke. After we sat down and lit our cigarettes, I started sniffling and wrapping myself in my sweatshirt, trying to look even sicker than I actually was. I did this not because I wanted pity (though there was probably that, too), but because once we came outside and there was no TV to distract us, my guard became uncomfortable, clearly feeling that he should be talking to me, the new guy, young and sick and away from home. But as soon as he saw how sick I appeared to be—so sick that I was totally ignoring him, lost in my own feverish thoughts—he felt better, thinking it was best to just leave me alone. He felt comfortable, so I felt comfortable. He took the opportunity to use the pay phone at the edge of the patio, winking at me as he went because it was against the rules.

A few minutes later an official smoke break began. The glass doors opened and my guard hung up the phone and ran back to me, putting his finger to his lips and smiling. Then nearly all of GSL's sixty-some-odd clients burst outside, restless from group, talking and laughing and flicking their lighters. Overwhelmed, I really pretended to be sick then. I bundled up and pretended to not notice the crowd, while actually listening to every word, scared and intrigued.

In spite of all my adolescent drug-dealing adventures I had, to that point, lived a pretty sheltered life. The only "criminals" I'd hung out with had been kids who were nearly as sheltered as I was. I'd taken trips to inner-city ghettos to buy drugs, but I'd never lived in any of those places (or even stopped to think what that would be like). I'd always bought my drugs and then left, thrilled by the dangerous little adventure I'd just taken, proud of how tough I was to risk doing it. But now, sick on the patio at GSL, my first adult rehab, I was surrounded by recovering junkies and adult criminals, the people I would be living with for the next nine months. I remember my first thought—lucid because I hadn't had time to adjust and develop an attitude that would muddy my thinking—my first thought was that it was shocking to see adults behaving like kids.

Men in their thirties, forties, and fifties were talking fuck this and fuck that, just like bad kids in high school. A guy who looked like my parents' old plumber was saying, "If Jeff had said that shit to me, man, I woulda fucked him up—I don't care if he's a goddamn counselor." Another guy was doing pull-ups on a wooden crossbeam, with a small crowd watching. When he dropped, after about eight, he told the crowd that he could have done at least ten more if the beam hadn't been so awkward to hold.

A woman in her early thirties, more than six feet tall and at least two hundred pounds, with her hair dyed black, was complaining about how the staff allowed men to wear whatever they wanted while women were prohibited from wearing anything provocative, specifically belly shirts. "I don't even wanna wear a belly shirt," she was saying, but then she smiled and became self-conscious. She turned the rant into a joke, poking fun at herself—her body, her intimidating appearance. "Of course *I* don't wanna wear a belly shirt. Can you see my fat ass in a belly shirt? But if Mya wants to wear a belly shirt, she should be allowed to wear a fucking belly shirt. Am I right or am I not right? Carlos, tell me I'm fucking right!" This woman, I would learn, was Wendy Kaplan.

For the most part people sat in groups, smoking in circles or crowding around the stone picnic tables, and it was clear that in many of these groups the coolest guys were the ones with muscles and tattoos, the guys who looked like convicts. Of these, most of the whites had shaved heads, the Hispanics thick mustaches. (There were hardly any black people at GSL.) They all wore khaki pants and flannel shirts over string T-shirts—the clothes I would ask my parents to send me about a month later.

About of a third of the clients at GSL were women. Sitting at the table nearest me, a woman with a high, cracking voice was talking loudly about having sex on crystal meth. She said her boyfriend used to "stunt-fuck" her for hours. She was in her early thirties and pretty. She had dirty-blond hair, green eyes, a wide smile, and faint freckles on her nose and cheeks that made her look like a lion. She saw me staring, and as I turned away she laughed, not unkindly. I got up and went back to my room. A few minutes later I heard my guardian come in.

When he knocked on the bathroom door, I said, "Out in a minute."

"Good, that's you," he said. "Man, you can't be leavin' me out there—if staff saw me without you, I'd get in big trouble. I'd have to write essays and shit, or maybe get up early on Sunday for extra duty."

"Sorry," I said. "I just got tired."

Days later, I was smoking on the patio toward the end of an hour and a half stretch (from nine thirty p.m. to eleven p.m., between the last group and bedtime) when everybody could smoke. There were only a few other people on the patio. One of them, sitting at the farthest picnic table, was a meth addict in his early twenties named Brian. Brian had told me a few days earlier that he knew my brother from when he was at GSL, saying that they'd been cool. He'd also said that if I needed anything I should just let him know. Those had been his words—"just let me know"—which he'd followed with a meaningful nod, as if we were in a prison movie, implying that he had pull at GSL. He didn't, though. Even I knew that. Brian talked constantly about the few months he'd spent in jail, but he'd never done serious time—he'd never been to prison—and you weren't really cool at GSL unless you had. There were about ten real convicts at GSL, and about thirty wannabes like Brian who looked up to them. (The rest of the clients were mostly alcoholics with straight jobs; they didn't care about being tough and therefore didn't understand why anybody would want to have been in prison.)

"Hey, Jersey," Brian called to me. "C'mon over here."

He was sitting with a woman at the far side of the table, and as I walked over, she whispered urgently to him and he laughed.

"What's up?" I said, standing in front of the table.

"You want a cigarette, homey?" he said.

I was already smoking one. As I held it up to show him, he laughed embarrassedly, and then said, "Dude, she's giving me a hand job."

The woman laughed, blushed, shook her head. She was at least six months pregnant.

"Cool," I said, smiling politely. "I guess I'll leave you to that."

"No, dude," he said. "It's cool. C'mon, sit down. You don't need to leave."

The girl, still blushing, elbowed him, and he laughed again.

"That's all right," I said. "I think I'm gonna go to bed."

After my week of detox was over, I moved to a different dorm and began following the schedule, going to all the groups and activities. We woke at six thirty a.m., and breakfast was followed by the Good Morning Meet, a GSL staple. It began with senior clients standing in front of the house (as we were collectively called) reading the schedule and any announcements from staff, and it ended with volunteers reading poetry, telling jokes, and singing songs. This was a morale boost, of course, meant to instill a feeling of community. And it worked. People listened to the poetry, roared at the jokes, and often sang along with the songs.

At first, before I knew anybody, this seemed bizarre to me. Everybody would assemble in the cafeteria, and I'd sit as far as possible from the performance area with my head down, tired and unhappy, and then all of a sudden the room would explode, laughing and clapping and singing a Bob Marley song. But eventually, once I made a few friends—like Wendy, the woman who wouldn't wear a belly shirt—I started laughing and clapping with everybody else.

A couple of weeks after I got off detox, Wendy volunteered to sing a song, and I couldn't help being nervous for her as she made her way to the front. Then she announced that she would be singing "Date Rape," by Sublime, and as I realized the risk she was taking, I squirmed with anxiety. Not only was "Date Rape" a long song with a very fast tempo, but also nobody else knew the words, so she would be singing alone. She took a deep breath, as if about to start, then looked up at the room and said, "Holy shit." Everybody laughed. "Okay," she said, "I'm gonna sing now. Promise."

A thirty-two-year-old convict on parole, Wendy would have been classically beautiful if not for her bad teeth, which were mostly rotted in the back, possibly from smoking crystal meth. She had a long neck and high cheekbones. Her eyes were narrow and dark. She wore dark eyeliner and lots of makeup, along with khakis, skater sneakers, and a pink T-shirt—punk-rock style.

I was sitting on the edge of my seat, before she'd even started singing, and I could feel the tension in my face from smiling. She took another deep breath, and this time didn't look up. Then she shocked us all. She could sing. There were a few murmurs of "Who the hell knew?" and then everybody was quiet as she sang the first verse, managing to maintain the melody, so that those of us who knew the song could hear it in our heads, even as the tempo quickened to rap-speed. At the end of the first verse, she paused and took a deep breath, made sure to not look at anybody and then kept going. She was trembling. It began to creep into her voice. Turning red, she stumbled over a few lines that were supposed to be funny and I thought she was going to stop, but she didn't, she kept going. She stumbled again and then kept going, staring at the floor but singing loudly, until she came to the last line, about a rapist who ends up being raped himself in jail—*Well, I can't take pity on men of his kind / Even though he now takes it in the behind*—and then she received a standing, laughing ovation.

The song was the last part of the Good Morning Meeting. Afterward there was a short cleaning session, and while the senior clients assigned everybody jobs, from mopping the floor (the hardest) to taking out the trash (the easiest), I ran up to Wendy excitedly, wanting to congratulate her. Once I was standing in front of her, though, and she was staring down at me, giving me her only halfway playful can-I-help-you look, I froze stupidly, unable to think of the words.

"You were fucking shaking, Wendy," I blurted out.

"Well, I was fucking scared, Jimmy," she said impatiently, and began to brush past me. As soon as she'd passed me, though, I turned around and literally jumped on her. I put my hands on her shoulders, pushing down as I jumped on her, and we both crashed into the wall. But before she could say anything, I shouted, "Wendy!" and playfully hugged her from the side, with my head down. I held her like that until she started laughing. She said, "All right, Jim-Jim—let me go." Then, without even looking at her, I ran to the other side of the cafeteria to find out what my job was.

Wendy had started calling me that—Jim-Jim—the first day we'd started hanging out together, the day we'd become friends. We'd been sitting in the lounge area with Luke, a barrel-chested convict with a shaved head, hoop earrings, and, sleeving his right arm and shoulder, a color tattoo of a woman with a machine gun standing in front of a wall of flowers. Luke had arrived at GSL only a few days earlier, having been paroled there directly from Chino Prison, but it was already clear that he would be one of the more popular convicts.

Wendy had asked me a question about drugs in New Jersey, about the way they're sold, and I'd been telling her about the inner-city drug blocks, exaggerating grossly (as I'd gotten into the habit of doing when it came to talking about New Jersey and who I had been there). I'd been exaggerating how dangerous the blocks were, and how much I knew about them. I'd actually been about to tell them that I used to sell dope on blocks that were more dangerous than Baghdad, when Luke interrupted me, saying, "That sounds real crazy and shit, but you know, dude, you don't have to lie to kick it."

"Did you just call yourself Kay-Kay?" I asked.

"What?" Luke asked.

"You just told me I didn't have to lie to Kay-Kay."

"No," Wendy interjected. "He said that you don't have to lie *to kick it*. It's a California thing."

"Oh."

"Who the fuck is Kay-Kay?" asked Luke.

"I guess you're Kay-Kay," said Wendy.

"I'm Kay-Kay? Cool. I'll be Kay-Kay—Big Daddy Kay-Kay."

"And I suppose I don't have to lie to Big Daddy Kay-Kay, now, do I?" I said.

"Nope. Why would you wanna lie to Kay-Kay?"

"Look," Wendy said. "It's Kay-Kay and Jim-Jim from New Jersey—the dynamic duo."

We went to lunch and sat together, and the nicknames stuck.

After the Good Morning Meeting and the morning cleaning session, we would have our first group of the day. The men would clear the long tables out of the cafeteria and arrange the chairs in a large circle, while the women set up in one of the lounges. The counselor leading the group would pick a topic—anger, fear, resentment—and one of the group members would raise his hand to share; then other group members would raise their hands and offer feedback. There would be a second group in the early afternoon, followed by an AA meeting (we would take turns reading from one of the twelve-step texts) and then, after dinner, an AA speaker meeting (an AA member who'd been clean for some time would come and "share his experience")—the last group of the day, from eight p.m. to nine thirty p.m.

I preferred the groups to the meetings, and I participated often, offering feedback that I convinced myself would be helpful to the person sharing. Had I been honest with myself, though, I would have known that the only reason I ever spoke was to enhance my image. For example, a client would say that he was conflicted about returning home to Rubidoux because of all the gang-related violence, and I would say, "Yeah, man. I know where you're coming from, but if you ask me, you gotta go somewhere totally new. I mean, look at me—I'm three thousand miles from home because it got too crazy back there. And I'm sure you're tempted to go back because of your family, and because it's fun—I know what it's like—but I don't see how you can do both, how you can go home and stay committed to recovery. I know I couldn't. Not yet, anyway." Who knows what I would have come up with if the women had been in the group with us, if Mya, the woman with the high, cracking voice who liked to get "stunt-fucked," had been sitting next to me?

There were a lot of romantic relationships at GSL. Many of the clients had come straight from prison, and even for the clients who weren't already backed up, ninety days was a long time. Of course we joked about this. "What do they expect from us? Men and women under the same roof; it's only natural!" We joked about it all the time, with phony enthusiasm, because we knew there was something more to this romantic phenomenon than horniness, something the counselors were always eager to explain. There is no easier (or less destructive) way to fill the void left by drugs—and to distract yourself from everything that's wrong with your life, everything you're supposed to be focusing on in rehab—than falling in love.

Mya started hanging out with us—Wendy, Luke, me, and a few others—after her last boyfriend at GSL got kicked out, partly for being too obvious about his relationship with Mya. (Relationships were against the rules, but, since there were so many of them, the staff often tolerated them until they became disruptive.) She was a thirty-three-year-old single mother who lived in a trailer park. I was an eighteen-year-old virgin who resented his upper-middle-class upbringing. I fell for her immediately, and it was just as distracting as the counselors had promised. During group, when I wasn't trying to come up with self-aggrandizing advice, I was counting the minutes until it was over and I could go to lunch and sit at the same table as Mya. But not next to her. I'd never had a girlfriend and I was shy. I'd hardly given her a hint as to how I felt.

Eventually I did tell Luke, and then every day after lunch, when we were in the weight room and he was teaching me how to work out, he would also give me tips on how to woo Mya. I didn't get anywhere with her, though, until Luke decided to act independently on my behalf. By this time both he and I had been at GSL for almost two months, and we were living in one of the cottages at the edge of the large field. It was Sunday morning, the only day we were allowed to sleep in. In the afternoon families would visit.

"Dude, with your hair like that you look kind of like a girl," Luke said.

I was just waking up, and Luke was sitting on the edge of my bed, handing me a cup of coffee and a cigarette.

"Fuck you," I said, putting the coffee on the nightstand. I tried to push my hair down, smooth it back, but it was no good—I was stuck looking like a fat girl until my shower.

"Don't trip, dude," said Luke, getting up off the bed. "We keep hitting those weights, you'll lose more weight, your face'll chisel up. You'll be all right."

I sat up against the wall and hit the cigarette. Smoking was prohibited in the cabins, but for the past week Luke and I had had the place to ourselves—two of our former roommates having graduated and the other having been kicked out for having sex in the toolshed—so there was nobody to snitch on us. We didn't even keep a serious lookout, since most of the counselors liked us and probably wouldn't have written us up if they'd caught us. We stashed our coffee cups in the unused dressers instead of returning them to the kitchen.

"I talked to Mya for you," Luke said.

"You what?"

"I talked to Mya, like I said I was gonna."

"What did you say?"

He laughed. He had narrow green eyes and crooked teeth.

"What the fuck, man? What did you say?"

"Don't trip, dude, it's cool."

"Dude, I'll tell you if it's fucking cool. Just tell me what you said."

I often said things like that—"I'll tell you"—to solidify our friendship. Nobody at GSL *told* Luke anything, but we were close friends, and friends can talk to each other however they want.

"If I tell you," he said, "you're gonna trip, so just don't worry about it. Trust me; it's cool."

"Fuck that! What did you say?"

"All right, you want me to tell you—I'll tell you. I called her into the lounge and I just asked her, so what do you think of Jimmy? And she was like, well, he's my friend. So I said, Jimmy wants to be more than friends—what do you think of that? She said that she didn't really know, that she liked you, but you weren't really her type; she said she was more into prison guys. And I was like, how's that been working out for you? You know what I'm saying? I told her, look—I told her what we were talking about—I told her, look, Jimmy's fucked before, but never sober, so why don't you just give it to him? Dude, you're freaking out, aren't you?"

"A little bit."

"See, I knew you would. But you don't even understand: I fuckin' hooked it up."

"What, did she say yes?"

"No, not to me. She just laughed and shit, but dude, I'm telling you, I hooked it up. You don't understand, girls in a place like this, they just want to be taken. You can take her, I'm telling you."

"Okay."

"Fuck that, *okay*. She's leavin' in what, like two weeks? You gotta take her now. I want you to go up to her and put your hand on the back of her neck and just start mackin' with her." He paused. "And you gotta do it soon, or else I'm gonna do it."

We burst out laughing.

I'm not sure how much Luke's talk actually had to do with it, but about a week later Mya and I, now both senior clients, were assigned to do "dorm searches" (to make sure rooms were clean, beds made), and we kissed in one of the empty rooms. After that I started writing her love notes, slipping them under her door at night. She always said that the notes made her cry. A few days before she graduated, she told me that if I chose not to go to New Standard after GSL, I could live with her.

Of course I was already considering not going to New Standard: For more than two months I'd been living with parolees and adult women talking about sex—how could I go from that to a "young adult school"? I convinced myself that I didn't need to, that I didn't need to listen to my parents' lawyer, who'd said that my going to New Standard was crucial if I wanted to stay out of prison. In the past, whenever I'd talked to him after I'd been arrested, he'd always told me how serious the charges were, how this time the prosecutor was almost sure to "jam me up," as he put it, unless he could work some sort of magic. And yet I'd never even been on probation. I figured he'd been scaring me then, for my parents, so he was probably scaring me now. I figured with a GSL certificate I could return to New Jersey, whenever they decided on a court date, and get off with another slap on the wrist. I would have figured just about anything to keep from going to New Standard.

For a while, though, it looked like I wouldn't have any choice. Mya graduated and I didn't hear from her. Luke had also suggested that we move together into a sober-living home, a kind of halfway house in Riverside—rent was cheap, we would both get jobs, and after a while, if I proved to my parents that I could stay clean without New Standard, they would probably even help with rent—but then Luke got kicked out for telling a counselor to go fuck herself, and I didn't hear from him, either. I didn't hear from either of them for about a week.

It was a long and unhappy week. Wendy was busy making plans for when she graduated, going on day passes to apply for jobs and talking with her parole agent about which sober-living she should move to. So she was never around to make me laugh or listen to me whine. I only had one other friend at GSL, and he, Brady, another convict who was also about to graduate, wasn't the sort to commiserate. Brady used to tease me about Mya whenever he got the chance.

One day, in the early afternoon, I was on my way from the weight room to the patio, arms flushed and throbbing, when I saw him coming up from the cabins. Brady was tall and fat with shaggy black hair that curled in front of his eyes, and he took big strides that went nearly as far side to side as they did forward. I called to him, "Yo, Brady!" and he stopped to let me catch up. I jogged down the sidewalk, passing Kelly M. and Angel P., who were lying on the grass, freshly cut from Sunday's chores. They were smoking, passing a cigarette back and forth in cupped hands, sneaking it because the grass was outside the designated smoking area. They were only about twenty feet from the patio, where smoking was allowed. Kelly, who had checked into GSL in order to regain custody of her children, had been getting into so much trouble lately that the staff might have kicked her out if they'd caught her.

"Can you fucking believe that?" I said, once I'd caught up to Brady. "She's always crying about her kids and shit, and now she can't walk a couple of feet to the patio!"

"What did I tell you, Jimmy—these whores are all stupid here."

Brady had never told me that before. But he wasn't really saying that he had: With Brady, "What did I tell you?" was just a good way to start a sentence.

"But don't be pointin' at her now," Brady said. "Yeah, she's a dumb bitch, and she's gonna get caught, but you don't wanna be the one to get her caught. Say staff's lookin' out that window and sees you pointin' at her. Sees the cigarette. She gets kicked out, loses her kids—she'll come kill your ass. Tell me I'm lyin'."

He was thirty-six, a bit of a loner; most everything he said to me sounded like advice. Yet it never felt condescending. He had a low, resonant voice, with only the slightest hint of a Southern drawl. Sometimes when we were sitting on the patio together, he would say my name three times—"Jimmy, Jimmy, Jimmy"—and then nothing more.

"Brady," I said, "you did all that time in prison—why didn't you ever start lifting weights?"

"I did a little, but I stopped," Brady said. "Long time ago. I didn't need to—I just grabbed 'em by the balls. Guys put all that muscle on, you just grab 'em by the balls, they'll listen like anybody else."

As he was saying this the pay phone rang, and I turned a little too eagerly.

"It ain't her." Brady laughed, patting me on the shoulder. "Mya already done found somebody else, Jimmy."

"Fuck you, whatever."

"Jimmy, Jimmy, Jimmy. You're gonna be all right. I'll find you some pussy when we get out of here. How long's it been since she graduated?"

"A week. A fucking long week."

"Yeah, I'll bet. Pussy will make the time fly in here—now you're wishin' you never got it. How was it, anyway? Was she any good?"

"I don't know. I never fucked her."

"You never fucked her?"

"No, we just went on dorm searches and kissed."

"You never fucked her? Well then you can forget about that. You know she's found somebody else."

"She said I could go live with her when I get out."

"Man, you can forget about that."

Brady and I didn't make plans to meet up after GSL. Brady didn't make plans with anybody. But on Christmas, the day before Brady's graduation and a few weeks before mine, I gave Brady my pair of black boots. He hugged me and said it was the best present he'd ever been given.

By that time Luke and Mya had each called me. Luke's parole

agent had forced him to check into another rehab, where he would stay for the next month. He gave me the phone numbers of both his girlfriend and his parents, and told me to call him when he got out. Mya was home, at a trailer park in Hemet, California. She still wanted me to come live with her.

When I told my parents that I wouldn't be going to New Standard, we had one of our *long* discussions. They respectfully asked my reasoning, I told them a bunch of juvenile nonsense about finding my own way, and they took the time to parse and refute each one of my bullshit arguments. They appealed to logic and wisdom and spirituality, until I lied and promised to think about it.

When I told the staff at GSL that I wouldn't be going, instead of arguing with me they held a secret meeting with all the clients who'd been to prison, asking each of them to talk with me one on one, to convince me that I should go to New Standard in order to avoid any chance of going to prison. Since I didn't know about the meeting, the first few talks were strange. I was shooting free throws alone on the basketball court when a guy named Marco, an enormous forty-year-old former weightlifting champion whom I'd hardly ever spoken with, walked onto the court and with almost no introduction started telling me about how prison had ruined his life. Later, a man named Derek came up from behind when I was walking up from the cabin—he slapped me on the back and said, "Hey, man, you don't want go to prison." I told him he was right. Eventually I learned about the meeting, and then it became a big joke: A convict would walk up to me and I would say, "I know all about it—you did your part." Embarrassed, the convict would laugh and walk away.

To my great surprise, though, Wendy took it seriously. Or at least she tried to. Smoking on the patio, she suddenly turned to me and said, "I think you should go to New Standard, Jim-Jim. I know you didn't ask me, but I'm telling you anyway."

"Oh, come on. You too?"

"Yeah, me too, Jimmy. Except I'm the only one of these fuckers who actually cares about you. But seriously, you should go. You don't want to go to prison. Prison sucks; and you only have to do, what, a year in the program? I know you're all like, 'I'm not scared of prison,' because you see all these dudes around here who just got out, but believe me, if they had the chance to avoid it they would, and most of 'em weren't talkin' so tough when they got sentenced. A year in a program? That's a sweet deal; you should take it."

"I'm not saying I'm not scared of prison; I just don't think I'm gonna have to go. I just think my lawyer's trying to scare me for my parents, so they can have me safe in this program. And fuck that program. New Standard. Bunch of fucking rich kids."

"You *are* a rich kid."

"Yeah, but I'm not like them."

"But you're still a rich kid. You have rich parents, and you should take advantage."

"I don't want to take advantage. That's the whole point."

"No, the point, Jim-Jim, is that you wanna fuck Mya when you get out. That's the point. And don't you even try to say otherwise. Don't you try to run game on me, Jimmy-James! You're going to prison for pussy, and you damn well know it, and all I'm saying is . . . all I'm saying is that it better be fucking good."

• • •

Of course it was good—Mya was my first. After graduating GSL, I lived with Mya in Hemet for one week. Then the only thing that could have happened that would have made me change my plans and go to New Standard happened: I ran out of money. I called my parents and checked into New Standard.

As soon as I got there, I learned that my brother wasn't there anymore. Joe had taken off as soon as he heard that I wasn't coming to New Standard, and now nobody knew where he was. That was just the first disappointment.

I hated New Standard. The schedule was easier than GSL, the rooms nicer, the food better—I suppose the New Standard staff figured that after GSL, students (as we were called) would be grateful to return to a new down comforter. But I felt as if I'd just gone from something "adult" and "real" to more spoiled upper-middle-class bullshit. And the staff treated us like children. I went from living with a thirty-three-year-old woman to asking permission to use the bathroom. From the first day, I plotted my escape.

I behaved well so that the staff wouldn't say anything negative about me to my parents, but every time I called my parents I calmly explained that New Standard was the wrong place for me, that the other students were constantly talking about getting high, and that the childish atmosphere was eroding my enthusiasm for recovery. At the same time I snuck phone calls whenever I got the chance, first to Mya, who had clearly decided that she wouldn't wait, and then to Luke, who said he would have a sober-living waiting for us whenever I could get out of New Standard. I told my parents I wanted to go to a sober-living, and after about two weeks' worth of phone calls we cut a deal: I would get a job and attend meetings and take classes at Riverside Community College, and my parents would send me money for rent. So in January of 2003 I moved into a sober-living home in downtown Riverside with my friend Luke.

CHAPTER 2. CRYSTAL METH

The sober-living home Luke found us was on Franklin Avenue just off Third Street, a block with crumbling curbs and broken sidewalks, dead grass and occasional palm trees. The house was faded yellow and had a front porch with a wheelchair ramp. Inside, it looked like the lounge area of a rehab, with cushy couches, an old TV with a circular dial, and everything mismatched and donated, from the coffee tables to the dishes. Aside from one other guy whose name I can't remember, Luke and I lived alone, as we had in our cottage. This other guy was never home during the day. When we saw him wheeling his bike through the hallway in the morning, we would ask him where he was going, and he would say, "Work." Then in the evenings the same thing would happen, except he would say, "Bed."

Luke and I were offered crystal meth within a week of our moving in. Since we didn't have jobs yet, we spent a lot of time smoking in the front yard, and one day a stocky Mexican with a shaved head walked past us and got into a car that was parked at the end of the block. A few minutes later he got out of the car and started walking back. He looked around cautiously. When he saw us, he stared for a moment and then walked over and shook our hands, asking if we'd just moved in. Luke said that we had, that I was from New Jersey, and that he'd just gotten out of Chino a few months ago. At this the guy smiled. He pointed to himself and said, "Folsom—six months ago. They call me César. This is my neighborhood." He said this last part so casually that I wasn't sure if he actually meant it as a warning. He might simply have been saying that he was a local. But maybe not. Then he asked us if we wanted some meth.

"Nah, we can't, dude," said Luke. "This is a sober-living house."

"I better get away from here, then," César said jokingly.

We laughed and shook hands and then César walked away; the word "Riverside" was tattooed on the back of his neck. As soon as he was gone, I felt a tinge of regret: I'd never tried crystal meth, and I was curious. Luke apparently felt the same. He laughed. "That dude probably had some good shit."

Afterward we both told our sober-living manager about our meeting with César, as if to prove our dedication to recovery, but deep down we both knew that recovery had had almost nothing to do with our refusal. We'd said no to César chiefly because it was the easiest way to end a loaded encounter, to respectfully keep our distance from a local gangbanger. Had we been more comfortable with César, I suspect we might have said yes.

Having been clean for nearly four months now, Luke and I had both said many times that we planned to stay clean. But announcing that you're going to stay clean is like announcing that you're on a diet. You say it with conviction, you understand just how important it is, but then you're confronted with a single damn cupcake and you simply can't imagine stopping after just one—or, more precisely, that you won't want to stop at all. With drugs, that failure of imagination may seem more dire, but that's only if you're not used to doing them. Once they've become a way of life, it's nearly impossible to imagine that one shot will make a difference.

Nobody else at the sober-living ever offered me drugs, so I stayed clean for a few weeks and even managed to get a job, through Wendy. Back at GSL, before she graduated, Wendy had given me the number to the sober-living she would be moving to in Glen Avon, and I called her there soon after moving to Riverside. The next day she picked me up in a sputtering 1984 Mazda RX7, and she took me with her to a telemarketing office downtown, where we were both hired immediately, given a script, and told to start making calls, for ten dollars an hour.

I talked to my parents often, bragging about my new life—about the friends I'd made and the job I'd gotten. I even proudly described the cheap food I was buying. The dish Luke and I ate most frequently was something called a spread, which Luke had learned to make in prison: refried beans, nacho cheese, and Flamin' Hot chili Cheetos all cooked together in a pot and then wrapped in a slightly toasted flour tortilla. My mom said it sounded disgusting, but otherwise she seemed pleased. At least I was working and safe in a sober-living house.

Soon after I got the job, my mom told me that she'd heard from Joe. She said that he'd started calling about a week after leaving New Standard, promising that he was clean. He'd said that he was living with friends in Riverside, working at a construction site. He'd been asking for money, but my mom wasn't sure if she should trust him.

"He asked for your phone number," she said, "but I haven't given it to him. I wanted to talk to you first, to feel it through with you, because I'm not sure how he's doing."

"Give it to him," I said.

"You're sure?"

"Yeah, I can handle him."

"Jim," she said, "part of me wants you to meet with him, because I'd like to know how he's doing—if he's on drugs, whether it's safe to send him money—but it's much more important that you don't do anything that's bad for you. You're still in a somewhat fragile state, and he can—for you especially—be . . . not so good."

"No, I'm sure. I'll be fine. Maybe Luke will even come along."

Joe called me the next day. Because I didn't want him knowing where I lived, I told him to meet me at the corner store where Luke and I shopped, about a block away from the sober-living. I waited at the edge of the parking lot for about fifteen minutes until Joe pulled up, wearing a black watch cap and slouching in the passenger seat of a 1982 Buick Regal with a huge rust stain on its hood. At first he didn't see me, and I didn't wave. I was considering turning around when I saw him start gesticulating wildly at the driver; then the Buick made a U-turn, screeched into the parking lot, and stopped in front of me.

"Yo, yo!" Joe yelled, getting out of the car, arms spread to hug me.

Joe had always been handsome, with a square forehead and a strong nose and chin—a chiseled face full of intensity. But not now. He'd become so thin that his face was unpleasant to look at: his skin was white as paper and looked creepily soft, like a baby's. Against the white, his grayish-blue eyes looked like contacts with too much color.

"What's up, brother?" I yelled back at him. "Man, you are fuckin' sucked up!"

"Yeah, I know, I know. I lost a little weight."

"A little? What are you, like a buck-twenty?"

"Nah, nah—no way. More like a buck-forty."

"Dude, you're out of your mind. You're like a hundred and twenty pounds, if that."

"Nah—well, maybe. Who cares? Fuck it. Ha, ha! C'mon, dude, let's go. Eh, yo, Hector, this my brother Jim. Jim, that's Hector."

I didn't even want to get in the car at first, but Joe insisted that we'd just get dropped off wherever we wanted—that it was "all cool." Hector seemed irritated to be driving my brother anywhere. He didn't even look at me. I said we should go downtown for lunch, and Joe said, "Cool, cool," but once I got in the car, Joe of course needed to make a stop, and Hector ended up letting us out at a decrepit house on Lime Street, about a mile from downtown. Happy to leave the car, I didn't argue.

"I just gotta get something from this house up here. C'mon," Joe said.

"Joe, I'm not going anywhere near that house."

"No, it's cool, it's cool. Well, fuck it—wait here—I'll be right back."

He ran to the door and knocked, only to get snubbed by an angry fat woman in shorts, smoking a cigarette. Then, after the door was slammed in his face, Joe picked up a bike with a missing tire from the porch and said, "All right, let's go."

"What the fuck are you doing with that bike?"

"It's my bike."

"What are you talking about?"

"What do you mean? It's my bike."

"Put it down, man. Let's fucking go get something to eat."

"Put it down? All right. You're right. Fuck it."

We started walking to town, and along the way Joe told me that he'd finally found a profession. "I'm a thief!" he said, laughing. "Look, I even got the clothes for it." He stopped so I could look at him. He was wearing baggy denim overalls over a white T-shirt.

"Don't I look like a construction worker? When I'm dressed like this I can walk up on any job site and just start grabbin' shit, 'cause I'm slick like that. And people pay money for that shit, yo. Power tools and shit. Tell me I don't look like a construction worker."

"You look like a junkie in baggy overalls," I said.

Joe laughed. "Whatever," he said. "I still get mad shit—I'm the best thief in Riverside. It's all up in Charlotte's house back there."

"You've got all your stuff in that woman's house?"

"Yeah, that's Charlotte. She's cool. I stay there sometimes. She won't try to keep none of my shit—she *best* not try to keep any of that shit. I got all my gear stashed up there."

We came to the main downtown avenue—University—and made a right. I asked him if he was doing meth.

"But I only smoke it," he said. "You shoot that shit, you start bugging out. Wait—stop! Yo, let me see your watch."

He'd put his arm out, stopping me on the sidewalk in front of a shoe store and a pawnshop.

"What? No, you can't see my fucking watch."

"Dude, I'll give it back. I just wanna go steal that TV over there. I got the perfect scam."

"No, Joe, we're not stealing any TVs. We're going to get lunch. What do you want to eat?"

It was easy to distance myself emotionally from Joe; I'd been doing it my whole life. I was actually enjoying bossing him around, feeling superior. I was the better son, responsibly finding out how messed up my brother was so that my parents would know what to do with him.

"Pizza," he said. "I haven't had pizza in mad long."

The pizza shop was in the Mission Avenue shopping complex, a cobblestone street filled with potted flowers and garish fountains. Surrounded by downtown Riverside, the shopping complex was supposed to be a pocket of luxury and safety—a glossy refuge—for the rich passers-through. There were fancy boutiques and art stores and a coffee shop with four-dollar cappuccinos. But no matter how fancy the town made it, the shopping center was still in downtown Riverside. Bums slept there at night, and as we walked to the pizza shop, I smelled piss instead of flowers.

I ate one slice of the pizza we ordered; Joe had the rest, wolfing the first three, hardly breathing, then slowing to a steady munch. He smiled dopily at me with a string of mozzarella hanging from his mouth. As the food settled in his stomach, he looked as if he'd taken a shot of heroin: His lower lip hung open, his eyes fluttered, and he struggled to keep his head up. With a sixth slice folded in his hand, he looked up at me as if he'd forgotten I was there. He tried to smile again but only managed to squint and show me the food in his mouth.

He was being overwhelmed by the food, and for a moment I felt sorry for him.

"See, man," he said, "I eat. I eat a lot. Look, I ate this whole pizza. You didn't eat shit. You should eat more. It's mad good. We'll get another one. But yo, look at me—I don't look like one of these sucked-up junkies runnin' around here; ya know what I'm sayin'. I ain't like one of them. Look how much I'm eating."

"Joe, I'm lookin' at you right now, man, and you look exactly like one of those junkies runnin' around here."

I paid for the pizza and told him I had to go. He said he'd call me, and I said, "Yeah, you do that," over my shoulder.

When I got home I told my parents that Joe was high and that they shouldn't give him any money. Weeks later Joe would be arrested and locked up in Temecula County Jail for possession of stolen property and a syringe.

For my nineteenth birthday Wendy took me to a tattoo parlor. She knew the artist, and her present, I suppose, was the cheap price I paid: eighty dollars to have the words "Dirty Jersey" tattooed in an Old English script inside my left forearm. This was on a Monday, midafternoon. We weren't at work, because we'd lost our jobs for poor attendance: Wendy had fallen sick for about a week, and I hadn't even tried to get another ride to work. After she'd gotten better, Wendy had resumed picking me up every day, but instead of going to work we'd go to the mall and to the movies and, a few times, to houses of Wendy's old friends, where a lot of the guys had tattoos announcing where they were from. This of course is where I'd gotten the idea for mine. It wasn't until after I'd gotten the tattoo, though, once Wendy's friends began asking what was on my arm, that I realized the bold statement I was making—that I was from out of town and I didn't care who knew it.

Sometimes Luke came along with Wendy and me, but not usually. He spent a lot of time with his girlfriend and his kid, sleeping at his girlfriend's parents' house about half the week. So Wendy and I spent most days alone together, often driving in comfortable silence. In a few weeks my parents would send me money for a car, and I would get a geographical sense of Riverside County, from Rubidoux to Perris, Corona to Colton; but until then, while I sat in the passenger seat of Wendy's car, I ignored the street signs and exit numbers, content to depend on Wendy for direction. Since the freeways in Southern California are often elevated significantly above the towns they connect—and since I had no idea where I was—I often felt, going up a freeway ramp, as if I were entering some sort of futuristic travel circuit, like the Jetsons, zipping about from one isolated place to the next. I gazed absently out the window, across three wide lanes and into the desert that lay between the exits, at the plain white crosses on a few of the mountaintops. Once, going east on the 91, I leaned over and bit Wendy playfully on the shoulder. She hit me, and we both laughed before falling silent again. Then she looked at me and said, "I wanna get high." She was giddy, barely able to keep from laughing, definitely serious.

Back at GSL, surrounded by enthusiastic counselors, and with the memory of withdrawal fresh in my mind, staying clean—recovery— had been, itself, a goal, a concept so often reinforced that it virtually became tangible. But this illusion of recovery as a goal fades in the real world unless you go to AA meetings and seek out people to keep reinforcing it. Nothing had actually changed since the last time Wendy or I had shot up.

"Well if you're gonna get high, then I'm gonna get high," I said.

"Jim-Jim!" she scolded, but she couldn't stop smiling.

"I'm serious, Wendy. I want to get high. I want to find out what this shit's all about, all this tweaking and sketching you guys keep talking about."

"What the fuck, Jimmy? I'm serious too, but why do you have to get high with me? You're—you're gonna make me feel bad."

"You'll get over it. You'll be feeling pretty good soon. So you know where we can go?"

"Fuck you, Jim-Jim. *Yes*, I know where to go. My friend Stacie's. It's like five minutes from here, in a mobile home park downtown. That is *the* place."

"Yeah?"

"Yeah."

The 60 and 91 freeways meet and do one of those complicated handshakes in the middle of Riverside. From there we exited onto Mulberry Street, and in a couple of minutes we were pulling up to the black gate of the mobile home park. Stacie buzzed us in. I'd never been to a trailer park before, and I was surprised at how normal and suburban it seemed. I'd assumed we were going to a trailer park like the ones in the movies, with tiny homes on wheels parked randomly on tiny plots of dead grass, each with a broken-down barbeque grill and a few stolen bikes; but instead Wendy and I were driving down narrow, smoothly paved lanes with an annoying number of speed bumps. The homes looked remarkably like real houses, only smaller and more rectangular; each had its own small backyard and a driveway with an awning. A few of the homes' windows, however, were eerily blocked out by nailed-up bedding or rugs.

After pulling into the driveway we walked in without knocking, and then Wendy introduced me to Stacie. Her appearance surprised me even more than the park's had. Since she was Wendy's friend, I'd expected punk-rock garb, tattoos, heavy eyeliner—something outrageous—but instead Stacie wore a plain T-shirt, tan capri pants, and glasses with gray frames. About five foot nine with wide hips and long arms, she had straight black hair that fell about halfway down her back. Her face was plain and boxy. She wasn't wearing makeup, and her skin looked coarse. Neither pretty nor ugly, in her early thirties, she seemed to have prematurely given up on the beauty race.

After the introductions Stacie led us from the living room through the master bedroom to the bathroom. Inside, there was a long, cream-colored double-sink counter, grimy and strewn with used cottons and translucent splotches of dissolved meth, and a Jacuzzi tub with an uncomfortable edge, where in the months to come I would sit and fix my shots. The toilet was located conveniently off to the side in an alcove. The smell was of both meth smoke and alcohol swabs: Stacie used to be a nurse, and she often swabbed her neck before shooting up in it. She kept the meth and needles on a shelf above the toilet in a small red lockbox which opened with a dial and a lever, like a child's toy chest.

Stacie took down the red box while Wendy and I silently removed our belts. After the shots were ready, Stacie offered to hit me. I said okay, tied off, and gave her my arm. Trying a new drug is always scary, but I forced myself to watch as Stacie stuck me with the needle. She pulled back on the plunger and then, once my blood shot through the chamber, slammed it home. I ripped off the belt. There was a tickle in my throat, and for a second I couldn't breathe. Grabbing at the counter, I doubled over and made a sort of noiseless, hollow cough. It felt even better than I'd expected, but at the same time the intensity of it caught me by surprise—like swimming in a rough ocean, enjoying it, and then all of a sudden you get taken under, crushed and tumbled, and you realize that you can't surface until it lets you. I dropped to the floor, eyes fluttering. I rolled my head against the thin, artificial-wood wall, mouthing the words "Holy shit. Holy shit." Parched, I could taste the speed.

That night, after Wendy dropped me off at the sober-living, I masturbated more than a dozen times. Lying in bed, watching a porno on my laptop computer, I would come and five minutes later be horny again. Throughout the night I must have watched the same DVD five times. I only ever stopped it when I was scared that somebody was outside my door: At three, four in the morning I would hear a squeak and flip the computer closed and then lie there, listening to myself breathe, until I became horny enough to start over again.

I had heard this discussed at GSL: the incredible sex drive, the paranoia. There was even slang for the different compulsive and paranoid behaviors: tweaking, rooting, and sketching. Sketching is meth-induced hallucinatory paranoia. Flipping the computer closed, tiptoeing to the door and putting my ear against it, then kneeling and peeking under it for feet, as if somebody were really trying to catch me jerking off—that was sketching. Mildly.

The next time Wendy and I went to Stacie's, I discovered tweaking. High and wanting to get higher, I was sitting on the bathroom floor looking for a vein. I tied myself off and a couple of veins popped up near the crook of my arm. I felt one, then the other—they were both plump and deep—then I felt each of them again. There was no difference between the two, but for some reason, as if I were comparing brands of cold medicine in a pharmacy, I couldn't make a decision. I ran my fingers along them, all the way down to my wrist. That was no good; those veins are small and uncooperative. The vein on the back of my hand between thumb and forefinger pulsated, and I stroked it and then followed its path up my forearm, marking where it forked by pressing my fingernail hard against the skin. Of course the marks disappeared, so I did it again . . . and again . . . and again. The belt around my arm came loose. I let the blood flow for a minute and retied the belt. I was sweating. My neck was sore. Before I knew what had happened, hours had passed, maybe four, and I never even took the shot. In the end Wendy called me out of my trance and told me it was time to go.

And so: To tweak is to become compulsively enthralled in an activity that can be as simple as tying a shoe, cleaning a glass, or finding a vein. Wendy used to steal colored markers and sketch pads and spend entire nights coloring. Some women pick at their faces until they bleed. Some guys work on cars. I traced my veins.

Rooting is similar to tweaking—actually, it's a form of it in which the enthralling activity is looking for something. Often the thing doesn't exist. For example, I would see a piece of lint on the carpet that looked like a meth crystal, and the next minute I'd be on my hands and knees, picking up the couch, crawling under the bed, rooting all over the floor.

Over the next few weeks Wendy and I began getting high regularly. Soon Luke joined us, and then it wasn't long before we were kicked out of our sober-living—basically for being slobs, which was understood to imply drug use. Of course, this was not what I told my parents when I called. Instead, I said that the managers were stupid and bigoted—that the real reason I'd been kicked out was that I was Luke's friend and Luke was a convict. I told them that it was actually a good thing, because downtown Riverside was a bad neighborhood, a dead end. I told them that with Wendy's help I had already gotten another telemarketing job (which was true, though we almost never went)—a job in Norco, just around the corner from Riverside Community College's Norco campus—so the smartest thing would be for me to find a room to rent in Norco. Then I would be able to go to work and go to school and I wouldn't have to put up with any more sober-living nonsense. But first I needed money. I needed money to stay at a motel for a few days, and for a car. Yes, a car. I had everything all lined up, just as I'd promised—school, job, safe place to stay—but now that I'd been in California for a little while, I knew that it was impossible to get around without a car. Without one I was bound to lose my job and be late for classes. Please. Nothing too expensive. I was starting a new life, couldn't my parents help me out?

Of course they could. They sent me fifteen hundred dollars for a 1988 Toyota Celica and additional cash for a room at a motel by the 91 freeway in La Sierra. I suppose I sounded convincing because I believed what I was saying: I still had good intentions. We all did, actually. Luke checked in to the motel with me (my impression was his girlfriend's parents didn't want him staying at their house anymore), Wendy joined us that night with some meth, and often when we weren't shooting up we were talking about how we all needed to start going to work and being responsible again.

We ended up staying at the motel together for about a week. There were only two beds in the room, though, and on the first night Luke made his intentions clear by lying on one and pretending to snore, supine and spread-eagled: no room for a bed buddy. So Wendy and I shared.

The first time, I laughed and grabbed her around the waist, aggressively pulling her into a spooning position, doing my best to appear comfortable being so close to her—though actually I was intimidated. The casual intimacy seemed so adult, something with which I *should* have been familiar; but it didn't take long for me to start enjoying it, though. She was bigger than I was, with a wide, inviting back and soft skin, doughy like a baby's. Pressing against her, I felt her warmth on my cheek, and then I began to enjoy it so much that whenever I shifted or moved or found a new place to rest my arm, on her hip or above it in the dip below her breasts, I felt that I was risking something, as if she were a snappish stepparent, eager to reprimand me and take away my newfound pleasure. But she never stirred. I nestled the side of my face in the diamond below the back of her neck and between the tops of her shoulder blades, gently rocking with the rhythm of her breathing. Throughout that week it was understood that when we spent nights together, we snuggled.

What I enjoyed even more, though, was the seediness of the motel. At night, when Luke, Wendy, and I parked the car and walked to the room in our khakis and string T-shirts, tatted up, we passed people hanging outside their rooms who were obviously there to get high. Some alone, some in groups, they drank beer, shifting shadily and sometimes nodding at us. It was especially fun when Luke or Wendy would make a wisecrack, like, "Check out Cheech Marin over there," or "Whoa, buddy, no more coffee for you," or "What happened to that dude's dome?" The familiarity of my friends' banter, their casualness as we passed these motel hoods, made me feel comfortable, and I would laugh and stick my chest out a little.

But everybody was scared of the cops. The motel we were staying at was a hot spot. Its management didn't seem to care who their tenants were, and it was cheap and close to the 91 freeway, so the rooms were packed with junkies. And yet La Sierra wasn't Rubidoux, or Colton, or even downtown Riverside. It was more upscale—there were malls and shopping plazas—and our motel was only a quarter mile from the town's tourist attraction, an amusement park called Castle Park. As far as the police were concerned, tweakers, tourists, and shoppers shouldn't mix, and so they regularly raided rooms and stopped suspicious characters in the parking lot.

On maybe the third night, Wendy stayed over at her sober-living and Luke started sketching. He turned quiet and started pacing back and forth, sticking his head out the door, shushing me even when I hadn't said anything. I hardly noticed him, though, since I was caught up staring at myself in the mirror, having lost about five pounds in the past few days. I stared straight on, in profile, quite taken with myself, until about midnight, when a bottle broke outside.

"Shhh!" Luke hissed.

"Dude, it's just a fucking bottle," I said.

"Shhh!"

He stood frozen, listening with his neck taut, like a woodland animal trying to place a snapped twig. Warily, he tiptoed to the door and slowly opened it. He poked his head out, looked both ways, and then shut it, locked and chained and dead-bolted it.

"Somebody out there?" I asked.

"No," he said.

But the fact didn't seem to comfort him. Standing sideways, he ducked his head a few inches to get in line with the peephole.

"Luke," I said, "I'm sure it's no problem. Somebody just broke a bottle."

"Cops come to this motel all the time," he said distractedly, still glued to the peephole.

"Yeah, but they wouldn't come for us."

He turned to me.

"You don't think so?" he asked, with such sincerity—as if what I thought really mattered—that I couldn't keep from laughing.

"Yeah, Luke, I mean, why would they come for us? I mean, how could anybody know that we were doing dope in here?"

He looked puzzled, as though he were trying to answer my questions. He probably was. I was a little puzzled myself. Although I'd gotten a sense of sketching from beating off at the sober-living, I'd never seen anybody else sketch before, and now here was Big Daddy

Kay-Kay, the hardcore convict, scared and obsessing over nothing. I watched in amused disbelief as he hunkered down into a half squat and returned to the peephole.

I took a shot in the bathroom and returned to the mirror.

Hours later Luke was still at the peephole, shifting his weight uncomfortably from one foot to the other. Then for a moment he broke away and stole a glance around the room, pausing briefly to gaze at the far wall—a mirror set above a desk and swivel chair—before returning to his watch.

"Man, that chair would be nice," he said wistfully.

If he had asked me to bring him the chair, I would have, of course. But since he was sketching, that was impossible. Lost in paranoid fantasies, he barely knew that I was in the room. At the time I thought it was bizarre and a little funny. Now I wish I had brought him the chair.

The following morning Wendy returned to the motel with a bottle of bleach. She had hepatitis C, we had only one needle, and according to junkie lore, bleach kills everything. A few rinses and we felt responsible. We were out of meth, though. So, after pouring some bleach into an Aquafina water bottle and handing it to me, Wendy told us to get in the car; she was taking us to Patti's house, introducing us to her connection.

Outside, the sun hurt my eyes. I'd been up for three days shooting meth, and my body ached. I was lightheaded, spaced out, fucked up. Getting into the car, I realized I was thirsty. I began to unscrew the Aquafina water bottle, but stopped myself with an I-can't-believe-I-almost chuckle when I noticed the slight discoloration.

We drove across the freeway overpass and past the La Sierra Metrolink train station, then made a left and took a few turns in a middle-class suburban neighborhood. Patti's house was on a street corner. An eight-foot fence around the side yard extended to within an inch of the sidewalk. We pulled around to the front and parked across the street. A chicken ran across the lawn. The grass was dead, full of dirt patches, and littered with greasy tools and a few baby toys. In the driveway there was a small, pale-green trailer home with its curtains drawn. It was connected to the house by a mess of cables running through the garage.

Mouth parched, I stepped out of the car, stared briefly at the house, and took a swig from the Aquafina bottle. Nothing will rip you out of dreaminess faster than physical pain, especially in your mouth. And what a pain. Searing flashes of acrid chemical burn. Reeling, I bent over and dropped my jaw. The bleach fell on the pavement in spotted clumps.

"No, you didn't . . . ," said Wendy.

"Rinse!" was all I could get out.

Laughing, Wendy hurried us to the door, then knocked once before pushing it open. When it thudded into the wall, its handle landed in a well-established hole. A step forward and we were in the den, inhaling clouds of meth smoke. There were people, couches, and a television to our right; a messy kitchen with newspapers on the floor in front of us; and a cluttered hallway to our left. My mouth was somehow numb and on fire at the same time.

"Patti, he's gonna go to the bathroom," said Wendy to a woman sitting on the longest of three tan couches arranged in an open rectangle. "He needs to wash his mouth out—he drank bleach."

Patti, in her fifties, was wearing a faded baggy T-shirt and shorts. She looked a bit like a miniature troll—very short, with a potbelly and a sharp nose. Her face was pale and lined with wrinkles, her hair short, gray, and dry. She leaned forward over a thick oak coffee table and dipped a pipe into a mound of meth.

"He . . . drank . . . bleach," she repeated, deadpan.

On one of the smaller couches was a younger woman, short, with black hair and a mocha complexion, weighing a bag of meth on a digital scale. "Well, what the hell did he do that for?" she asked.

"I don't know," said Wendy. "You'd have to ask him."

"Who is he?" Patti whispered, as though I weren't there.

"Oh, that's my friend Jimmy from New Jersey I was telling you about."

"And he drank bleach," said Patti.

"Yeah—well, I don't think he actually swallowed it—and this is my other friend, Luke."

Wendy pointed me down the hall. On the way I stepped over two, three, four Pomeranian dogs, one of whom nipped at me and barked as I closed the bathroom door. The floor was littered with newspapers and soda cans and cardboard tubes from the insides of toilet-paper rolls, and in the corners were bundles of damp clothes. I rinsed my mouth, gargled, spat, rinsed again. The water did nothing. I hadn't just put a foul taste in my mouth; I'd burned layers and layers of mucous membrane. I stood, staring into the mirror, sloppy and unhappy, halfheartedly cupping water with one hand and splashing it toward my mouth, watching my shirt get wet.

Wendy knocked on the door; I gathered myself and let her in. She asked if I was okay, and I told her that I was, that my mouth was just a little fucked up. Then she took out two needles, and we each did a shot before walking back to the den, navigating past the dogs in the hallway. We sat on the couch, and Wendy introduced me to Patti and her friend, and then I had to explain—as cheerfully as I could, because there was no sympathy in this room—why I had drunk bleach.

"I was fucked up," I said.

Everybody laughed.

I fell quiet after that, worried that I'd somehow permanently scarred my mouth, while Patti packed and lit a bowl full of speed and then passed it to Wendy.

The room was filthy. Whenever I moved my feet, I felt the granular scrape of dirt on the wood floor. Even in the dim light I could see the thick coat of dust on the TV and the coffee table. And this was the cleanest room in the house. Beyond the den there was so much trash that it took me a while to realize what I was looking at: piles taller than men, looming over the far couch, *occupying* the dining room. Busted furniture, tattered rugs, broken toys, old clothes, jars, cardboard boxes, dresser drawers, newspapers, rusted trinkets. The trash extended through the kitchen to a sliding glass door that led to the backyard, where there were larger piles reaching all the way out to the fence.

Once the bowl was finished, Wendy asked me if I wanted to buy some speed from Patti. I did, a fat twenty sack, which I thanked her for, distractedly. Between the trash and the bleach I was overwhelmed—so overwhelmed that it wasn't until about a week later, when I stopped by Patti's alone for another sack, that I realized I'd been given a crystal meth connection.

CHAPTER 3. BABYSITTING MEGAN

We all checked out of the motel when Wendy found me a room to rent in Norco for four hundred dollars a month. Luke, needing a place to stay, called one of our old counselors from GSL, who ran a sober-living on Mission Avenue in Riverside. The counselor had an available room, but Luke didn't have any money, so I gave him a couple hundred dollars when Wendy and I dropped him off (in my car, since Wendy's Mazda wouldn't start). Then we drove to Norco, to my room, and paid the first month's rent.

The homeowner was an immensely fat Mongolian woman in her fifties, with thin lips and strikingly white skin. As I carried in my stuff—a trash bag full of clothes and a laptop computer—she told me in slightly choppy English that the last boarder, a nice girl, had kept strange hours and had nailed a blanket over the only window in the room, blocking all light from the outside. "I think this girl's on drugs," she said.

"Yeah, they do that," I volunteered, proud of my newly acquired expertise. "They call it 'sketching'—paranoia. Crystal meth."

"So you know about this?"

"I know about this."

She began to speak, then stopped. There was a pause. I had already paid the first month's rent.

"I mean, I don't *do* it," I said. "I just know about it. I used to do it, a little bit, some time ago, but not anymore. I'm a student."

I waved my hand vaguely in the direction of Riverside Community College.

"When's the last time you use drugs?" she demanded, but a nervous smile belied her aggressive tone. She was an immigrant, not used to asking questions, while I, a rich American kid, felt as entitled as . . . a rich American kid.

"It's been years now," I said. "I'm in recovery."

I had an impulse to reach into my pocket and show her the Narcotics Anonymous coin that had been given to me at my graduation ceremony from GSL, but I had lost it months ago.

"That's what the last girl said. She says, 'I am in recovery,' and I believe her."

"Well, all I can do is promise you," I said, smugly ending the conversation.

I didn't even feel bad about lying, having convinced myself, as liars often do, that the lies were merely technical—that it was all *essentially* true. Even though I'd shot up every other day for the past month, I still planned on going to school in the fall. Since junkies don't go to school, I wasn't a junkie. I wasn't a junkie, so I was telling the truth. Besides, all she really wanted to know was that I wasn't going to steal from her.

In a short while I would have a simpler way to rationalize my lies. The day after I moved into my room, Wendy and I drove to her sober-living in Glen Avon and discovered that she had been kicked out for failing a drug test, and that the sober-living manager had forwarded the results to her parole agent, who now wanted to see her ASAP. Wendy had used a drink sold in head shops that's designed to clean your system of drugs. Obviously it hadn't worked, despite the double-your-money-back guarantee. After she stopped crying in the driveway, I was able to make her laugh by asking if she thought her parole agent would be willing to a write a note to the company as proof of the product's failure. We packed all of her things into my car. Then Wendy called the parole office and was told that if she turned herself in right away, she would only have to do a few months at the CRC correctional facility, which happened to be in Norco, only a few miles from my new room. We each did another shot, and then I drove her to the parole office. On the way, she asked me if I would send her money in prison. Of course I would. She also asked if I would send her a package of food, clothes, toiletries—she wasn't exactly sure what the prison allowed, but she would call me at Stacie's in a few weeks and let me know. There was another thing: Would I pay part of Stacie's phone bill so that she would accept Wendy's collect calls? Of course I would. I would watch her things, and send her money and a package, and accept her phone calls, because she was my best friend and I loved her. At the parole office we hugged. Then she went back to prison.

Now I had a mission that would justify everything that needed justifying. My best friend was in prison, and I needed money to take care of her—that is what I told myself the next day when I called my parents and asked for more money. They weren't pushovers this time. I'd gone through a lot of money quickly, so they wanted proof that I really had a job; they understood that I couldn't support myself, but they wanted to know what I was doing with my time. So I took one of my few paycheck stubs to Kinko's and altered the date, dollar amount, and check number before faxing it to my parents. And I didn't feel guilty when they sent me the money (and a cell phone so they could reach me), because I needed it for Wendy.

I also needed to stop by Stacie's house for Wendy, to arrange the deal regarding Wendy's collect calls from prison. I called and then drove over and paged Stacie from the black gate. She buzzed me in, but when I knocked on the door, nobody answered. In the past, whenever I had come here with Wendy, she had always walked in without knocking. Should I now? The door was unlocked. I pushed it open and stood still for a minute, suddenly aware that there might just be a world of difference between coming to a place like this with Wendy and coming here alone. At least I was coming *for* Wendy. I passed through the cluttered foyer, the washer and dryer on my left. In the living room a blond-haired, shirtless man with a prison tattoo running across his ribs of a near-naked woman on a horse nodded at me and said, "What's up?" He was lean, about six feet tall. There was laughter coming from behind the bedroom door.

Alone on the couch sat a nine-year-old girl with lightly freckled cheeks and red hair that was so light that her eyebrows were almost invisible.

"I'm Jimmy," I said to the man.

"Yeah, from New Jersey, right? You're Wendy's friend, taking care of her while she's down. Stacie was telling me. That's cool. I'm Danny White from Riverside. Wendy's my homegirl."

Danny was handsome, with short hair and a closely cropped goatee. On his way out he put his flannel shirt on—slowly, so that I could stare at his huge tattoo. He then gave me his cell phone number, saying that if I needed help getting Wendy's stuff together I should give him a call. I thanked him and he left.

I was alone with the little girl. She was on the couch, staring at the television. Above the couch, hanging on the wall, there were portraits of her: one alone, a few with Stacie. There were other portraits too, in the same commercial style—glossy with a dreamy blue background—portraits of guys who looked like they'd just gotten out of prison. It was bizarre.

Stacie poked her head out of the bedroom.

"I thought that was you," she said. "This is Megan. My daughter."

Megan didn't turn from the TV.

"C'mon in," Stacie said.

In the bedroom the smoke stung my eyes and fogged my vision, but I adjusted quickly. A dark-haired girl was sprawled on the bed, lighting a pipe and ignoring me.

I asked Stacie about accepting Wendy's phone calls, and she said I could accept as many as I wanted so long as I paid her back. Okay. Simple enough. What else? I asked if she could get me forty dollars' worth of meth. She could; she just had to run around the corner. Did I mind waiting here? No, of course not. I asked her if she would spot me enough for a shot until she returned, and she said she would; she even had a fresh needle.

We went into the bathroom and made up two shots. She hit me first, and then, as I sat on the floor rushing, I watched her hit herself in the neck, the only vein she still trusted. Standing on tiptoe, she held her breath and leaned over the counter, bringing her face inches from the mirror. Body taut, eyes fixed in perfect concentration, she contorted her head to the side and puffed her neck out like a frog. With her left hand she probed the targeted skin; with her right she held the needle, poised for insertion. But she couldn't find the vein in time—couldn't maintain the tension—and, with a frustrated exhalation, she fell away from the mirror and let her heels drop to the floor. She shook her head and took a few deep breaths, staring blankly at the sink. But in another instant she was at it again—feet arched, fingers probing, midriff pressed hard against the counter's edge. This time she found it. Blood burst into the chamber. She plunged it back into her neck and then swiftly pulled out the needle and set it down. Clutching the counter, staring at her dilated pupils in the mirror, she rolled her shoulders back and shuddered. Then, before I had even regained control of my breathing, she straightened up and gathered herself. A veteran.

"Whew . . . wow . . . that was good," she said. "All right, I'm gonna go get that—you wait here."

"Okay," I nodded.

"Are you all right?"

"Yeah, yeah, I'm fine. It's just . . . good."

"But you're all right?"

"Yeah, definitely."

"'Cause, don't forget, Megan's out there."

"Oh. Okay."

"I'll be right back—she'll watch TV. Just don't let her come back here. She won't, but don't let her."

"Okay."

Stacie left me in the bathroom while she and the dark-haired girl said bye to Megan. They slammed the door on their way out. I sat on the floor, breathing, blinking, rushing. Stacie's car started, then sputtered down the street. The rush had hit me hard, settling in my crotch—I wished I was back in my room in Norco with my laptop—but I kept my pants on, didn't even rub myself. I could hear the TV through the wall. It was about ten p.m.

After ten minutes or so I decided hiding was silly, and I walked into the room and took a seat on the couch with Megan, at the far end. You never really know how high you are until you're supposed to act straight. My pulse was pounding in my ears. I was sure that my face was twitching uncontrollably. I pressed my lips tightly together and tried not to blink. Megan didn't look at me, though. She was absorbed in the TV, and I quickly pretended to be too.

Hours passed. Stacie didn't have cable, so by about midnight there was nothing on but infomercials. Every time a light flashed from outside, I lifted the blinds and peered into the street. Usually there wasn't even a passing car—just a light being turned on in one of the other mobile homes, or maybe nothing at all. I would pretend that I'd gotten up for water or to go to the bathroom; then, sitting down, I would sneak a glance at Megan to make sure she hadn't noticed me peeking through the blinds, window-sketching.

Stacie had said she was going "around the corner." I wondered if she had been arrested or gotten into a car accident. What would I do if she had? I didn't even have a phone number for her. I couldn't just leave, could I? Leave this girl sitting on the couch when something might have happened to her mother? In a few hours I would probably be sober enough to call the cops, but when should I call? At four in the morning? At what point was this an emergency? And if I did call, if a cop came to the house—who the hell was I?

Suddenly Megan turned to me. She asked me to make her punch. She said there was Minute Maid in the freezer and a pitcher under the sink. She liked it sweet but not too sweet.

I found a wooden spoon in a drawer and used it to break up the frozen concentrate in the glass pitcher. I broke it up thoroughly and then spent some time mixing the juice, trying to make the feeling of responsibility last. It was too sweet for me, but she liked it. This too made me feel adult and responsible.

"Good," she said, smacking her lips. "It's good."

"Shouldn't you be in bed?" I asked.

"No."

I thought about telling rather than asking her to go to bed, but decided against it.

At around two thirty a.m., as the illusory lights from the street became more frequent, I asked her if she was all right, and she looked at me as though she hadn't the slightest idea of what I was talking about. I got up and sat back down. I paced around, looked in the refrigerator, and peeked through the blinds again, slyly so she wouldn't notice. She was watching a commercial for some abs machine—"just fifteen minutes a week"—and the tinny noise from the TV echoed throughout the trailer and exaggerated the emptiness. I needed to do something. I went into my pocket, found the number Danny White had given me, went into the kitchen, and called him.

"What's up—who's this?" he said.

"It's Jimmy from New Jersey," I said. "We just met at Stacie's."

"Oh, yeah, what's up? Everything all right?"

"Sort of. I mean, I'm calling you 'cause Stacie went out to get something, you know what I mean? She said she was goin' around the corner, and she's been gone for like five hours. So . . . I don't really know what to do."

"She took off with your money?"

"Well, yeah, but I don't even care about that. I mean, it's hardly any money. It's that she left me alone with her daughter, Megan. It's almost three in the morning and I don't know this girl and I don't know if her mother's coming back or what, you know what I mean? So I was wondering if you had some way of reaching her."

"That's fucked up," Danny said. "Here, let me see if I can find her. I'll call you back."

When I came back to the couch, Megan asked me where her mom was.

"She'll be back any minute," I said. "She's just at a friend's house."

"You don't know where she is."

"Of course I do."

"No, you don't!" She was shouting at me. "If you knew, you wouldn't be looking out the window every fifteen seconds!"

I looked at her dumbly.

"Who'd you just call?" she demanded.

"A friend of mine."

"No, you didn't. You were calling to find out where my mom is because you don't know."

She was looking at me crossly—that playfully irritated look kids use to mock and mimic their parents. But she was serious.

"Who? What? What do you mean, who did I call? I called whoever I wanted to call. It's none of your business who I called." I tried to laugh. "Look, I'm sure she'll be home soon."

"No, you aren't!" she shouted. "This is ridiculous! I'm supposed to spend the weekend with my mom and she stays out all night! I should have stayed with my grandmother! You know what . . . I'm gonna call her!"

"No, no, your mom will be home soon. You can't call your grandmother—it's three in the morning—"

"It's three in the morning and I'm all alone in a house with some guy I don't even know!"

"I'm a friend of your mom's—"

"I don't know you!"

There was a long pause. I saw the lights of a car driving by but managed to stop myself from looking out the window. I didn't know what Megan's calling her grandmother meant, but I felt compelled to stop it from happening. I didn't know what any of it meant. A child was yelling at me, and though I didn't know why, I felt that I deserved it.

"Look, just give her another half hour," I said. "If she's not home by then—"

"Fifteen minutes."

"No, come on, give her a half hour—"

"Fifteen minutes!"

She looked at the clock and then at me, making sure I saw her check the time.

We bargained for the next hour. Every time I thought she might have forgotten about her threat, she would call out the time remaining in the countdown. When the countdown ended, I would plead for more time, and she would whine, "You said ten minutes half an hour ago!"

Finally, at four thirty a.m., a car pulled in the driveway with a definitive scrape of metal against concrete. I felt like an idiot: I'd been jumping at the window every time a squirrel farted, as if I'd never heard the distinctive sound of a car pulling into a driveway. Car doors slammed. Stacie and the dark-haired girl walked in, followed by a guy I'd never seen before. They were all talking loudly, cheerfully. Megan didn't even turn to look at them.

I wanted to be angry with Stacie. I had imagined that there would be a confrontation when she arrived, that Megan would run to her and ask where she'd been, or that Stacie would immediately launch into an apologetic explanation. But clearly that wasn't going to happen. Laughing, Stacie nodded at me, and the whole party headed toward the bedroom. I was the only person who seemed to think that anything was wrong. Even Megan didn't seem to care. She just stared at the TV. Part of me wanted to protest and make Stacie aware of the anxiety she had caused, to somehow grab that anxiety and show it to her before it was all swept away by the happy chatter. But part of me also wanted to just go with it, to shoot the meth Stacie had probably just returned with, to stop caring.

Stacie signaled for me to follow her into the bathroom. She handed me back my forty dollars and introduced me to the guy she'd returned with, a Samoan named Maki, who sold me a generous bag of meth before doing a shot himself and then leaving. Once he was gone, Stacie began preparing her own shot and handed me a needle. The dark-haired girl stayed in the bedroom and resumed smoking her bowl.

"You said fifteen minutes," I said, hands shaking in anticipation as I crushed up the speed.

"Yeah, Maleah's parents called and we had to go by her house," she said flatly.

Stacie had been doing meth for so long that it was usually hard to tell when she was high, but now it was obvious. She kept looking around the room, speaking in short bursts as if she were allotted a fixed amount of time for talking and didn't want to waste any of it.

"That was hours ago," I said. "I mean, Megan's been worried—"

"Oh, she's fine," Stacie said. "You want me to hit you?"

I did.

In the following weeks I began buying meth from Patti in La Sierra, and soon I discovered the reason for the piles of trash. I called her house and her son—Garrett, a convict with a tough reputation—answered the phone. He told me that she wasn't home but I could come over and wait for her. She should be back soon, she was out Dumpster diving. I didn't know what he meant by 'Dumpster diving,' but Garrett didn't sound like he wanted to chat. When I got there—a ten-minute drive from my room in Norco—Patti had already pulled up in her Silverado, its bed loaded with junk.

"Ha!" she shouted when she saw me. "You're just in time to help me unpack. This here's the good stuff!"

"That's why I'm here," I said.

"I know it. Grab that big bag over there."

Dumpster diving is essentially rooting, except on a much larger scale. Patti would get high and then drive all over Riverside, stopping in front of people's houses and at Dumpsters at the back of stores, throwing whatever looked valuable into the truck. On meth everything looks valuable.

I carried in trash bags (mostly full of clothes), a child's toy chair, and a tiny, broken chest of drawers. Inside, seated on the couch and surrounded by her bounty, Patti lit a pipe and began inspecting each item. She declared most things to be junk, then threw them over the couch and into the dining room. Others, she told me, were "nice" or "a find." She would set those aside for an hour or so, until one by one she inspected each of them again and said, "On second thought . . ." In the end everything joined the piles.

I didn't mind helping Patti unpack or even waiting while she sorted through everything. I liked Patti. She sold me speed at incredibly cheap prices, since I was taking care of Wendy while she was in prison, and a few times she had insisted that I sleep on her couch when I'd been up too long to drive. Also, it's a general rule that if you do something personal with a drug dealer before buying the drugs—anything, really, other than stopping by or meeting on a street corner—you get a better deal.

She gave me an exceptional deal once, when I came over and she was dry and she invited me to accompany her to meet her dealer. We drove to a hardware store with a huge parking lot, and Patti left me in the truck for a few minutes while she got in and out of a black Nissan Maxima. On our way back she took a different route, avoiding main roads. I found this to be smart of her, professional, but then abruptly she pulled over, hopped out, and began throwing clear plastic bags that had been set by the curb into the truck bed. "Come on!" she shouted, and I got out to help her.

"This is the good stuff!" she said excitedly.

To my surprise it really did look like good stuff: mostly shoes and clothes, not too worn.

"Nicely done, Patti," I said, as we climbed back in the truck.

"That looked like the *good* stuff!"

We were on a narrow two-lane road in one of the richer neighborhoods of Riverside, lush with palm trees and green grass. There were large modern houses, fancy brick, with long driveways. The lawns on both sides sloped upward, so we were driving in a shallow valley. As we drove, I noticed that there were clear plastic bags at the bottom of many of the driveways and that their contents were similar to those of the bags we had just thrown in the truck bed. Sneakers, especially, bulged.

"Patti, I think those were donations," I said.

"I think so too," she replied sulkily.

But it was clear she had no intention of giving them up.

Soon I received my first phone call from Wendy at Stacie's, and after she yelled at me for not having been to work since she went to prison, Wendy asked me to take down a list of things to send in her package. I was supposed to hold on to this list for about a month, since Wendy couldn't actually receive a package until then. But I would always lose it and have to take down a new one every time Wendy and I spoke.

Then I would hang up the phone and put the list in my pocket, and Stacie and I would go into her bathroom, where she would take down the red box and we would get high. Usually, I supplied the dope and she supplied the needles. Of course this was an unfair trade, but Stacie would make up for it by selling some of my dope for me. For example, a friend of hers would stop by and ask where he could buy a twenty bag, Stacie would give me his money and then take half of what Patti had given me for twenty dollars and give it to him. The bags Patti sold me were so generous that Stacie's friends were always happy. Eventually, as I got to know them, I began selling to them directly. Then I started buying larger quantities from Patti.

"So for the half ounce you're gonna give me two hundred now and another two hundred when?" Patti asked.

We were sitting on the couches, meth on the coffee table, Pomeranians at our feet. There were, I'd learned, eleven of them: Gremlin, Checkers, Suzy, Suzy Black, Champ, Melvin, Princess, Jaws, Fred, Bam-Bam, and Mr. Max.

"I should have it within a week," I said. "Two at the latest."

"That's cool."

"I'd be good with a quarter now, but you know I gotta start getting this package together for Wendy."

"Jimmy, I know you're taking care of Wendy. I trust you. You don't have to keep on saying it. But I do have to ask: You've been around for a very short time—how do you know you can move it?"

"I'm good at meeting people."

back in the house but refusing to go. She didn't want me around Garrett. They didn't get along; they professed to anybody who'd listen that they hated each other (though it was understood that if you stole from Patti, you'd have to deal with Garrett). Patti always said that she would kick Garrett out if it weren't for Sonny, who evidently still had the last word (probably because his pension paid the bills), even though he lived in a trailer in the driveway. Sonny had moved out of the house some time ago. He didn't get high—just drank—and I guess the meth, dogs, and trash had at some point become too much. Now he was walking back to the trailer, telling Garrett how fucking stupid he was: "You want the cops out here again?" He slammed the trailer door. I took a step toward Garrett and Patti shook her head and went back inside.

"What was that about?" I ventured.

Balding but still handsome, Garrett was about five-foot-nine, wide and brawny, with no tattoos. He liked saying that tattoos didn't make you tough.

"Nothing," he said. "He's just a fucking punk. You see the way he was covering up?"

"Yeah, I hate it when they do that," I said. "It's frustrating—you can't get a solid shot in."

"Exactly," said Garrett. "That's it—it's frustrating. He's a punk. He tries to tell me that he's keeping our stereo. We both came up on it, fuck what he's saying, and now he says he wants to keep it. So I say pay me for it, fool. And he says no, like I'm just gonna get beat."

"Are you serious? What did he think you were gonna do?"

"I don't know. He knows I can whoop him."

We were talking back and forth, excited, he from having just been in a fight, and I from talking with him.

over him: He turned silent; his eyes dropped.

my friend, too," he said. After a pause, he looked

"He's around here all the time. You've seen him her

me to confirm that Dwight was in fact his friend.

"All the time," I said. "Almost every time I come here. ...g on the truck and shit."

Between buying dope at Patti's and selling it at Stacie's, shopping for Wendy's package and shooting crystal meth in my room, I didn't even realize that I wasn't doing any of the things I had planned to, that I didn't have a job and I wasn't going to school. I would start the day with one goal, buying jeans or shampoo for Wendy, but to do that I would first need to get money. I would need to sell some drugs, or buy some drugs so that I could sell them; and of course when it came to drugs, things always got complicated and ended up taking much longer than expected, because everybody involved was tweaking. Even if I did manage not to lock my keys in my car or lose track of time masturbating, even if I showed up at Patti's at the agreed time to pick up an eight ball, she would likely have forgotten and be out Dumpster diving. Or her connection would be missing, out tweaking somewhere. Shampoo would have to wait. And wait it would, for days, because when it came down to it I was in no rush. I had quickly come to enjoy hanging out at Patti's and Stacie's.

And then, maybe a month after the first time, Stacie left me alone with Megan again. The previous night I'd crashed in Stacie's empty

, slept maybe twelve hours; when I woke, I walked into the
.itchen and Megan was there and Stacie wasn't. It was morning, a daz-
zling day, sunlight streaming into the kitchen. Since I'd hung out with
Megan a few times over the past month, when she'd visited from her
grandparents', it wasn't an urgent situation. Not yet anyway. Megan
told me that Stacie had run to the store for milk or something, and I
poured myself a glass of water.

"I have a question for you," said Megan.

"Sure. What?" I said.

"What's in the box?"

She looked up at me innocently. Her mouth was half open, reveal-
ing the bottom row of her small, white, perfect teeth. She ran her
forefinger along the edge of the kitchen counter.

I knew that it was all a game to her. I had learned, over the past
month, that in the course of growing up as Stacie's daughter Megan
had been exposed to far more of life-around-meth than I had. Years
before I came to Riverside, Stacie and Megan were living in Oregon
with Stacie's fiancé, Jacob. Jacob had a best friend named Steve who
was like an extended family member to Stacie and Megan. One night
Steve stayed up too long on speed. He sketched out and stabbed Jacob
to death. Megan was home. Some years after that, while Wendy and
I were at GSL, Wendy was given a day pass to attend the funeral of a
friend; that friend, Evan, had been shot through the lung and killed
in Stacie's TV room by Megan's father, Darrin. This happened in front
of Megan.

I knew that by now chances were that Megan knew exactly what
Mommy and her friends did in Mommy's bathroom. But with those

light green eyes looking up at me, with that mock-impatient tap of her tiny foot, it didn't really matter what I knew and didn't know about Megan.

"What box?" I said.

"The one above the toilet. The red one."

Slowly I began to recognize that this conversation was inescapable. A little girl had hit me with the most loaded question I'd ever been asked, before I'd even taken my morning piss. I stared at her, unable to fathom that I'd just been trapped. It was like being stung by a butterfly.

"The red one above the toilet . . . ," I repeated slowly.

"Yeah, you know it. I'll show you."

She started toward her mother's bedroom.

"No, no, that's all right. I know what you're talking about."

"So then what's in it?

"I don't know. I've never looked inside it. It's not mine."

I had three needles in the box, bought with Stacie from her diabetic friend.

"Well," she said, lowering her voice, then pausing for effect. She looked down and dabbed coquettishly at the floor with one of her tiny feet. "I've looked inside the box."

"Oh yeah?" I challenged her. "What's in it?"

"Well . . . it was like . . ."

Her voice was barely audible. She moved closer to me, and her face went from playfully mischievous to genuinely upset. All of a sudden she was acting as though I were an adult and she a child with something to confide. The shift was astonishing. Everything that I had assumed was tacitly understood between us—that she knew exactly what was in the box, and that she had, just two seconds ago, been screwing with me—none of that mattered anymore. She'd decided to change the game and I had to go along. You simply can't wink and say, "Come on, you know the deal," to a nine-year-old.

"It was like . . . pointy things," she said, sadly furrowing her brow.

Now I was supposed to intuit what these pointy things were.

"Pointy things?"

I shook my head and also furrowed my brow.

"Yeah, like . . . needles," she said.

"What? You mean, like, to inject yourself with?"

I started to make a clarifying demonstration with an imaginary needle on myself, but stopped short, remembering my track marks, and so I ended up stiffly working an invisible retractable pen in front of her face, saying, "Like this?"

"Yeah. What are they for?"

"I'm not really sure. I imagine medicine, if anything."

"My mom takes medicine?"

"I'm not really sure. I think so. I mean, I'm sure it's nothing bad."

Megan looked at me silently, seemingly sad and confused.

"You're sure it's nothing bad?" she asked.

"Yeah, of course."

"Promise?"

"Yeah, of course."

"Okay, but you have to promise me something else."

"What?"

"That you won't tell my mom I looked in the box."

I liked secrets, but what I liked even more was playing at the role of a responsible adult. I actually looked forward to telling Stacie, not because I wanted to show her what a bad parent she was, but because it would be serious, dramatic. The adults would be talking.

"Megan, I can't promise you that."

"Oh, c'mon, she'll get so mad at me. Please! She'll yell at me."

"Well, I will promise you that nobody's gonna yell at you."

"Promise?"

"Yeah, I promise she won't get mad."

CHAPTER 4. MAKI

I called my parents every week and continued sending them forged paycheck stubs so that they would keep sending me money. Also, since they valued creativity, I read them poems that I'd written in my room while tweaking. I didn't know the first thing about poetry, but I did think I was very smart—intellectually equipped to answer life's grander questions—and so I'd written page after page of highly abstract, richly ridiculous metaphoric maundering. Even before I'd begun doing meth, inventing bad metaphors had always made me feel smart. Provided no one actually scrutinized the metaphors, I could sustain my belief that I saw connections where nobody else did. On meth it got much worse: Every metaphor I came up with, no matter how meaningless, seemed apt and brilliant—in the same way, I imagine, that everything Patti came across while Dumpster diving seemed desirable. Garbage is, after all, garbage. But my parents wanted to encourage me, encourage my creativity, so they offered only the gentlest criticism. "It's good . . . it's great," they would say. "If you could make it just a little more . . . grounded." Then I would hit them up for more money.

I told them that Wendy had been unfairly sent back to prison for breaking curfew at her sober-living. She'd been doing her best, trying to get her life together, and the sober-living manager hadn't given her a chance, I said, playing on my parents' liberal sensibilities. I told them that I would need a little extra money this week so that I could send her a package in prison. *Did you know, Mom, they don't even give the prisoners shower shoes?*

I spent most of my money on drugs, a little on Wendy (I'd sent her a hundred dollars so that she could buy food and toiletries at the prison canteen, though I'd bought hardly any of the items on the list for her package); and occasionally Luke asked me to help him with the rent at his new sober-living. He didn't have a job, and his girlfriend was regularly giving him a hard time because he couldn't support their three-year-old daughter. I would stop by and Luke would be on the phone, his girlfriend shouting on the other end, using the word "diapers" in every sentence. "Oh, so you have time to go to the bar with your brother, but you can't come over here to change your baby's diapers? So you've got money to go hang out with your friend Jimmy, but you can't buy diapers for your kid?" Once, after he hung up the phone, Luke used the word on me.

"Dude, do you think I can borrow some money?" he asked. "I need to buy diapers for my kid."

"How much do you need?"

"Like a hundred bucks."

"How about I just buy you the diapers? I'll get you the biggest box they have."

"Dude," he said, "that's not the—"

"I'm fucking with you—I'll give you the money. You wanna get high?"

"Fuck it. Why not?"

Luke didn't approve of my new lifestyle, of my driving from dope house to dope house, selling meth to people I didn't know. But because he hit me up for money and occasionally got high with me, he couldn't protest too loudly. I would tell him about something crazy that had happened at Patti's, and he, bent over a line of meth, would just tell me to be careful. A few times, though, when we were high together, Luke ended up going with me to Stacie's. He said he wanted to watch my back, which would have been helpful—had he actually done it—because I was beginning to have trouble with Danny White, the convict I'd met the first time I babysat Megan.

Danny was at Stacie's all the time. He'd seen me selling meth there, and he was clearly resentful that I, a nineteen-year-old upstart from out of town, was doing so well in Riverside. Danny was in his late twenties; he'd grown up in Riverside. He wanted me to both look up to him and be scared of him. He was constantly telling me how serious this town was, and how it was a good thing that I was taking care of Wendy in prison; otherwise people he knew probably wouldn't let me operate so freely. I assumed he meant himself. He said that there was a loosely connected network of convicts in Riverside, a network with rules and arrangements. Stacie was a part of this network, and Stacie's mobile home was a "*convict* squatter pad," he told me, implying that I was getting a little too comfortable. The convict network meant that even though Danny didn't know Stacie very well, she would immediately welcome him and give him a bed until he got back on his feet. Then, once he made enough money selling meth and doing whatever else, he would look after Stacie and get her high. That, he said, was the way things worked.

But in spite of all his efforts to impress and intimidate me, I didn't look up to Danny, nor was I afraid of him. I saw him as a hustler, not a strong man. And so it wasn't until he began bringing a friend of his to Stacie's, a big Hispanic convict who called himself Big Manny from Fontana, that I felt intimidated and wished that Luke really would watch my back.

At Stacie's, however, Luke acted strangely. We would be getting high in the bedroom, talking with Danny and Stacie (Manny rarely spoke), and then all of a sudden Luke would leave. He would say he had to make a phone call or get a drink from the kitchen, and when I would come looking for him, he would be gone. Often he wouldn't return until morning, when he would walk in unannounced, holding either money or jewelry that he had not had before leaving. I assume he broke into houses, though I could never get an explanation out of him. He would say, "I just had to go, dude. Don't trip." It must have been a meth thing, a sort of thrill-seeking tweak.

Whatever it was, while Luke was gone, I would be left alone with Danny and Manny, and Danny would try to pressure me into going in with him on some dope—that is, he would want me to give him money and then wait at Stacie's for him to return with a bag for us to split. Of course I didn't want to do it, and the first few times, possibly because Luke could have returned at any moment, Danny didn't push very hard. He said I would be helping him out, insinuating that it would be disrespectful if I refused, but he didn't go further than that.

Ironically, it was when Luke was there that Danny finally convinced me to front him the money. Actually, he convinced Luke and then Luke convinced me. Danny had called my cell phone, asking me to meet him at Stacie's. He'd said that he wanted me to split a half ounce with him at four hundred dollars (a good deal), and that he would already have the dope, since his connect was willing to front it. Luke was with me at the time, so I drove right over to meet him. When I got to Stacie's, though, Danny said that his connect wouldn't front him the dope after all, and now he needed me to front him the money. He'd been up for a few days; he had a frantic, desperate look to him. When I told him I wasn't sure if I wanted to do it that way, he said that he'd already asked his connect to hold on to the half ounce, and that if I didn't chip in—as I'd said I would—he would look like a sucker, unable to come up with the cash. He might even lose the connect. Why, he asked, was I bullshitting him?

There were reasons to give Danny the money—I needed a half ounce, I didn't want him as an enemy—but the harder he pushed, the more I suspected he was trying to screw me. I was getting ready to say no and leave, when Luke, who knew I was conflicted, said he would sort it out for me. He called Danny aside to talk privately, and a few minutes later he told me to give Danny the money. He said that Danny had sworn "on his skin"—some sort of convict honor thing—that he would return with the dope. Luke said he was convinced that Danny wasn't lying and that if he was, Luke would handle it personally. I was not convinced, even with Luke's assurances, but if I had said so at that point, I would have been implying that I didn't have any faith in Luke. I gave Danny the money and he didn't come back.

At first Luke was furious, saying he would fulfill his promise and smash Danny as soon as he saw him, but then in the morning, when I dropped him off at his sober-living, Luke did what he always did the

morning after a night of using meth: he turned sullen, regretting having gotten high. He complained that I was getting him involved with
the wrong people. He had a family, he told me, and he didn't want to
go back to prison. He waited until the next time we saw each other to
ask for diaper money again.

Over the next few days at Stacie's I talked about what had happened constantly. I always talked about things that embarrassed me
(in this case that I'd been exposed as an amateur and—if I didn't fight
Danny the next time I saw him—a coward), as though if I used the
right words I could convince whoever was listening, as well as myself,
of a version of the story that would keep my image intact. One of the
first people I tried to convince was Maki, the Samoan. He was often at
Stacie's, selling meth or stolen checks or credit-card numbers.

"I don't even know what to do," I said to him. "I mean, I'm just
trying to put something together for Wendy; I'm not trying to get all
involved in shit out here. And Danny's supposed to be Wendy's homeboy. I thought he was cool."

"You don't know what to do," he repeated amusedly.

Maki—lean and muscular and about six feet tall—had a voice that
was surprisingly high and soft. A tattoo of vines, castles, demons, drag-
ons, and women sleeved his chest and shoulders like a breastplate.

"What do you mean, you don't know what to do?" he repeated.
"You gotta smash him. You can take Danny, right?"

He looked me over with his jet-black eyes, the same color as his
close-cropped hair.

"Yeah, you can take him," he said. "You got to anyway. Nobody's
gonna respect you if you don't. No girls are gonna respect you."

He surprised me with how nonchalant he was, with his indifference toward Danny, the way he could just say, "Yeah, you can take him," offhandedly giving me the benefit of the doubt. What confidence. I'd never heard him talk about smashing anybody before. He'd always been so polite, holding doors open and saying thank you and excuse me; when leaving Stacie's he would often thank her and everybody in the room for our hospitality.

"But that's the thing with this motherfucker," I said. "I wasn't trying to get involved in shit like this. I got charges back in New Jersey—I'm trying to lay low out here. But now this faggot, he's gonna have me doing some dumb shit. And that's the thing; I'm not trying to do that out here. Of course I'd try and smash him if I was back home, but all I'm trying to do out here is take care of my homegirl till I gotta go back."

"You're in So-Cal now," he said, not looking at me. "You gotta do what you gotta do."

That was the end of the conversation. I was not satisfied that I'd convinced him of anything.

After Maki left, Stacie, who'd been listening, as usual, told me she didn't want me starting anything with Danny.

"Jimmy, I'm worried about you," she said. "Wendy asked me to look out for you, and I don't want you getting into trouble out here. Promise me you're not gonna start anything."

Wendy had asked her to do no such thing and I knew it, but I didn't want to argue. I was gratified that she seemed to think I needed to be talked out of seeking revenge.

"So what am I supposed to do, just let him get away with it? That money was for Wendy—I need that shit."

"But you don't even know what happened."

"Oh, come on. Of course I do. What do you think happened?"

"I don't know, Jimmy. I don't care what happened. I just don't want you getting in any trouble; it's not worth it. I can help you get the money back."

"How?"

"I can actually, probably, get you a lot more than you lost, if what I'm thinking works."

"How?"

Stacie said she had checks, three stolen checkbooks, actually, lifted by a tweaker from somebody's mailbox and then traded to her for dope. She wanted to know if I had a checking account. I did, an empty one with Bank of America that my parents had insisted I set up when I got my first telemarketing job. I'd never used it, didn't even know how.

She wrote me three checks from the stolen books for about fifteen hundred dollars (a thousand for me, five hundred for her), and then gave me specific instructions. I was to deposit the checks at the bank counter, immediately withdrawing however much I was allowed to take before the checks cleared; then I was to withdraw the rest from an ATM. Finally, I should go to a different branch of the bank and close the account within three days.

"Three days," she said. "That's very important."

The idea, as she explained it to me—the absurd idea that Stacie must have guessed I would believe—was that if the checks went through and debited money from somebody's bank account, then I would somehow be safe from prosecution, all evidence of my involvement in the fraud having been eradicated when I closed the account. Having never cashed a check in my life, let alone committed check fraud, I had no idea that people got arrested for this sort of thing all the time. So it sounded good to me. Why wouldn't that work?

The other possibility was that the checks would bounce. Stacie said—and yes, I believed her—that if I closed the account within three days, that magic number, I would not be in debt. The bank would lose track of me, forget about the money.

The checks did bounce, luckily, and instead of being arrested for check fraud, I ended up merely owing the bank about fifteen hundred dollars. But I was in no position to confront Stacie, because when I got all that money, I shot a lot of dope and forgot about closing the account in three days. Of course it wouldn't have made any difference if I had closed the account, but try telling that to Stacie. I could hear her in my head: *You didn't follow instructions and now you want to blame me? I try to help you out for Wendy and you accuse me of taking advantage of you?*

Besides, I probably wouldn't have confronted her even if I had followed her instructions. I preferred to pretend that I had not been a sucker—that Stacie and I had been partners and I'd made off with a grand. Nobody needed to see my credit statement. Come to think of it, what did I care about my credit anyway?

And this way I didn't have to fight Danny. I'd gotten my money back, more actually than he made off with, so what did I care? I could pretend to believe the story he told when he returned to Stacie's, about how he'd had to go into hiding because gangs were hunting him.

"Jimmy," Danny said, "I would never just take off on you. I know you're taking care of my Wendy while she's down. That's not how we do it out here. This was some other shit. I'm just glad you got the money back so you can get that to my homegirl."

So everybody was happy (except my parents, who, months later, would pay my debt).

Maki was whispering on his cell phone, rubbing the back of his neck, pacing vigorously in Stacie's living room. Because he was sweating I should have known to at least shut up, if not go quietly into the other room: Maki, I'd been told, was a sketcher—somebody who, when he "sketches," becomes especially paranoid and volatile—and if a sketcher is sweating for no apparent reason, there's a good chance he's sketching. But I was too high to be reading any signs. A few days earlier I'd met a guy at Stacie's with whom I'd traded meth for some tar heroin. Now, having just done a shot of both, I was feeling numb and cocky.

Lori, Maki's girlfriend, was talking with Stacie by the bedroom door. White, with curly dirty-blond hair, she had thick thighs and wide hips and a face that, though handsome, looked hard and unforgiving.

Maki flipped the phone shut and prepared to leave, but he was too high to concentrate, and as he scanned the room for his things, he became visibly frustrated, even a little desperate.

"Hey, Maki," I said. "What was that you were saying on the phone? A teenth?"

"What?" he said.

He peered at me, not quite comprehending.

"Yeah," I said, "you told the guy you had a teenth. I was just wondering what that is. Some kind of denomination of dope?"

Maki peered at me for another moment as if I were out of focus. Then his face hardened. He took a step forward and squared himself in front of me, rigid and tense.

"What? You fuckin' two-eleven my conversation?"

I froze with half a smirk lingering stupidly on my face.

"Maki," said Lori, shaking her head. "Come on—no."

Turning to Lori, Maki took a step back. He then looked at me and chortled.

"Dude—it's just—I'm not from around here," I said. "I'm trying to get the . . . the . . . lingo."

Lori was already halfway out the door, urging Maki to follow. He turned and looked at me with an expression of amused disbelief. "You're fucking crazy," he said, laughing.

Once he was gone I turned to Stacie. "Jesus, he fucking flipped out," I said impassively, trying to pretend that I wasn't shaken.

"Well, yeah, Jimmy—he's a sketcher. I don't know how many times I told you, don't fuck with sketchers. And you know damn well what a teenth is—you just sold me one."

"I know what a *six*teenth is—half an eight ball—but you guys got all these crazy denominations out here. A teenth. One-point-seven-five grams. Why not just sell grams? That's how we do it in Jersey. Anyway, it doesn't matter. I was just fucking with him. I wanted to see how he'd react. It was funny. And what was that shit he said, 'two-eleven'? What the fuck is that?"

"It's the police code for robbery."

"Oh, so I robbed his conversation."

"Yeah, we don't do that out here either. Especially not with sketchers."

"All right, sure. But, c'mon, it was funny. I did not expect him to react like that."

It didn't take long before I learned what to expect from Maki. I walked into Stacie's living room one day to find Stacie and Lori frozen, staring. A man I'd never seen before was squirming on the couch, his face twisted into a terrified grimace. Maki was jabbing at him with a screwdriver, stopping only inches from his chest. Knees slightly bent, standing on the balls of his feet, Maki looked as though he were playing a sport. Jab, jab. Jab, jab. Suddenly the guy squealed and clutched the cushions and thrashed his head to the side. I couldn't tell whether Maki had actually poked him with the screwdriver or if the guy had just been overwhelmed with terror.

Maki was taunting him with the same soft tone that had once seemed so benign—"So you don't wanna pay me, huh, is that how it is . . ."—and I gathered that Maki had given him a stolen check to deposit, but that the guy's bank had refused any payment until the check cleared—which, of course, it never would. Maki didn't believe him; he thought he'd just kept the money. I was sure he was telling the truth. Maki told the guy he owed him six hundred dollars and then left him trembling on the couch.

Weeks later, in the late evening, Maki and I were at Stacie's, and I asked him if he could get me some heroin. He said he could; he just needed a ride to his place in Colton and then to his connection. Colton is in San Bernardino County, about twenty minutes north of Stacie's on the 215 freeway. Running alongside the stretch of freeway before the exit was a chain-link fence in front of a dirt road which was lined with tiny ramshackle houses—roofs thatched, shutters askew. We got off the freeway and Maki had me turn into an alley of sand and dirt bordered by matted weeds and needle grass. We crunched down the drive, kicking up dust clouds; on our left was a stone wall, about three feet high and crumbling. Maki pointed for me to park. I turned off the headlights and waited for my eyes to adjust.

"Come on in," Maki said. "I just gotta get something real quick."

Maki lived in a shack that had once been an outbuilding at the edge of someone's backyard. There was a tiny front room, a bathroom, and then a bedroom, all messy and cramped. Width-wise it was so narrow that if I had stretched my arms I could have almost touched both walls.

I stayed in the front room while Maki moved me around in the narrow space, patting my shoulders to direct me out of his way. He opened a drawer and immediately shut it.

"Just gotta get this thing real quick," he mumbled. "Where the fuck is it?"

He was jumpy, his breathing tight and sporadic. He walked into the bedroom and picked up a lonely pillow from the foot of the bed, and then I knew that he wasn't looking for anything at all.

"Let's go," he said, herding me toward the door.

"You find it?"

No answer. Outside it was dark, and I could barely see the ground in front of me. I had a sudden premonition that I would be sliced open and my insides would spill out of my body. I put a hand on my stomach, as if to confirm how tender and sliceable it was. I thought to attack him first—he would never expect it—but now that we were alone in a dark alley I realized just how scared of him I was. Even the blow I fantasized striking him with did no more than glance off his head and send him into a sadistic rage. I walked toward the car, pretending all was cool, trying not to look at him.

"Wait," he said.

I turned around. Maki was standing a few feet back, at the edge of the alley, where the porch lights from neighboring houses didn't quite reach. I could just make out a hand raised in the air and a leery, half-bewildered look on his face.

"What? You want me to—"

"Just don't fucking move, man," he said exasperatedly.

He looked as though he were listening for something.

"All right—"

"Shhh!"

He bugged his eyes at me and shook his head, seemingly astounded that I would talk again. He took a step toward me, pressing his hand into the side of his face and then clutching at the back of his skull.

"I don't know, man," he said. "I like you, dude. I mean, I think you're all right, but they keep tellin' me things, dude—like, like, they want me to get you."

"Who?"

"You know *who*!" He couldn't believe that I wasn't following him. "You *know* who. All of 'em, dude—they all want me to get you. But I don't trust them."

"Maki—"

"But I don't even know you either, dude."

"Maki, you know me," I said. "I've always been straight-up with you—"

"Yeah . . . yeah . . . ," he mumbled, shaking his head, drifting into a trance. Then suddenly he looked up and said, "You still want that tar?"

"Well, yeah—"

"Here, just gimme the money. You said you wanted like an eight ball, right?"

I hadn't, but I went for my wallet anyway, scared and eager to believe that we might be getting heroin after all, that nothing bad was happening. As I fumbled in my pocket, Maki took another step forward out of the dark.

"An eight? Yeah, sure, I think I got that," I said, leafing through the bills in my wallet. "That's a hundred, right? Yeah, I got that."

Everything in the alley, from the brush to the broken wall, was murky and shrouded.

"A hundred for an eight ball?" he said. "I guess I can do that for you. But—I don't know—is that all you got?"

With a deft movement, a graceful invasion, he placed his hand lightly on my wallet and looked at me apologetically.

"You don't mind," he said. "It's just, I don't even know you, dude. You could be anybody. I don't even know who you are." He didn't snatch; he hovered with his hand on the wallet, waiting.

"Oh, yeah—sure!" I said, handing him the wallet and indicating with a wave of my hand that I had hesitated only because I hadn't understood. "Go ahead, man. I don't give a fuck. It's cool. You don't know me; I'm not from around here. I know what it's like, man. You gotta cover yourself."

"So you don't mind? That's cool," he said, seemingly relieved, as he walked around the car and got in on the passenger side. I got in, started the engine, and turned on the lights. In my wallet were six twenty-dollar bills and a few ones, all of which Maki removed, fanned, and then set on his lap for a few seconds, considering. He put five of the twenties in his pocket and the rest of the bills back in the wallet, which he then handed back to me after briefly examining my driver's license and Social Security card.

"Where am I going?" I asked, pulling out of the alley.

Maki directed me along back roads I'd never taken, toward downtown Riverside, in the direction of Stacie's trailer park. Sitting in a crouch, leaning against the door with a foot up on the dashboard, he would tell me to turn at the last minute and then give me a bug-eyed, exasperated look when I slammed on the brakes. Every time we made a turn that took us closer to Stacie's, I would begin to ask where we were going for the heroin, but he would cut me off, groaning and clutching at his head.

"Maki—"

He put his foot down and opened the glove box. He rummaged through a few papers, holding my registration up to the light for a second before shoving everything back in the box and then clicking it shut with a frustrated sigh, as if that should have explained something but hadn't. He pointed me a turn closer to Stacie's.

"Maki, where—"

"Dude, I don't know what to do!" he said, frantic again. He let out a little high-pitched screech and grabbed his head with both hands. "I don't trust any of these people. I don't know you. I don't have any money. Fuck, dude! I don't know who I can trust. Fuckin' Lori's daughter's missing. I don't have money to find her. And I can't trust any of these fuckin' people."

"Maki, I've always been straight-up with you. I mean, for as long as you've known me, haven't I done straight business?"

"Yeah . . . but I don't know you, dude."

"Well, what about Lori? You trust her, don't you?"

"What? Fuck, no!" he said, as if it were the most absurd thing he'd ever heard. Then he shook his head and laughed. "*Fuck*, no! Make this left."

We were only a few blocks from Stacie's.

"You know I wanna help you out," I said. "I'll be coming up with some cash in a few days—I could lend you a little something to find Lori's daughter."

"Oh yeah, that's cool. But man, I don't know. I don't know if I even wanna find that little bitch. She ain't my daughter—you know? These motherfuckers. Just, just pull over here. I'll straighten this shit out." We were outside the trailer park. "Yeah, I'm gonna go in here and straighten this out. I'll call you in a little bit about that."

Maki got out of the car and walked down the street. Again I thought to attack him, to run after and tackle him, and then take my money out of his pocket and spit in his face. I thought about it as I drove away—I would think about it for the rest of the week.

I called Luke from my cell phone and he told me to come over. Usually to get across town I would have taken University and enjoyed passing the gritty street scene: the tweakers and the hookers outside cheap motels, the skinny kids in their hoodies smoking cigarettes. Usually I would have felt proud to be at home there, comfortable among thugs. But on that night, shaken and vulnerable, I made an early right and took mostly back roads, passing my old sober-living before making a left onto Market, then a right onto Mission.

I had some meth safely hidden in my boxer briefs where the fabric overlaps to make the fly. And when I reached Luke's, he snorted a few lines while I did a shot in the bathroom. Then I told him what had happened, though I made it sound a little more ambiguous than it had actually been. Embarrassed at having been taken, I tried to make it sound as if there was still a chance Maki might give me heroin for the money I'd given him, but Luke saw right through me.

"Sounds like you got beat, dude," he said.

"I'm not sure," I said. "I think I should call over there."

We went into the kitchen and Luke gave me the phone. I called Stacie's and asked for Maki.

"What's up?" he said.

"*What's up?* I'm sayin'—what's goin' on with that?"

"With what?"

"With that thing. I'm still tryin' to get that. You got my money."

"What are you talking about? The money you lent me?"

"I didn't lend you that. That was for—"

"Oh, dude!" he said. "Don't do this. Why are you gonna bullshit me, man? You said you'd lend me that for Lori's daughter. You wanna take it back? Don't do this now."

"I did not lend you that!"

Luke shook his head. He was leaning heavily with both hands on the counter, triceps bulging.

"I told you I would help you out when I got more money," I said loudly, feeling confident with Luke next to me. "But that bill was for tar."

There was a long pause.

"Look." Maki laughed softly. "I don't give a fuck about you, dude."

"Oh, is that right?"

"Yeah, man. I don't give a fuck about you."

"Fuck that dude," said Luke. "Tell him you want your money."

"Ya know what, dude?" I said toughly to Maki. "Don't even worry about it. I'll see you when I fuckin' see you."

"What did you say?"

"I'm gonna see you whenever the fuck I see you," I said threateningly. "Don't worry about it."

"Meet me at my house," he began, but he broke off, seething. "Meet me at my house—*right* now."

"Relax—we're not makin' a Western here," I said. (Uncle Junior said that to Mikey Palmice in the first season of *The Sopranos*.)

"A what?" said Maki.

"I said you're not calling the shots. I'll see you when I see you."

I hung up on him.

Luke immediately volunteered that he had my back. He said that over the next couple of days we would go looking for Maki, and we would get him together. Throughout the night we got high and smoked cigarettes with rolling tobacco from a can (the way we had in our cottage at GSL), and Luke, talking a mile a minute, told me stories about prison—about the fights he'd been in and the crazy people he'd met. Every time he finished a story, he turned to me and said, "Yeah, don't trip, dude. This Maki ain't nothin'." At about five a.m., I passed out.

When I woke, Luke was in the kitchen cooking one of his prison spreads. He looked sullen.

"I can't do this anymore," he said, handing me a plate. "Sorry, but I got a kid. I got a girl. I can't do this."

So over the next couple of weeks, I avoided Maki, carefully calling Stacie's before I went over to make sure he wasn't there. But one day he just answered the phone.

"Hey, you want Stacie?" he said. "Wait a minute, who's this? Jimmy?"

"Yeah, what's up, man?"

"Not much, dude. How are you doin'? I haven't seen you around here. I wanted to talk to you."

He sounded as though he wanted to forget about what had happened. I wasn't sure if I could trust him, but since I didn't have Luke to back me up anymore, I was happy to play along.

"Yeah," I said. "I wanted to apologize about the other day."

"No, dude—don't even worry about that. It's cool. But I heard you got some fat sacks—you're hookin' it up."

"Yeah, I'm movin' a couple things."

"I might have to see you for something. My connect dried up."

"Oh yeah, sure—I remember you used to take care of me."

"Yeah, I'd really appreciate that. If you could just hook it up when I see you, that'd be really cool."

"No problem."

That was how we left it, though I still didn't go over to Stacie's that day. In fact, over the coming weeks I would keep calling to make sure he wasn't there. I would also start carrying a knife.

CHAPTER 5. WENDY'S PACKAGE

There was a guy about my age, maybe a little older, who was known at Stacie's as Computer Sam because every time he came over he sat at her computer for hours and hours, scamming and tweaking. Sam was taller than I was, thin and handsome with a cleft chin, sandy-blond, almost clean-cut in his Keds and khakis and short-sleeve button-downs. He had no tattoos. From the first time we met, I knew that I could take him.

He was sitting by the computer while Stacie and I were arguing. Half an hour earlier Stacie had called and told me to stop by, saying she'd come up on a stolen credit card, but when I'd gotten there she'd said that something had gone wrong and now she didn't have the card.

"What the fuck, Stacie? I thought you said you had it."

"That's not what I said."

Normally I wouldn't have minded so much, this being typical of Stacie, but a couple days earlier I had spoken to Wendy, who'd asked about her package, again. When I'd confessed to not having bought a single item on the list she'd given me, there'd been a terrible silence, broken only by the insect whine of the jailhouse phone and the depressing roar of too many voices in the background. So the guilt was fresh. With a stolen credit card I could have made enough money to drive straight to Target and get Wendy her package once and for all. Stacie had gotten my hopes up.

"Yes, you did fucking say that! Why else would I be here? I'm beat; I've been up for like three days. I was on my way to my room to crash when you called me. I haven't been there in weeks, and that fucking chink of a landlady probably went through all my shit and called the cops, and—"

"She can't do that," Stacie interrupted, predictably. The rights of convicts, squatters, and tweakers were important to Stacie; in prison she'd have been the jailhouse lawyer. "That's your room and property. It would be inadmissible."

I couldn't tell whether she'd stated this dubious fact on principle, or to take the wind out of my sails. Probably the former, but I was still left stuttering, having exposed myself by going on a rant, giving her the option of which point to challenge. Everything was always a fight with Stacie.

"Yeah, but I might have warrants in New Jersey—"

"It wouldn't matter because—"

"Fuckin' Christ, Stacie. Never mind. Just never mind. Can you at least hit me in my neck?"

We went into the bathroom. I handed Stacie some dope so she could mix two shots. Spoons, needles, bleach, cotton swabs, and the red lockbox were scattered across the double-sink counter. Waiting, I sat on the edge of the bathtub and picked at a dried splotch of toothpaste, not really mistaking it for dried meth, but hey, you never know.

Stacie stood behind me, tilted my head to the side, and said, "Puff, don't flex." Then she slid the needle into my neck. *Whoa.* The rush was instant: pinpricks of euphoria all over my face, chest, and legs; warmth in my neck and crotch. I dropped to my knees and put my forehead against the carpet, savoring. While Stacie did her shot, I crawled back over to the bathtub and leaned against it. The off-white, smudged caulking that ran along the bottom was peeling.

When we came back into the living room, Sam was still at the computer.

Now high and invigorated, I was ready to fight again. I started in on Stacie, accusing her of doing nothing to help her friend Wendy, of doing worse than nothing, of tricking me into driving across Riverside when I could have been making money to put toward the package, just so she could get a free shot. Also, she'd been breaking my balls, demanding I pay her phone bill because of all the collect calls from Wendy. "Why should I be the only one paying for Wendy's phone calls? But fuck that for now—that's beside the point. Right now I wanna know how we're gonna make some money for Wendy's package. Are you gonna help or what?"

"I might be able to help," said Sam.

He was sitting on the floor, cross-legged, surrounded by the parts of the computer he'd just disassembled. The motherboard lay on the carpet, its intricate circuitry shimmering in the lamplight. I found this irritating. *What, does he think he's a surgeon or some shit?*

"Oh, I hope you don't mind, Stacie," he said. "I had to take this thing apart—I found glitches."

"I don't know anything about computers," said Stacie. "I trust you."

Naturally, that irritated me more. And he was wearing this restrained, puckish grin, as if he knew something we didn't.

"So how can you help?" I said.

"You're talking about Wendy Kaplan, right?"

For a moment I didn't say anything; I just stared at him, letting Wendy's last name hang awkwardly in the air.

"Yeah," I said. "How do you know her?"

"I've known her for a while. She used to live at Lauryn's house—"

"Who's Lauryn?"

"Oh. I live at her house," he said, stammering slightly.

"I know Lauryn," Stacie interjected. "She's cool. Wendy used to live over there."

"Yeah," said Sam. "Wendy and I go back—we're friends."

"Oh, so you're friends," I said, pleased and a bit surprised by how natural this all felt. "Well, that's good, because she's my *best* friend. I mean, I'll do fuckin' anything for that girl, you know what I'm saying?"

"Yeah," said Sam.

"Cool," I said. "So how can you help? I need like three hundred bucks for this package. You wanna throw in some cash?" Sam laughed. "What? That's fuckin' funny?"

"Oh, no, no," he said. "The only thing that's funny is me having cash. I'm broke."

"Well, you know what we're talkin' about here—you know she's up at CRC and we're tryin' to get this thing together for her. So how are you gonna help? I mean, I ain't tryin' to be all in your shit, but you said it, not me; we were talking over here, you know what I'm saying? Now I got some dope I'm trying to move—you know anybody around here?"

"No, yeah, sure, I mean . . . look, I wanna help Wendy out—and I can probably even help you sell some dope later—but what I was talking about is checks. There should be some good checks over at Lauryn's, and if you get her high I can get her to cash 'em. I'll get her to pay for the whole thing."

"There *should* be checks?"

"Yeah, I'm sayin', they're not mine. I don't want to promise that they'll be there, and then they might not be."

"No, no, that's cool," I said. "And you know what, I'm sorry; I don't mean to be breaking your balls over this. It's just, we're talking about my best friend, so I get a little crazy. But that's cool if you're gonna try and help. Just do me a favor and make sure you call me when you get back to your place, Lauryn's or wherever. That's where you live, at Lauryn's, right?"

"Yeah, sure."

"So you're sayin' you're gonna call me when you get there, right?"

"Yeah, sure."

"Now you do know what you're saying, right? 'Cause this means I'm not gonna be callin' or goin' to see some other people about tryin' to move this dope, or whatever, 'cause I'll be waiting for your call instead. You know what I'm sayin' to you?"

"Yeah, but I can't guarantee the checks—"

"Dude, I didn't say anything about the checks. You said you don't know, so I can't hold you responsible for them. But you are sayin' you're gonna call me, and that's all I'm sayin'—that I'm gonna be waitin' for that call. All right?"

"Yeah, all right—I'll call."

"Cool, cool. So you wanna get high?"

After we went into the bathroom and I made up two shots, I tied off my arm and searched for a vein, running my fingers down my forearm and wincing as I poked at oblong bruises, yellow and purple, freckled with marks that looked like scratched mosquito bites. Frustrated, I cursed, and Sam offered to hit me. I asked him if he was sure he could do it; my veins were hard to find. He assured me he could, bragging, as junkies often do about their skills with a needle. After I retied my arm and gave him the needle, he found a vein and the chamber filled with blood. Then he lost it—lost the vein—right at the critical moment. He took the needle out of my arm, set it on the counter, and looked at the floor. I laughed and told him not to worry about it. I told him to do his shot and to go home and to call me when he got there.

When he left, I called Stacie into the bathroom and she managed to save the shot, hitting me even though the chamber was already bright red.

"By the way," she said after taking her own shot, "you know Wendy fucking hates that kid."

"Really," I said. "That's good to know, because if he doesn't call I'm gonna go over there."

"What are you gonna do?" she said.

"I'm gonna make him help pay for Wendy's package."

"Good. You should, running his mouth like that."

Hours passed and Sam didn't call, so at about five a.m. Stacie called Lauryn and introduced me as Wendy's friend. I asked if Sam was there. Lauryn said he was. Her voice was high and nasal. When I asked whether she minded if I stopped by she said that she didn't, that Sam had told her who I was, and that she was actually about to invite me. She offered to give me directions. At first I was suspicious of Lauryn's eagerness to have me over, but then I decided to run with it, figuring that Sam had told her I had lots of meth and that she, being a junkie, would blindly believe I wanted to share. *Why would a guy I've never met want to drive across town to get me high?* No. *Why WOULDN'T a guy I've never met want to drive across town to get me high?*

I left Stacie's at about six a.m. With the early birds going to work I felt safe, inconspicuous, my car blending in on the road. I wondered if I could arrange it so that I only ever drove at this hour. Stacie had lent me a copy of Pink Floyd's *Dark Side of the Moon*. The song "Time" came on, and when I heard the line "Ticking away the moments that make up a dull day," I began to ponder time. I didn't know what day it was. Did I care? Should I? Weren't days just an artificial construct designed to control us, to constrain us to neat, safe little schedules, to keep us from thinking and living? What did time matter, anyway? Nothing to me. I wouldn't even know what time it was if it weren't for the police—a need to be at least remotely aware of the straight world so as not to be caught by it. It occurred to me that my thoughts were neither original nor interesting, and I wished I had some acid. I used to have some really good thoughts on acid. Then I remembered the time I had run from the cops while tripping on acid, the time my pants fell down and my parents had to pick me up, and I smiled at what a little kid I had been.

On Fourteenth Street I passed a high school with a large track and football field. I stared at the purple scoreboard—HORNETS 00, VISITOR 00—and the car drifted steadily to the right until, just before I would have hit the curb, I yanked the steering wheel and swerved well into the next lane. A car honked. The woman driving hissed at me, her face contorting as she turned to the window and showed me her teeth. I looked around; we were the only cars in sight. I laughed at her, but she had already pulled ahead of me. I fingered the knife in my pocket and thought of ramming her into the divider and dragging her, while she kicked and screamed, out of the car and under one of the bushes, where I'd show her my knife, smiling, and then run the tip of the blade from her temple to her chin—not to hurt her, just to scare her, to rip her out of her safe little coupe and give her the fright of her life.

When I reached the address Lauryn had given me, I parked at the curb and stared at the house for a few minutes, unsettled by how normal it looked: light blue clapboard siding, stunted shrubs in front of a bay window. If Sam and Lauryn lived in a house like this, they might not be junkies at all but recreational drug users, so removed from the thug-tweaker lifestyle that the threats I intended to make might not mean anything to them. They might look at me with horrible faces and call the police. But that, I realized, was absurd: Sam had just disassembled a stolen computer while sitting on Stacie's floor; Lauryn had invited me over to get high at five a.m. They were both junkies.

I called Lauryn from my cell phone, and a paunchy woman in checkered pajama bottoms and a brown T-shirt waddled out the front door. She beckoned to me and then went back inside, closing the door behind her. When I reached the door, I hesitated, unsure whether to knock or just walk in. I knocked but then immediately changed my mind and, compensating for my indecision, emphatically swung the door open and stepped forward like a TV detective making a bust.

Sam was sitting on the floor again, another motherboard next to his knee. Lauryn, her face pale and puffy, was standing at the edge of the kitchen, holding a turquoise coffee mug. She seemed uninterested—in me, in everything.

"What's up, man?" said Sam, wrenching himself away from the computer. "This is Lauryn. Lauryn, this is Jimmy, Wendy's friend."

"Hi," said Lauryn.

"Hey, Lauryn," I said and then, determined to get to business, turned to Sam. "You didn't call me."

"Oh yeah, I got it wrong," he said. "Sorry. Those things were no good."

"No, dude, I don't think you quite understand," I said. It was a line I'd wanted to use for years. "You had me sittin' over there at Stacie's jerkin' off while I'm waitin' for you to call me. I mean, we talked about this. Didn't I make myself clear? Whether the thing comes through or not, I don't care, just so long as you call me so I'm not sittin' around. You know what I'm saying? I'm over at Stacie's tryin' to get Wendy's package together, setting up this thing and that thing, lining up sales, and then you open your mouth and I put all that shit on hold. And now I'm just sittin' there, waiting for you to call me—'cause you said you would. And you're supposed to be Wendy's friend."

"Aw, man, you shouldn't have stopped doing anything—"

"Well I did. And I did it because you said you would call. Remember, I said, 'It doesn't matter if it comes through—you're not responsible for that—just make sure you call me.' You remember that? I said it like three fuckin' times, and you nodded along. You said you'd call. And so basically I lost money, dude, 'cause of you."

"You mean you missed some sort of opportunity," he said. "Can't you just, I don't know, call them now? What kind of thing was it that you can't—"

"No, I can't call them now, but that's beside the point anyway. And what kind of thing? Honestly, dude, that's none of your fuckin' business."

I felt a little rush as I said that—*none of your fuckin' business.* Then I continued with greater confidence, speaking to him harshly and pedantically, because if he was ever going to tell me to fuck off, that would have been the time to do it. "What kind of thing? That's between me and whoever I'm dealing with, and really that's got nothing to do with this. The only issue now is that I lost money for Wendy's package because of something you did."

"I don't understand," Lauryn said.

Sam rolled his eyes. It was clear that he rolled his eyes often around Lauryn.

"Look, Lauryn," I said, "I don't know what this has to do with you, except that Sam says he lives here. Is that right?"

She nodded, and for the first time I wondered about the nature of their relationship. Sometime later I would find a contract in the house, handwritten by Lauryn and signed by Sam, stating that Lauryn would allow Sam to live in her house on the condition that he had sex with her three times a week.

"Well, the thing is, Lauryn," I continued, "Wendy's my best friend, and she's up at CRC right now, and she needs a package. I'm tryin' to put that together. And basically I'm tryin' to help her out, and I'm gettin' jerked around here—maybe not on purpose, but that's beside the point. The point is, I was clear, and money was lost, and she still needs to get that package."

"So you want us to help you get Wendy's package?" Lauryn said.

"Yeah, sure. I'll help."

She turned to Sam, who, picking up on her lead, nodded and said, "Yeah, of course I'll help Wendy."

"What kind of stuff does she need?" asked Lauryn.

Confused, I gave her Wendy's list: jeans, T-shirts, socks, underwear, ivory pressed powder and matching cream foundation, Lash Discovery black mascara, liquid eyeliner, purple and pink eye shadow, plum lipstick, ThermaSilk shampoo (and gel and conditioner), Fifth Avenue perfume, Nivea lotion, coffee and creamer, hair clips, and a whole lot of candy. I had never actually considered what was on these lists that Wendy kept dictating to me; the only time I ever even looked at one was in the moment I was taking it down. And then, after a brief scan, I would always shove the list quickly into my pocket, frustrated and daunted by the prospect of shopping for all these items that were utterly foreign to me, of exploring aisles in a giant store and asking a salesclerk a question that might make me look stupid.

"I know where I can get that," Lauryn muttered to herself, running a finger down the list.

"She's a thief," Sam explained.

"Oh," I said.

I didn't know what my next move should be. I had just begun

to feel comfortable in my new role as extortionist when Lauryn had offered, as though it were her idea, to help get Wendy's package. Since I'd never extorted anything from anybody before, I didn't know that this was the way it worked—that at this point I should actually have been encouraging the shift in mood, allowing them to say whatever they wanted in order to save face. I didn't know that I was supposed to observe their maneuverings with detachment, concerned with one thing and one thing only: leaving with exactly what I had come for. Instead I felt cheated when Lauryn *offered* to help, as if we'd been wrestling and she'd gone limp right when I was about to win.

But at the same time I was relieved that they were cooperating, because now that Sam and I were face-to-face, I realized (unhappily) that my backup plan of beating him until he found some way to come up with the money I wanted was total fantasy. It simply wasn't in my nature, no matter what I'd told myself during the ride over. Besides, Lauryn and Sam had been playing this game longer than I had. They knew how to placate me: They weren't going to give me exactly what I'd come for (cash), but they would offer me something so that I wouldn't feel forced to become violent. They were better weasels than I was a tough guy.

"Cool," I said. "You really think you can get all of this stuff?"

"Yeah, I can go right after Dale has his cereal and leaves for school."

"Cool, cool," I said. "Who's Dale?"

"My son."

"Oh. How old?"

"Eight. He's eight."

"Oh," I said.

And just then Dale trudged down the hall, wearing white and blue Power Ranger pajamas. He was small for eight. He had brown hair and lots of freckles. Sam nudged me and then pointed to my arms, which were bare, bruised, and tracked. I folded them and smiled at Dale, who didn't look at me. He seemed to make a point of not looking at me. He gave his mom a perfunctory hug, then sulkily poured himself a bowl of cereal and took a seat at the kitchen table, clearly feeling that it was unfair that he had to get up for school.

After Dale had finished his cereal, gotten dressed, and walked out the door, Lauryn changed into a baggy green dress.

"Sam said you had dope," she said.

"Oh, did he?" I replied in an ambiguous tone, either playful or haughty, depending on her reaction. She stared at me, looking like a depressed mother who'd just sent her kid off to school and who now wanted to get high. I went with playful.

"Yeah, of course we can do a shot. You're helping Wendy."

"Thanks," she said. "There's one other thing, though. I can get all the stuff on that list, but I'm gonna need you to drive me around, unless you wanna wait here while I borrow your car."

"Sure, why not?" I said indulgently. "Borrow the car."

I spent the day there, watching TV and getting high, while Lauryn drove around stealing. Every few hours she stopped at the house to unload her dress, and by about midafternoon the living room was strewn with cosmetics, toiletries, lingerie. Some of the things, Lauryn admitted, were for her rather than for Wendy, and this irked me, because every time she'd stopped in we'd done a shot with my dope. I was beginning to get the impression that Lauryn would have been out stealing today whether I'd come over or not, and that picking up a few extra things for Wendy was no more than a small inconvenience, well worth all the meth I'd been supplying. Which meant I wasn't extorting anything at all, now was I?

I took it out on Sam, reminding him in my toughest voice that I was in charge here. But he, too, had a way of making me feel that I was the one being played.

"Lauryn should be back soon, right?" I said.

"I think so."

"Well, she's only gotten like half the shit on that list, and I can't be hangin' around here for days. So I'm saying, that shit's gotta be done by tonight."

"Yes, sir."

"Sir?"

"Oh, what, you don't like being called that?"

"No, I don't fuckin' like being called that. Ya know why—'cause I'm not fuckin' stupid. That's why. As if I don't know you're mocking me. Don't call me that fuckin' shit again."

"Sorry, sir."

"What, are you fuckin' kidding—," I growled.

"Oh, no, no—I didn't mean—it's just a habit."

"Well, fuckin' break it."

"Okay."

In the early evening Lauryn returned from her last trip of the day. She asked to do a shot, and as we walked down the hall toward her bedroom, I could feel Sam staring after us. In the bedroom the ivory carpeting was covered with clothes, from sweat-shirts to panties—overflow from the walk-in closet. Lauryn sat on the edge of her water bed, while I sat in a black swivel chair and set up the shot on a desk that was covered with sketch pads and markers. When I asked her for a spoon, Lauryn told me to open the farthest drawer and look toward the back.

"I was able to get almost everything," Lauryn said. "Just not the jeans and T-shirts. I wasn't in a place I could do that."

"All right, cool," I said. "But I think those are important, so you gotta get that tomorrow."

"Okay—well, I don't know. I don't understand. Why do I *have* to do anything?"

"*You* don't have to do anything. It's Sam."

I turned away from her to crush the crystals with the plunger, and also to work up the energy to repeat my dubious rationale.

"I already explained all this," I began, as if that granted it some validity. "But the point is, I was over at Stacie's, tryin' to figure out a way to come up with the money so I could get this package. Sam jumps in on my conversation, sayin' he's got these checks over here. Then he doesn't call me to say he doesn't have them, so I end up not following up on these sales I had lined up. Look, the point is, it's on him—not you. I mean, it's cool you're doin' this, and I do appreciate it—as Wendy's friend—but that doesn't change the fact that it needs to get done. So if you wanna put it back on him, that's your choice, but somebody's gotta get the thing."

"No, I don't want to put anything on him. It's just that . . . well, he's been saying this is all my fault."

"What?"

"He's been saying it's something I did. He's been blaming it all on me."

"What? Fuck that. Yo, Sam! Come here, man!"

Sam, probably thinking I was going to offer him a shot, ran down the hallway.

"What's up?"

"I'll tell you what's up," I said. "I just wanna clear up—between the three of us—what's going on here, because you're telling her some fucking bullshit. I'm here 'cause you ran your mouth—not her. She didn't do a fuckin' thing but help. She did what needed to be done. So don't go tellin' her that this is her fault, when you know it's yours."

"Yes, sir."

"What did you fuckin' say?"

"Oh, sorry—"

"No, ya know what—get the fuck outta here. Go play with your computer or some shit. Just get the fuck away from me."

Sam shot Lauryn a look and then closed the door, jiggling the knob to make sure its bolt had latched. Then the front door slammed.

"He'll be back," said Lauryn, shrugging. "Is that ready?"

I handed her a shot. She tied off her arm and then plunged the tip into her puffy white skin. Blood ballooned, she slammed it back, and her eyes rolled up into her head. With one hand she clutched at her bed sheets, breathing heavily, her tongue curled around her front teeth; with the other she massaged the inside of her thigh through her dress. She ground her buttocks into the water bed and a few times, slowly, as if she were trying to keep from doing it, bucked her pelvis.

Then, as the rush passed, her eyes lit, jaw still trembling, she looked at me and said, "Your turn."

"Can you hit me?"

"Sure," she said, leaning forward and groping my arm.

She ran her fingers along the tracks and bruises.

"Ouch," she said.

"Yeah, I've been having trouble hitting myself. Stacie sometimes goes in my neck."

"Well, I could probably hit you here, but it's gonna hurt—you really messed yourself up. You know, when you reuse needles, you bruise more. But if you want me to go in your neck, I'll try."

"I don't want you to *try* anything," I said, laughing. "I don't want to be your guinea pig for neck-sticking."

"Well, there is something else we could try."

"What's that?"

"Some guys go in their dick."

There was a pause, though not a long one.

"Okay," I said. "Yeah. You wanna do it?"

"Sure."

She looked down at my crotch as if to say, "What are you waiting for?"

I was already half hard and actually eager to do it, eager to try anything new, but I was shy and I couldn't quite bring myself to just take my dick out. So, after fumbling around unfastening my belt, I pulled my pants down around my thighs and then gingerly opened my boxer fly, just enough to show Lauryn the part where I thought the vein would be thickest.

"C'mon," she said. "I've seen 'em before."

I laughed and pulled the shorts down.

"It has to be really hard anyway, or I won't be able to hit it." She grabbed me. "You know, I used to be a nurse, and they told me there's this spot that's really sensitive, kind of like a guy's G-spot—I think it's right there. Yeah, doesn't that feel good?"

"Wait a second—stop," I said. "No, I mean, it feels good, but let's just do the shot first."

She shrugged and took the needle and laid its tip, angled to pierce, on the skin beside the bulging vein. I had imagined that it wouldn't be that bad, that once I had overcome the fear it wouldn't be so different from shooting up anywhere else. Not so. The point resting on my dick—a pinprick that anywhere else had actually become a turn-on— turned my stomach to knots, and it was all I could do not to smack her hand away. And yet I had to maintain a hard-on. With her free hand Lauryn stroked me and stretched the skin, coaxing the vein.

"Do you just want me to flick it?" she said.

"Whatever you think."

"Yeah, I'm gonna flick it."

"Then fuckin' do it already."

She held the needle in place with her left hand, and with her right she locked the ring finger behind the thumb as though she were playing marbles. *Flick!* She popped the end of the chamber, but not quite hard enough: The needle punctured the skin but not the vein. The pain, though sharp, felt somehow internal; it reverberated in my anus and up into my intestines with eye-bulging—*wow*—intensity. But I wasn't ready to give up. Neither was Lauryn. She kept hold of me and pursued the vein, while I, gripping the arms of my chair, wriggled and grimaced and curled my toes. I could feel every adjustment beneath the skin.

"I . . . I think I got it," she said.

"You *think?*"

"No, I got it. There it is."

"Then fucking go!"

She hit me for about half of the shot. Then she lost it, lost the vein running along my cock. I yelped like a kicked dog and she knew to take it out. We watched the spot where she'd missed swell and then quickly harden into a bubble about the size of a blister. The sting, how-ever, soon passed, eclipsed by the orgasmic sensation of meth rushing through my crotch. The pressure was actually better than an orgasm, and as the rush worked its way to my throat, I grabbed Lauryn's wrist and put her hand back on me. I came quickly—even though, a few times, she failed to avoid the hypersensitive "miss bubble."

Hours later, night had fallen and I was alone in the living room, sitting on the couch with a few stuffed animals and too many of those little decorative cushions, staring at a blank television that was sur-rounded by videos you could tell were in the wrong boxes. This would be the fourth sleepless night in a row, which would mean how many hours? Seventy-two? No. More. A hundred something. Fuck. I knew that I was beginning to sketch. I knew that I should go into the bath-room, shoot some heroin, and pass out while I was still able to distin-guish the real noises from the ones in my head. But that's the thing about sketching—it's like sleep: You can feel it coming, but you're never aware of crossing the threshold.

A car passed in front of the house, its lights streaming through the blinds and then disappearing, fading with the sound of wet tires rolling over wet asphalt. No, it didn't. No such thing had happened, and I knew it. I knew that I had imagined the car, the lights, and the sound, but I got up to check anyway, just to confirm what I already knew. After I peeked through the blinds and sat back down, I felt proud of myself because I'd been right—there had been no car—and, what's more, it wasn't even raining.

Sam walked through the front door.

"What's up, man?" I said. "Where you been?"

"Just went for a walk, down to this girl's house. You all right?"

"Yeah. Whad'ya mean? I'm fine."

"Nothing. Do you know where Lauryn is?"

"I think she's in her room."

He walked to the bedroom, and even after its door had opened and shut I heard his footsteps thumping and then pitter-pattering down the hallway, echoing as another car drove past the house. Somehow I managed to get up off the couch and walk to the bathroom to do a shot of heroin—at this point the most sensible option.

The bathroom was directly across the hall from the bedroom.

Before sitting on the toilet to cook the shot, I dropped my pants, because that's what you do before sitting on a toilet. I put a few chunks of tar in a spoon and added some water. I lit the lighter. The tar bubbled and the gas from the lighter *hissed*. Sam and Lauryn were whispering in the bedroom. Their voices were tense, struggling to remain whispers. I let the lighter die so I could hear them, but as soon as I did, they stopped talking. I told myself that I was being stupid, that I should take the shot and then everything would be okay. I lit the lighter again. Immediately I heard Sam's voice. He was angry. I put down the lighter and the spoon, but this time the voices didn't die. Sam had a gun. He was going to kill me.

I pulled my pants up and put my ear to the door. I was breathing too loudly, though, to hear what they were saying, and when I held my breath my pulse drummed out their words. There was just the back-and-forth, him talking, then her, the emotional rise and fall; but it was perfectly clear what they were talking about. Sam was furious. He had a gun. And he was going to shoot me. Lauryn, it seemed, was trying to talk him out of it, but without success. Sam was going to come out of the bedroom any minute and kill me.

I took my knife out of my pocket and snapped it open—loudly, meaning for him to hear it, because I was no coward. The sound of it was sharp and piercing, and when it died there was total silence. They had heard me and stopped talking. Now was the time. I put a hand on the doorknob, intending to rush across the hall and into the bedroom, to not give him the slightest chance, to knock him over and stab him and keep stabbing him until he had stopped moving. I began to turn the knob.

"Sam," I said through the door. "It doesn't have to be like this, man."

My voice sounded so scared and yet so clear and real that I was no longer sure I'd heard Sam talking at all. Still holding the knife, I took a deep breath and stepped through the door. Sam came walking toward me. I closed the knife and put it back in my pocket. He was coming from down the hall, from the kitchen and living room. He hadn't even been in the bedroom.

"Are you all right?" he asked.

"Yeah, yeah, I'm fine. What do you mean?"

"Nothing. Did you say something from the bathroom a second ago?"

"No. What the fuck are talking about? I didn't say anything."

"Nothing. I'm sorry. I just wanted to make sure you're not sketching out or anything."

"No, I'm good."

"Cool. There's also—I wanted to ask . . . I mean, I know you've already been very generous, but do you think you could hook me up with one more shot?"

"Yeah, sure. Why not. Let me just finish my shot first."

"Thank you, thank you, thank you."

CHAPTER 6. MY ROOM

The next morning Lauryn finished stealing everything on Wendy's list, and that day, after sending off the package, I drove home to Norco. Home was the second-to-last house before a dead end that tapered into a stretch of sand, dirt, and brambles. For a while I sat in the driveway, staring at the flat-roofed one-story house, at the brick porch with its three splintered wood columns. Having hardly slept in five days, I was so tired that it was tempting to just pass out in the car. But that would have given my landlady one more thing to complain about, one more thing that she could add to her ever-growing list of my *strange behavior*. I could hear her already:

"Why? Why would you sleep in your car when I give you nice bed? Doesn't make any sense. It's strange behavior. You say you're tired—you work—but we are all tired. We all work. You think I don't work? You don't see me sleeping in my car. Are you on drugs?"

Prior complaints included: "Why do you climb in your window? I gave you key. Maybe you don't want me to know what time you come home, but I know. Believe me, I know. You come home at four in the morning, and that's fine—just come in the door."

And: "Why would you put blanket over your window? When you first come here—remember—I told you the girl that lived here before does the same thing, and you tell me that people on drugs do that. Remember?"

She'd also been pretty unhappy the time I'd rooted through her kitchen and laundry room. I'd gotten high and, remembering that my landlady was a nurse, gone on a junkie's treasure hunt, rummaging through drawers for needles and pills with the same narrow, maniacal persistence that I'd had while searching for my veins in Stacie's bathroom. Then, mid-root, I remembered that the last boarder, the "nice girl," had nailed a blanket over her window and therefore must have been a tweaker. *If she's on meth, she's probably just as horny as I am.* I rooted through the sofa for the nice girl's number, assuming that if I found it she'd happily meet me for sex.

"Jimmy, please, I have to ask you, do not search drawers in my kitchen. I think maybe you think since I am a nurse I have some drugs hidden, but I do not keep that in my house."

"No, no, I'm not looking for drugs. I don't do drugs. And I'm sorry I looked through the drawers—it's just that I have a condition. I'm OCD," I said, automatically assuming, because of her accent, that she was a moron. I'd also simply gotten worse at constructing lies. This was inevitable, considering that believable, preferably true details are what sell a lie: a fabric of truths and easily-could-be-truths woven from everyday experiences to support and hide the one thing that didn't actually happen. Which of course made selling lies nearly impossible for me, because, living on meth, I wasn't having any everyday experiences. I had nothing with which to weave—no separate, acceptable, mundane stories in which to hide the transgression—so my big fat lies were just out there. *I have obsessive-compulsive disorder.* At the same time, though, I was oblivious to how outrageous the lies were. I'd grown used to telling bad lies with a straight face.

"What's this OCD?" she asked.

"Obsessive-compulsive disorder. I'll start doing something, and I can't stop. I mean, I should be able to control it. I'm sorry; I should have told you when I first moved in. But I can pretty much guarantee you it won't happen again."

"But you say it's a condition—so how can you not do it?"

"I can usually control it. That was a rare thing, the other day; hasn't happened in a long time."

"You know, I am a nurse."

"So you should know all about it."

"Yes, but I don't think you have this thing. What you call it? O—"

"Obsessive-compulsive disorder. You don't even know what it is, and you're telling me I don't have it. What, you think I'm lying? Why would I lie about that? You wanna talk to my doctor back in New Jersey?"

"What's his name?"

"Steel, Dr. John Steel."

"You call him."

"What, *now*? I can't call him now. It's ten at night over there."

"I knew you would not call him—"

"It's ten at night!"

"Yes, but I knew you would not call him anyway. But that does not matter. I don't care. I don't care about this, what you call—"

"OCD. Obsessive-compulsive disorder. Well, it's good to know you don't care about it," I said, actually offended. Another result of lying so often was that it didn't feel like lying anymore; when called on it I didn't feel any shame. It just seemed that the person was being nasty.

"Yes, I do not care about this obsessive-compulsive disorder. I only care you do not search my drawers. And it's good you do not try to deny it this time, because I know. I know the next time. I saw you. I have hidden camera."

This was an unfortunate thing for her to say, since it gave me an excuse to flip out. Furiously I told her that hidden cameras are illegal, that it's illegal to film somebody without his knowledge. She told me that they were not illegal and that anyway, now I knew. I threatened to sue. She said I had no grounds. And that sent us back to the issue of hidden cameras and their legality, which I told her didn't really matter, because I wasn't really going to sue. I liked her too much to sue. It's just that I was upset about all the mistrust and, frankly, bizarre accusations—I flat-out didn't understand them—but I was sure that we'd be able to work it out once we'd both cooled down. I told her I liked her a lot, she reciprocated, and then, before she could finish her "but," I walked away, firmly repeating that we would work it out once we'd both cooled down. It was important that we work it out.

Another reason it was unfortunate for her to tell me she had a hidden camera was that it gave me a motive, as well as an excuse, for rooting through her house whenever I got the chance. By that time I had become pretty paranoid—I didn't need somebody to tell me I was being watched, or filmed, or followed, or stalked in order to believe it. So after she actually said, "I have hidden camera," I of course got worse. I suspected that the camera was only the tip of the iceberg and that she went into my room whenever I wasn't in there. I began setting traps. Before locking the door one night I got on my knees, reached around the door and into the room, and carefully placed an open container of Minute Maid orange juice in the door's path. I'd seen this done in a spy movie and felt proud for having remembered it.

I also suspected that my landlady regularly called the cops on me, and that one day they might be waiting for me in the house. She really had called the cops once since I'd moved in. Not on me, though—on Luke. I'd walked in the door and she'd started shouting about my big friend with tattoos and earrings, and how she'd called the police and filed a report because he'd nearly given her a heart attack. Later I found out from Luke that on a night that we'd gotten high and I'd let him borrow my car, he had driven to my house at five in the morning to retrieve his flannel jacket from my room. When I told him that my landlady was furious, that he could have gotten me kicked out, and that I would have happily brought him his flannel if only he had asked for it, he did what he always did whenever I asked him about where he'd been and what he'd been doing while he was high: He told me not to trip.

Between Luke and the hidden camera and my lies about Dr. John Steel (not to mention that I hadn't paid the woman for the last month), coming home had become such a pain that I'd been sleeping at Patti's as often as she would have me. I'd also been staying at the cheap motels on University and Magnolia, where I could shoot up and watch porn and tweak in privacy all night long.

But now, sitting in my car, staring at the brick porch, I was so tired that all I wanted was to go to my room and pass out. I only hoped that my landlady wasn't home. I got out of the car and walked to the front door—wide, heavy oak. Its purely decorative handle was copper-tinged and located awkwardly in the center, a point of minimal leverage. I unlocked the door and pushed it open. The landlady wasn't home. I walked down the hall to my room, opened the door, and spilled Minute Maid orange juice all over the carpet.

I stood there for a while, staring at the darkened carpet. First I thought, *How stupid and paranoid of me,* but then I realized that my landlady could have already fallen for the trap and then reset it. *Either way, the police aren't here now, and I should probably clean that up or it'll start to stink. But how do you clean a carpet?* I'd seen several ads for carpet cleaners in the past weeks while tweaking through the classifieds section of the newspaper. *Carpet munchers.* I regularly tweaked through newspapers in search of disguised ads for prostitutes who would accept either meth or stolen credit-card numbers in exchange for their services. *Pussy lickers.* I called ads for escorts and listened to people prattle about automatic transmission and only sixty thousand miles, about buying American and Ford durability. I tried to guess the code word that would make them put the prostitute on the phone.

I was a sleep-deprived nineteen-year-old boy who'd recently started having sex and who was living on the strongest aphrodisiac in the world.

When I had first moved in, the room—an average-size guest bedroom with double bed, nightstand, walk-in closet, and one long, horizontal window—was immaculately clean. Sheets laundered, carpet vacuumed, window Windexed. Now the sheets were filthy and the window was crudely covered. The floor was practically invisible, covered by the junk that I had thrown around my room while rooting. Some of this junk was mine—clothes, food wrappers, papers relating to GSL and to scams I was trying to run with Stacie, boxes of pornographic DVDs—but most of it was the stuff Wendy had trusted me to keep while she was in prison: purses, ID cards, CDs, Walkmans, lotions, sketch pads, colored pencils, jewelry, clothes.

During many of my more sexually charged rooting sessions I had found and used certain intimate articles of clothing. Then, after finishing, I'd frantically hidden them, swearing never to do that again. But of course I had done it again—and again—until over time I'd become inured to the shame. I had stopped caring enough to hide my best friend's soiled panties, so now they were strewn among the rest of the garbage on the floor: red-and-pink sequined reminders of what a depraved little shit I'd become.

I kicked off my boots and crawled onto the side of the bed that wasn't covered with junk. My laptop was also on my bed, the laptop on which I watched pornographic DVDs and wrote the poetry that I read to my parents. Recently I'd been watching more and writing less—I hardly ever read to my parents anymore—and yet I'd come to value the poems I'd already written more than ever. As my life had begun revolving more and more around getting high, as I'd abandoned notions of cleaning up tomorrow and getting a job—as I'd begun to admit that I was a junkie—the poems had, in my mind, remained the one *good* thing I'd held on to. I thought they were brilliant, and I even fantasized that they would be found after I died of an overdose, that people would say that the world had been robbed of a genius. They would say this when they read the lines "A watched pot never boils / Make straight lines, not coils / What's to be done with the time in between?" Junkies have few places to invest their vanity.

I wanted to take one last shot of heroin before I let myself pass out, to make the sleep warm and cozy, but at some point after I tied off my arm and before I hit myself, I fell asleep. Hours later I rolled over and pricked myself with the needle.

CHAPTER 7. BRADY AND THE HOUSE ACROSS THE BRIDGE

I was driving through downtown Riverside when I heard my name shouted from the street. The voice sounded familiar. In my rear-view mirror I saw a man on a bike waving to me, pedaling hard. I pulled over and got out cautiously, but when the guy lifted his head, I recognized him immediately. It was Brady from GSL. He kept riding until he was a few yards away, playfully threatening to run me over, the way a kid would, before swerving to the side and braking.

"Jimmy, Jimmy, Jimmy," he said, brushing his shaggy brown hair out of his face.

Brady had a way of grinning with his eyes, a part of his rascally charm.

"What's up, brother?" I said warmly.

For a moment we smiled at each other, not saying anything. I was trying to decide whether or not to tell him I was getting high, when he said, "I relapsed."

"Me too."

We laughed. I looked down and saw that he was wearing the black Timberland boots I had given him for Christmas.

"Wait a minute, Jimmy," he said. "You relapsed? On what? Wait, don't tell me. You look like you lost forty pounds. Jimmy, don't tell me they got you on that speed out here. I thought you were a heroin junkie."

"I was, but your heroin sucks out here. And your speed fucking kicks ass."

"Didn't I tell you? And look, you're slamming that shit, too. Lemme see your arms. Jimmy, Jimmy, Jimmy. You been at it for a little while now."

"Couple months. Can you see the ones on my neck?"

"You stick that needle in your neck?"

"I don't. This girl Stacie, Wendy's friend—you remember Wendy— she hits me. She used to be a nurse."

"They all used to be nurses, Jimmy. You fuckin' her?"

"God, no."

"Ugly?"

"No, not really. More like . . . asexual, if you know what I mean."

He laughed.

"That's what I like about you, Jimmy. Who else would say that? Fuckin' asexual."

"It is what it is, man," I said. "Fuckin' asexual. But come on, what are we doing out here? You need a ride? Throw that bike in the trunk; let's do something. I got some dope on me if you know someplace we can go."

"I know a place in Rubidoux," he said. "My boy Chuck's house.

That's where I was ridin' to. I was gonna ask you to drive me anyway."

After we put the bike in the trunk, Brady got in the car. He rapped the dashboard with his knuckles.

"How long you been goin' now?" I asked.

"I was doin' good for a while," he said. "I'm workin' as a mechanic, and I was clean for like five months. It was just last weekend I smoked a couple bowls. But I was okay, you know—back at work on Monday, worked the whole week. It's Friday again." He smiled. "So how's Wendy? You said this other girl's a friend of hers."

"Wendy's locked up."

"That sucks. Where?"

"Over at CRC in Norco. Short time, like four months. I just sent her a package. I'm supposed to go down by that other girl's place later—she said she came up on some credit-card numbers with addresses for the Western Union scam, you know, where you call and have cash sent—"

"Everybody knows the Western Union scam, Jimmy. Have you tried flowers? You know you can use a credit card to send flowers to yourself with cash as a gift."

"That's a good one."

"Yeah, it is. But you can count me out for all of that shit. Jimmy, I'll tell you right now, if you're going to meet some chick with stolen credit cards, you can drop me off. I ain't tryin' to be nowhere near any of that. I got a job, I'm doing good, it's the weekend, and all I wanna do is smoke this bowl. That's it. So if you could just drop me off in Rubidoux, I'd really appreciate it."

"Fuck that, man, I'm not dropping you off anywhere. I'm not

really trying to do that shit either. It's just that I still gotta put money on Wendy's books and pay for her collect phone calls and whatnot, but either way there's no rush. I don't have to be there any time soon. It's probably bullshit anyway. Stacie, her friend, does this all the time: calls me over, something about checks or a credit card, and then by the time I get there it's too late or I misunderstood, and meanwhile we just happen to be getting high with my dope. Fuck her. Let's both go to Rubidoux. Let's go get high at your boy's. Just tell me where to go. It's good to see you, man."

When it came to giving directions, Brady was spacey, and he had a bizarre tic: Every time we reached a stop sign, I had to turn to him and ask, "Left? Right? Straight?" and every time he would reply, "Forward, Jimmy—never straight."

"So you want me to go forward?"

"No, I'm just saying, it's 'forward,' not 'straight.' Here, I want you to make a right onto Mission and take it across the bridge. There'll be a trailer park on the right there, as soon as you get off the bridge."

On Mission Avenue we passed through Mount Rubidoux Memorial Park, then drove under an arching stone overpass and onto a four-lane steel bridge with a sidewalk where you could stand and look out across the dry riverbed. Rubidoux, a slummy desert town, seemed tinted rusty gold from all the dirt and sand.

"Home sweet home," said Brady.

"You said you were working. Around here?"

"No, over in Riverside—a garage on Fourth Street. I'm livin' over there too, at my sister's, but this is home sweet home. Born and raised. So you said you got some bunk heroin out here?"

"No, I said the heroin out here *is* bunk. That tar, it's bullshit. Why? Can you get me some?"

"Why would you want me to get you bunk?" he said, laughing.

"You work with what you got, dude. C'mon, don't fuck with me— can you get it or not?"

"Chuck probably can, and it won't be no bunk, neither. But how 'bout the pussy out here? You think that's any good, or is that bunk, too?"

"To be honest, I've actually gotten an embarrassingly small amount of it."

"Well, you ran into the right guy. We'll have to change that. But what, you haven't gotten any?"

"Aside from Mya—you know I went and lived with her after GSL—"

"How was she?"

"Loose."

"Yeah, I could have told you she was a slut."

"And there was one other. You remember Rachel from GSL?"

"Ugly, fat Rachel?"

"Yeah, exactly. Ugly, fat Rachel. It's actually a funny story. I'm over at the Memory Motel on Magnolia at like five in the morning, high as a kite, and I see Rachel in the parking lot. I'm like, what am I gonna tell her? How am I gonna explain being at the fucking Memory Motel at five in the morning? She's walkin' up to me, grinning, lookin' all stupid and shit; and then I'm like, wait a minute, if she's here at five in the morning, ain't no way she's still clean. . . ."

Brady, nodding along with my story, gestured for me to turn left into the Palm Woods mobile home park, which, unlike Stacie's, did look like the sort of trailer park they have in movies. We pulled onto a dirt road, parked, and got out, and then I followed Brady past a seemingly abandoned trailer toward a green mobile home with white trim. Its sideboards and windows were filthy. A two-foot-high white picket fence with a little swinging gate bounded the tiny, dried-out front lawn, and as we passed through the gate, Brady indicated, with a raised eyebrow and a tap on my shoulder, that it needed to be kept shut.

"So we go back up to the motel," I continued. "We do a shot and I get her to give me head. It was good, too. Fat girls give the best head. Then she says she's gotta go take care of a couple things, but I keep the room for an extra day and we agree to meet back early that night. Meanwhile I do a few things. I go to that girl Stacie's house and wait for a call from Wendy; then I hook up with Luke—you remember Luke from GSL—yeah, we've been hanging out, getting high and shit. The thing about Luke, though, is that whenever he smokes speed he gets fuckin' weird. I mean, every time. We'll get high somewhere, and at some point, usually pretty quick, he'll get real quiet and say, 'I gotta make a phone call; I'll be back in fifteen minutes.' Of course there's a phone wherever we are, but before you can say anything, he's gone. And the weird thing is that when he comes back, hours later, he's always come up on something—money, jewelry, something. I don't understand it, but he does this every time. He did it over at Stacie's the one time I took him there. Took off and came back at like six in the morning with like two hundred bucks and a story, said some nigger selling rock tried to jump him, and Luke beat him and took his money. I don't know. But anyway, after I talk to Wendy, I pick up Luke and take him back to the motel. As usual, he gets high and takes off. Then Rachel shows up . . ."

The rickety front door swung open and out burst a shirtless Vietnamese midget covered in prison tattoos. He hopped down the front steps, took a sharp pivot, and rushed out the gate and down the street, belatedly throwing a hand in the air to greet Brady.

"Did he shut the fence?" a man shouted from inside, a whiny voice.

"Nope," said Brady. "I'll get it."

"That fuckin' little gook!"

"That was Pan," said Brady, referring to the midget. "Chuck lets him live here. You were sayin', Rachel shows up . . ."

"Rachel shows up," I repeated distractedly. "Yeah, that's right. Rachel shows up. She's got dope. I've got dope. She's smokin' it, I'm bangin' it. I got some tar, too; I'm bangin' that shit, getting fucked up. She decides she wants a shot, too. I hit her. And now she's all fucked up, horny and shit. So I start fuckin' her. I'm fuckin' her in the ass—wait, no, no—I get her to give me head again first. That's right. I blow my load, she swallows it, and then I go to the bathroom to kinda clean myself off; and you know, at that point I don't give a fuck; I couldn't care less about her. So I walk out, and she's all high and horny and shit, lying on the ground, sucking on her fingers and, you know, playing with herself; and she's looking at me like she wants me to do something. I don't know what to do. I'm just standing there. So I just kinda reach with my foot—sock on, mind you—and I start . . . massaging her—"

"With your sock on," said Brady, opening the front door for me.

"Swear to God, dude. Anyway, I do more speed, get horny again, and I end up fuckin' her all night, in the ass, watching porno, a fucking meth marathon. Well, at one point, like seven in the morning, I'm half nodding, can't even get it up anymore, and she wants to get off. So I finger-bang her, and she comes so hard that she straight passes out. Out like a light, pants off, just lyin' on the bed. Like half an hour later someone knocks on the door. It's Luke. He's back with some shitty little necklace he got from God-knows-where, and I tell him Rachel's passed out in the room. I'd already told him about getting head from her in the morning when I first picked him up, so he's like, 'Leave me alone with her.' He's dead serious. I'm laughin' and shit. I don't care. Taco Bell's just about to open, so I go across the street and get one of those Nachos Supreme things, and when I come back, Luke's gone. Shit looks the same. Even her purse is still there. I get my shit together and go. Later when I see Luke, I ask him what happened, and he says he tried to get her to give him head, but she wouldn't wake up. So he took his dick out, and he's like smackin' it against her face and shit. She still won't wake up, so he says he just beat off, and nutted on her, and then left."

"Chuck, this is Jimmy from New Jersey," said Brady. "Jimmy, this is Chuck."

"So your friend just nutted on her and left, Jimmy," said Chuck, laughing.

At less than five feet tall, Chuck was puny and ill-proportioned—he had a potbelly and a large bald head, yet his arms and hands and legs were like a child's, thin and smooth—though he wasn't quite a dwarf. He was sitting in a brown recliner so large that he looked like a parody of a king.

"Yup, nutted on her and left," I confirmed, looking around for a place to sit. I settled on a child's wooden rocking chair next to a dusty old TV and a top-load VCR.

"Jimmy here's looking for some tar," said Brady, who upon entering the room had pounced on a long dresser draped with a black quilt and now sat packing a bowl of speed. "He's good people. I met him up at GSL."

I took out my own bag of speed, indicating that I would pack the next bowl—that I was, in fact, good people.

"I know he is," said Chuck. "Of course he's good people if you're bringin' him here, Brady."

Sitting on the recliner next to Chuck was a cruddy terrier with greasy curls—the reason, I gathered, for the fuss about the gate.

"Junkie Jack's around here with Cliff and Todd somewhere," Chuck said. "Probably in the shed shootin' up right now."

"I'll talk to him," said Brady, taking a lighter out of his pocket to spark the pipe.

A meth pipe is a glass tube about six inches long and a half inch in diameter, with a bubble and a small hole at one end—the chamber—where the meth crystals melt before vaporizing and then traveling up the tube into the smoker's mouth. Brady put his lips to the end of the tube, flicked the lighter, and took a deep hit. Smoke whirled in the chamber like a tempest in a crystal ball, clearing through the tube when Brady's cheeks dimpled, then billowing with a fresh fury when he relaxed and focused the lighter's flame.

"Chuck," I said, "who was that little guy who ran outta here a minute ago?"

"You mean the houseboy," Chuck said, as Brady handed him the pipe. Chuck took a huge hit of his own and then exhaled ostentatiously, pursing his lips and tilting his head to the ceiling, before explaining, "He's a gook."

"Oh," I said. "Okay."

There was a pause.

"Well, where does he sleep?"

Chuck's mobile home was far smaller than Stacie's. Aside from the living room, there was one bedroom, a kitchen, and a bathroom.

"In the shed. Why? What would you do with a gook?" said Chuck.

And we all roared with laughter as the room filled with smoke.

"Yeah, he's a fuckin' gook, all right," came a strange, gruff voice approaching from the kitchen. The words flowed like a river, one continuous rumble. "Hey, what's up, Brady, Chuck?"

"Hey, Jack," said Brady to a gaunt, tall man in faded jeans and a dirty T-shirt who swayed, leaned against the doorjamb, and then took a long stride into the room. "This is my friend Jimmy from New Jersey."

"I'm Jack," said the man. "They call me Junkie Jack round here— you can call me whatever you want."

Short with bushy eyebrows and a mane of receding white hair like Albert Einstein, Junkie Jack had a faded tattoo of a dagger running up the left side of his neck.

"Jimmy here was looking for some tar," said Chuck.

"Oh, yeah?" said Junkie Jack. "Tar. I can help you out with that. Friend of Brady's is a friend of mine. What do you want, twenty? I can break you out a twenty right now."

"How about a gram?" I said. "What can you do a gram for?"

"Gram—I'd like to help you with a gram, but that's like all I got. I normally get 'em for forty, but I'm not a drug dealer, I'm Junkie Jack. Whad'ya got there?"

He was pointing to my bag of meth, a healthy sack of dope, about an eight ball. I handed it to him, unworried, judging that he didn't want a fight any more than I did—that he appreciated what we all had here at Chuck's: a home that was friendly to junkies, where everybody was grateful for a safe place to get high. How could he not appreciate it, with Junkie for his first name?

"It's good shit," said Chuck.

"Looks good," said Jack, handing it back to me. "Tell ya what, I'll sell you the gram, but then I'll a be left with nothin'—guy just came around, ya know what I'm sayin'? So you give me forty—that's what *I* paid for it—and then you break me off a little piece so we can do a little shot."

"How about we do a little bit of both?" I said, holding up the meth.

"Now you're fuckin' talkin. How 'bout we do a lotta both? Go up and down"—he made an undulating wave in the air with his hand—"up and down. You need a point? I got lotsa points. C'mon."

He waved for me to follow him into the bedroom, where he sold me the gram and we each did a mixed shot. When we came out, Brady and Chuck were smoking another bowl. I lit a cigarette and held the pack out, offering. Junkie Jack took one and rumbled a warm thanks. I said I had to be somewhere, consciously choosing to leave on a high note in order to make a good impression. Chuck said I was welcome any time. Just before leaving, I took out my bag of meth and dropped a few crystals down on a small wooden table next to Chuck's recliner, casually explaining, "For the next bowl." As I walked out the door, I heard Brady say, "Hell, yeah, Jimmy's a good dude. He gave me these boots. They're the best boots I've ever had."

CHAPTER 8. AT THE CONCHA LINDA

Brady never went back to work. He called me in the middle of the following week, asking if I could get him a quarter ounce. I felt guilty. I thought I was responsible for his now full-blown relapse, and I even tried to talk him into cleaning up and going back to work—tried and failed. Over the next couple of weeks we started getting high together, and I never tried again. We went over to Chuck's regularly (where I found a regular heroin connection in Junkie Jack), and when one of us ran out of dope to sell, we each found sales for the other.

Brady also hooked me up with a girl he knew, a stripper who smoked meth. About two weeks after Brady and I ran into each other, I called her and took her to the cheapest motel in downtown Riverside, the Concha Linda, an old Spanish colonial revival–style three-story building with a circular annex in the back. It was morning when we checked in, and I was happy and excited—fully equipped with meth, heroin, needles, and a stripper—but by the early afternoon, after some bad sex, she was gone. She'd said she was going to the store for a soda and she hadn't come back.

So now I was alone in a strange motel room at midday, watching porn on my laptop, with showy little piles of meth and heroin in the ashtrays, needles on the nightstand. There was a queen-size bed and a round mahogany table with four mismatched chairs; the bathroom had no door, and the walk-in closet held a vacuum cleaner and bucket of soapy water. I stayed there all day—got high, masturbated, wrote a few poems. That night Danny White called my cell phone, saying he wanted to hang out and get high, meaning he wanted to smoke my dope instead of his own. I didn't mind, though. Danny and I had gotten along well since the time he had taken off with my money and I had pretended that Stacie paid me back. Besides, I'd been in that room for almost twelve hours, and I was getting lonely. I gave him directions to the motel, and he said he was coming with his girlfriend.

Danny arrived at a little before midnight, wearing jeans and a string T-shirt under an unbuttoned flannel shirt, showing off the tattoos on his chest. He was carrying a blue butane blowtorch. His girlfriend was a pretty redhead with brown eyes, named Nicole.

"Dude, I gotta give you credit," Danny said, taking a seat on the bed and lighting the torch. "I've been runnin' around this town since you were in diapers, and I never knew this place even existed."

"Thirty-five dollars a night, too."

Danny took a glass tube out of his pocket and blew a meth pipe by melting one end and blowing through the other to create the bubble-shaped chamber where the meth would sit. While the glass was still hot he poked an airhole in the chamber with a toothpick—the last touch. Then he leaned back and admired his work.

"Can we pack this?" he said. Then he laughed. "You don't even understand, dude—I blew a fucking pipe in Colton this *morning*. It was perfect, and she fuckin' lost it. I can't believe you lost that pipe, baby. I've been wantin' to smoke all day, but dude, we've been driving since, what, nine in the morning. From Colton to Fontana to La Sierra, saw Big Manny; then we got fuckin' pulled over—"

"You got pulled over? Then how the fuck are you not locked up?"

"That's what *I'm* sayin'! Dude, she keisters the dope, but they find residue in a baggy, so I'm thinkin' it's over. They got me cuffed. I'm tellin' her I love her and shit, already sayin' good-bye. I mean, this is highway patrol. But then, and I couldn't believe it, they fuckin' let me go. I couldn't believe it. We've just been lookin' at each other all day, like, *How the fuck . . . ?* I don't know what they're up to, maybe planning some big shit. But anyway, we're driving all over the place after that, moving all the shit 'cause we don't wanna be carrying it, and I never even got a chance to smoke! And somehow, at the end of the day, after I paid everybody back for all the fronts, I got almost no money and less than a half teener of dope. I don't even know how I pulled that off. So I say lemme call Jim. I know he'll help a brother out."

"You know it," I said. "It's right over there—in the ashtray."

"You wanna grab that, baby?"

Danny slid a few crystals down the tube, making sure one caught in the pipe's neck—a dip just before the chamber where, customarily, the last hit is saved for whoever supplied the dope. He then took a giant hit before passing the pipe to Nicole, who pursed her lips almost daintily as she lit the lighter and approached the tube. When she was finished, she pondered the taste by tapping her tongue against the roof of her mouth.

I told them about the girl Brady had set me up with, how easy she had been and then how she had just taken off. I made a joke out of it, laughing and calling her names as I walked around the room smoking a cigarette. Danny and Nicole thought it was hilarious. They packed another bowl. Then Brady called.

"What are you doin', Jimmy?" he said.

"I'm at the Concha Linda with Danny and his girl."

"Danny White?"

Danny and Brady had been in Tehachapi together. They were friendly, though not friends.

"Yeah, c'mon by," I said. "You remember where it is. Where I was the last time—room 137."

"I know it. I'm practically there."

After hanging up, I asked Danny if he minded if Brady stopped by. He said that he didn't care, that he didn't have any problems with Brady and it was my room regardless. About fifteen minutes later Brady knocked on the door. I let him in and immediately told him that the girl he had set me up with was nuts.

"What did I tell you, Jimmy?" he said. "They're all fuckin' nuts."

Everybody said hello, and then they rearranged the chairs to let Brady into the circle.

"This is just about dead, Brady," said Danny.

"Pack another one," I said. "It's right over there, in the ashtray. Go ahead, keep packing 'em. I'm gonna do a shot."

"Jimmy, Jimmy, Jimmy," said Brady when he saw the heroin.

The room was filling with smoke, and I had that feeling you get when people you've known separately are hanging out and getting along. I figured if I could just get a little higher the situation would be perfect, so I went into the bathroom and finished off the heroin with a shot that looked like creamy chocolate milk. I thought I would throw up, but the lump in my throat receded, and after a few minutes of clutching my knees and staring at the floor, the nausea passed, and I floated back through the smoke and lay down on the far side of the bed. Brady asked me if I was all right.

"Of course," I said, "but I might just pass out here, so you guys stay as long you want."

"Go for it," said Danny, laughing. "I'm gonna pack another bowl here, this time from the emergency stash, 'cause—no offense, Jim—what you got here is good, but I wanna taste some of this rocket fuel."

"Whad'ya got there?" said Brady. "You think this is better?"

I began to nod.

Lamplight shimmered in the smoke, which sailed past me at a steady, disorienting pace, and then it was the room that was moving. "This one's done," I heard; "one more?" and then, "Why not?" I lost track of it all, feeling warm and cozy. There was laughter, and flicking lighters, and Danny's voice coming from somewhere, a dream, maybe, or a muffled radio, noise from an infomercial at two in the morning:

"Check this out—Brady's so fuckin' scandalous, he hit the neck of my pipe."

It was a joking tone, must have been, some friendly ball-breaking, because hitting the neck of a pipe is not a big deal. It's like asking for a sip and taking a gulp. That's all.

"No, I didn't," said Brady.

"Oh, c'mon. Yeah, you did."

"No, I didn't."

"Well, did you hit it, Nicole?"

"No."

"So then, you hit it, Brady—'cause I know I didn't."

"No, Danny—I already said, I didn't hit it."

"Well, check this out, Brady—there's only three of us here, and I know I didn't hit it, and my girl's sayin' she didn't. So then if you're sayin' you didn't, you're callin' my girl a liar. You're disrespectin' my girl. And you better not be disrespectin' my girl, Brady, or you'll get fuckin' smashed up in here."

When I heard the word "smashed," I managed to lift my head off the pillow. They were still sitting, Brady in his chair and Danny on the edge of the bed leaning toward him.

"All I know is I didn't hit the neck of your pipe, you son of a bitch," said Brady.

He leaned back and slouched all the way into his chair so that his shoulders rested against the back cushion, as if to say, *See? Look how relaxed I am—and that's the end of it.* I was lying on my back, only half conscious, straining to keep my head up. Over there, somewhere, the feeling was incredibly tense, but only over there. I was warm and cozy, dimly aware, and when Brady leaned back, I figured it was all okay. I closed my eyes and didn't see Danny pick up the blowtorch and use it to split Brady's head open.

The sound was like a muffled cymbal, and the blowtorch fell to the floor.

I jumped up. Brady was backpedaling across the room, stumbling and covering his head, while Danny threw wild punches at his shoulders and forearms. They moved together in a frenzy of arms and grunts, bumping into the table and knocking over chairs, Brady with a shocked look on his face that said he just wanted this to stop. When for a split second Danny cornered him against the wall, they instantly twirled around and started across the room again. It didn't seem possible for them to stop moving.

I surprised myself by getting behind Danny. I grabbed him around his chest and arms, pulled him across the room, and said, "Calm down."

"Brady, don't you ever fuckin' disrespect my girl!" Danny shouted. He didn't struggle much. He took a few deep breaths and then seemed to realize I was holding him. "Get off me!" he growled, though it was understood that he was done fighting.

"Keep it down, man," I said as I let him go. "It's late at night. This is my fucking room."

Danny mumbled a sorry, then told Nicole to get whatever stuff they'd brought. Brady stumbled to the bed and sat down. He blinked rapidly with his mouth hanging open; he rocked and pressed his palm against his forehead while Nicole picked up the blowtorch from a corner of the room. Halfway out the door, Danny looked back at Brady, then shook his head and left. Brady kept rocking on the bed.

"Are you all right?" I said.

"What do you think?" he snapped.

He jumped up and went into the bathroom and a few moments later I heard him, a scared voice—"Oh, fuck!"—and I knew he had just looked in the mirror. He came back into the room, and there was a line, practically black, that ran from his right eyebrow to his hairline. It was speckled with blue paint chips.

"I gotta get to the hospital," said Brady.

"Can you drive?"

"No. I don't even have a fucking car here. I got dropped off."

"Oh. Well, then let's go."

I gathered all my meth into one bag and stuck it up my ass—the only place I trusted while driving through Riverside at one in the morning—then I grabbed my laptop and leather jacket and walked with Brady to the car. The streets were mostly empty. A car here and there, but it would pass and then we'd be all alone, two guys on a wide California road, one of them with bloody hair and a foot on the dash. *What am I doing here? That's actually a good question, officer.* The lights took forever.

"Which way are we goin' here, Brady? Left? Right? Straight?"

"Forward, Jimmy—never straight."

I laughed. He smiled. He directed me down Mission Avenue and had me pull over at a house just before Commerce Street. I knew the place, a sprawling yellow house that had been converted into a sober-living and then practically abandoned. Now it was just a bunch of two-room apartments rented to junkies. No questions, no maintenance; a get-high spot with whores on the front porch.

"I thought we were going to the hospital. What are we doing *here*?"

"Gotta stash my dope at Molly's—c'mon."

"Who the fuck is Molly?"

"C'mon."

Molly was a pitifully dumb girl who weighed barely a hundred pounds and whose apartment wasn't really hers anymore; she'd let the junkies in with no way of getting them out. But there weren't too many people there when we showed up: three or four who all knew Brady. They jumped up and asked him what had happened, got him ice and told him to sit down. He said he was sure he had a concussion and that he was on his way to the hospital. He was just here to stash his dope, but fuck it, why not smoke one more bowl? They all cheered. Then, while smoking, they reminisced about all the fights Brady had been in, about the time Brady had overpowered a guy who'd tried to pistol-whip him. I stood just outside the circle and watched Brady smoke and smile, wincing whenever he adjusted the ice on his forehead. One bowl turned to two, and someone suggested Brady take Tylenol. I argued that he shouldn't, not with a concussion. The argument lasted a while. "You don't know what you're talking about." "No, you don't know what you're talking about." They all smoked another bowl.

An hour later we were on Fourteenth Street driving toward Riverside Community Hospital, worried that someone would call the cops on us when we got there.

"You can just drop me off at the door," said Brady, "or . . . maybe wait for me."

"No," I said, "I'll come in with you. But what are we gonna tell 'em?"

"I walked into a shelf."

"Where?"

"At my house, in my garage."

I laughed. Brady's owning his own house seemed so absurd to me that I thought he was joking. But Brady wasn't laughing. He was dead serious. And why not? What was so unreasonable about a forty-three-year-old man, a mechanic, owning a little house where he could stay up late watching TV and fetching beers from a fridge in the garage? A little drinking, a little stumble, and bam! Perhaps a month ago this had been a plan of his, saving enough money to buy a little house. Perhaps it still was. Surely he would have laughed if I'd told him that I still planned on going to college.

"I guess we'll tell 'em it was painted blue," I said.

"What?"

"The shelf in your garage—it was painted blue."

At the hospital Brady filled out forms, and we were led to an open room with operating stations divided by curtains. The nurses kept asking Brady, "Is this your friend?" and I became paranoid, wondering why they were all so interested in me, until I realized that the nurses were testing his memory. The doctor soon came. He asked Brady what had happened—"Jesus Christ! What happened to you?"—but he didn't even wait for an answer. After injecting an anesthetic into Brady's forehead, he held the wound open, examining it with a flashlight. I could see the skull. The doctor told Brady that he had a concussion and there would be a scar, but that otherwise he would be okay. Then he left the nurses to do the stitching. This took about an hour. As the situation began to feel less like our drama and more like their work, I started to nod, and one of the nurses gave me a chair, thinking that Brady's skull was making me queasy. Then another nurse commented on the blue paint chips, and I got to tell her that the shelf in Brady's garage was blue.

After he was all stitched up, I drove Brady back to his sister's. He thanked me and said he'd be in touch. When I got back on the road I started to fall asleep. I didn't think I could make it to Norco, so I decided to go back to the Concha Linda and pass out until checkout and maybe then I'd spring for another night. I drove down Market Street and began to turn into the parking lot.

"There he is," I heard someone say.

Four people were walking from the annex into the parking lot toward my car: Nicole; Maleah, the dark-haired girl I'd met at Stacie's; and in front of them Danny White and Maki. For a second I thought about backing out of the parking lot and driving away, but they'd already seen me. They were waving. Maki was walking over, smiling, nodding, *What's up?* I nodded back. He was only a few yards away. I hadn't seen him since the time we'd driven to get heroin. We hadn't talked since I'd apologized for threatening him and he'd said it was cool, but then again I hadn't trusted him . . .

"What's up, dude?" Maki said.

He was only a few feet from the car.

"The lot's full," I said. "What's up, man? I gotta park on the street."

Maki walked to the sidewalk and watched me struggle with a spot. Two false starts, and on the third try I was still several feet from the curb. I opened the door and looked down doubtfully.

"Jimmy, you're good. Don't worry about it," Maki said.

"You think so?"

"Yeah, you're fine—leave it." He leaned through the passenger window and shook my hand. "So what's up, dude? I haven't seen you at Stacie's."

"I've been kinda tryin' to stay away from that place," I said. "It gets kinda crazy over there."

"Yeah, I know what you mean," he said. "But I'm sure you'd be cool. I was just over there. We were actually talking about you. Danny said you had dope. I need to re-up. Remember how you were sayin' you'd hook it up?"

"Oh, yeah, sure," I said. "I mean, I don't know about a whole re-up; I only got like an eight ball. But, fuck, I'll sell it to you."

"You can hook it up, though, right? You know I'm tryin' to flip it."

"Yeah, of course."

Danny walked over to the sidewalk.

"Hey, what's up, Jim?"

"What's up, Danny? Look, just meet me at the room—I'm just gonna get this thing closer to the curb—and that way we're not all waitin' on the street."

They paused for a half second, glanced at each other. Then Maki said sure, and they walked back through the parking lot toward the annex. The two girls followed. I was glad that the girls were there, because if Danny and Maki were planning on trying something, why would they have brought the girls? Still, I slipped my wallet, full with about three hundred dollars, under my laptop in the trunk of my car before walking through the parking lot to my room.

It was about six in the morning, and the reception desk was empty.

"Where's Brady?" asked Danny.

"I dropped him off," I said. "We were in the fucking emergency room all night."

"Is he okay?" Danny asked.

"I guess."

Maki and Danny and the girls crowded behind me as I fumbled with the lock. Then, high and exhausted, I opened the door and made a beeline for the bed, as though it were somehow safer there. I turned and lay on my back with my hands clasped behind my head. Danny was closing the door. The girls had not come in. Maki, still smiling, was standing over me with a knife.

"Jimmy," Maki said, seemingly giddy, holding the knife tightly next to his hip. "I would love to stick you so fucking much right now."

For years I'd fantasized about what I would do and say in a situation like this. I'd seen myself as either a wild man, overpowering my attackers and making them beg for mercy, or as a cool customer, calmly convincing them that hurting me would be impractical. And though I had always known, even in high school, that these were in fact fantasies, I had never guessed just how different the reality would be. I didn't *decide* not to fight. Rather, I became so scared that everything I did seemed involuntary. The blood drained from my face, and I didn't realize that I was inching backward on the bed until my back was pressed against the headboard.

"Get up," said Maki, and as I stood, my hands just went up over my head. Maki grabbed one of my arms and turned me around. He reached into my jacket pocket, took out my knife, and sneered.

"Take it off—slowly," he said, pulling at my jacket. "I swear to God, Jimmy, if you even fuckin' move fast . . ."

His hand was trembling on my shoulder as I worked my arm down the sleeve. I was worried that I might flinch.

"Danny," I said, "you wanna help me with this jacket, so Maki knows I'm not trying anything?"

"No, I think he's doing just fine," Danny said. "You see, in Riverside this is what we call a shakedown. Now we're gonna search you."

I finished taking off my jacket and dropped it on the bed. Then Maki searched my pants pockets with his free hand, throwing the motel and car keys, along with change and cigarettes, on the bed. He reached into my back pockets, which were empty. Then he pulled at my pants.

"Take 'em down," he said.

I undid the button and pulled my pants down. Then I realized that I was standing in my boxers and that I'd been forced to take off my pants.

"Where the fuck have you got it?" Maki said angrily. "Where's the dope?"

"It's in my ass," I said.

"It's what?"

"That's where he keeps it," said Danny.

"Get it," said Maki.

I pulled out the baggy.

"Don't give me that shit," said Maki. "Put it in a tissue or something. Where's your wallet?"

"It's not here," I said.

"Where is it?" said Danny.

"It's at my friend John's house. I dropped it off on the way over here."

"So I'm doin' all this shit for a fuckin' eight ball!" said Maki.

"All right," said Danny. "If you dropped it off, you don't have it, but we're all gonna take a drive somewhere and search your car, so—"

"It's in the trunk."

"Pull your pants up."

"And put your jacket on," said Maki. "Look, Jimmy, we're gonna walk to your car now, so if you try anything—if you make any noise—I will stick you so fuckin' fast."

When we reached the parking lot, Maki put his arm around my shoulder and skipped enthusiastically to show the few cars driving by that we were friends having an outrageously good time. But I was sure that nobody was looking. Again I thought to run, but it just didn't happen.

The girls were waiting by Danny's car. They wouldn't look at me.

Danny gave his car keys to Nicole and my keys to Maleah. Then he said that we were all getting in his car and that Maleah should follow in mine. Maki herded me into the backseat, then got in and faced me with the knife.

"Go to the park," Danny told Nicole as he climbed in the passenger side. "No, not on Market. Turn around—you can go straight all the way to Fourth. I'll tell you when to turn."

Nicole began to make a U-turn, but Maleah had already pulled out behind her.

"That dumb bitch," said Danny. "Back the fuck up!"

"Sorry!" Maleah screamed. She was crying.

Danny shook his head, then turned to me.

"All right, Jim," he said. "We're goin' to Fairmont Park. Do you know Fairmont Park? No? Well, I do. And the reason I know is 'cause

I've lived here in Riverside since I was a kid. I know every inch of this town. Maki, too—he grew up here. You been out here for what, like six months? You're runnin' around here sellin' eight balls and quarters and shit—fuck, I wasn't selling quarters when I was your age. But ya know, whatever, that's cool; you came up fast 'cause of Wendy. Whatever. Personally I don't think she did you any favors, 'cause I don't think you're ready for it—and this is what happens—but you'll get your shit together. Knowin' you, you'll probably come up again real soon.

"As far as what we got here, whatever's between you and Maki, that's got nothin' to do with me. That's you and him. As far as we go, you've been good with me and you're takin' care of my Wendy, and I always said that's cool, but she doesn't have anything to do with this. This is about my girl being disrespected in your room."

"I didn't disrespect your girl," I said.

"No, you didn't. But you did let Brady disrespect her under your roof. That's your room—you gotta control that shit."

"All right," I said, "I don't really . . . okay. Look, Maki, I apologized to you before for getting out of line. I'm apologizing to you now."

"That's cool, Jimmy," said Maki. "You know I never had any problems with you."

"Yeah," said Danny, "and if you wanna leave it at that, at an apology, then that's cool. This can end right here."

"But if you call any of those fuckin' people you run around with," Maki said, "I will find you, Jimmy."

We pulled up to a picnic area that overlooked a lake. Danny told me to wait in the backseat for a few minutes while everybody else got out. Maleah pulled up and I heard the trunks open and close, and then Danny called me outside.

"All right, Jimmy, this can be it, right here," said Maki.

He was holding my wallet, counting the money.

"Do you think you can give me twenty bucks?" I said.

"Yeah, ya know what, Jimmy—I can do that for you."

Maki handed me a twenty and my car keys, and then they all got into Danny's car and drove away. After the car disappeared, I turned and looked at the park. It was a gorgeous day, a gorgeous view. A family was sitting at a picnic table, parents and two children; a man was running on a path that went around the shimmering lake. It was an idyllic scene, and I stared at it numbly for a while. Then I remembered that my laptop had been in the trunk of my car. I checked and it was gone. My poems were gone.

CHAPTER 7. ALONE WITH THE BUSHMEN

In the following weeks I became obsessed with retrieving my stolen poems. Whenever I was getting high with anybody who might have even heard of Danny White, I would tell that person to deliver Danny a message: that he could keep the computer and I would let the whole thing go if only he copied my poems to a floppy disk and had them delivered to me. "That's it," I would say. "You tell him."

Of course, I also needed to recover the lost money so I could go on shooting dope.

"Mom, I have to tell you something. I was walking out of Maxi Foods with my friend Brady. You remember Brady—from GSL, I was telling you—the mechanic, staying at one of the sober-livings in Woodcrest. I told you we've been going to meetings . . ."

"I think I remember you telling me about a Brady."

"Anyway, we were walking out of Maxi Foods last night and these Mexicans jumped us. Brady tried to fight, and one of them hit him in the head with a bottle. I had to take him to the emergency room. They got all my money and my computer."

"How many were there?"

"Hi, Dad. Four."

"Jesus Christ, Jim. Are you okay?"

"Yeah, I think so. It's just I was at the emergency room all night and I'm exhausted. A little shaken up."

"You sound shaken up. I'm so sorry that happened to you. And they got the computer?"

"Yeah . . . my poems."

"I'm sorry. I'm really sorry . . . but Jim—I have to ask—we haven't heard from you in weeks—"

"I work all day, then go to meetings. I have friends. I haven't wanted to trouble you—"

"Trouble us?"

"No, I'm just saying. I'm enjoying being independent. This kind of shit happens when you're on your own."

"Not necessarily. Never happened to me or Dad."

"Well, out here it does. But that's not the point. I mean, I wouldn't even be calling to worry you if I didn't need money for rent."

"We sent you money for rent."

"I've been using that to live on, food and stuff. I was gonna use my paycheck to pay the rent, but now it's gone, over six hundred dollars. I mean, I hate to have to ask you—I like being independent—but I don't know what else to do."

"No, of course. I'm just glad you told us. And it's never any trouble for us when you call. Please call more. Can we send a check?"

"Western Union would be better, only because the landlady's been asking me. I didn't see her before and then I ran low on cash. I'm sorry. I know it's a fortune."

"It is, but we'll do it. Just tell me—are you sure you're okay?"

"Yeah, I promise. I'm fine. Happy, even, aside from this."

"Is Brady okay?"

"Yeah, he'll be fine."

With a half ounce of meth from Patti, I got back on my feet: dealing, shooting up, crashing on her couch. Then, a few weeks after the robbery, one of the regular heroin junkies over at Chuck's—Todd, a shady character—told me that Stacie was selling a Toshiba laptop for two hundred dollars. Todd said that if I gave him an eight ball to barter with he was sure he could bring me back the laptop within an hour. I had long suspected Stacie of being a passive participant in what had happened. I was sure Danny and Maki had plotted at her house, and I didn't doubt that she'd had advance knowledge. It was quite possible that she would now be selling the computer. But I had learned a little something over the past months in Riverside, and even though I'd been up for three days, I wasn't about to hand over an eight ball and hope for the return of my computer. I told Todd that I'd go over there myself, that I appreciated his concerns about it being dangerous for me, but that this was something I had to do. Then I drove to Luke's to see if he would back me up.

Luke didn't want to go. Again and again he reminded me that he had a kid—that he wasn't trying to do this sort of thing anymore. I in turn reminded him of all the money I'd given him since GSL, money that he'd often said he needed because of his daughter. "How can you ask me to do all this shit for you because you have a family, and then refuse to help me out the one time I need you . . . because you have a family?" I was relentless, shouting, cursing. "You're supposed to be my big brother!

Remember that? And the one time I fucking need you . . ."

"Fine," he said finally. "Just fuckin' have me back here in a couple hours."

Walking to the car, I called Stacie and asked if Danny and Maki were there. She said that they weren't and wouldn't be any time soon; not only had she banished them from the house several weeks ago when she heard what they'd done to me, they were both back in prison, having been picked up recently for parole violations. I said, "Sure," and hung up. I checked the trunk to make sure I'd taken my baseball bat.

On the way over, Luke asked me if I had any dope, because if he was going to be doing this shit he might as well fucking do it. I handed him a screwdriver from the center console and told him to take the face off the speaker by his right knee. Luke removed the half ounce I'd gotten from Patti. He dipped his driver's license into it and dropped a few crystals on a CD case, then cut himself a fat line and sarcastically offered to do the same for me.

"Oh yeah, I forgot," he said. "All you wanna do is shoot this shit."

We parked in a lot around the corner from Stacie's. Luke put the dope back in the speaker, and I took my bat out of the trunk.

"You gonna hit somebody with that?" Luke said snidely.

"I hope not," I said.

I knocked on Stacie's door, holding the bat behind my leg. There were stabs of fear, flashes of what might happen if Maki and Danny were really inside, but mostly I thought about getting my computer back. I was obsessed, and after three sleepless days, with shadows whispering and faces beginning to look alike, that obsession had become a driving force, powerful enough to overcome fear and reason. Stacie opened the door and I brushed past her before she could see the bat.

"Are they here?" I said.

"Who?"

"Danny and Maki."

"No, Jimmy, I told you, they're locked up. Why do you have a bat? Luke, what's wrong with him?"

I checked all the rooms and closets for Danny and Maki. *What's wrong with him?* The only other person there was Lori, Maki's girlfriend, who warily assured me that Danny and Maki were both back in prison. She said they'd had a falling out over the money they'd stolen from me and now Maki was gonna smash Danny. "Yeah, right," I said, and opened a closet door, bat poised to swing. *What's wrong with him?* When I was satisfied that neither Maki nor Danny was in the house, I started searching for the laptop, in cabinets, under beds; I buried myself under old clothes in Stacie's bedroom closet. Then, with a shock, I realized I'd left the bat next to the bed. I threw the clothes aside, stumbled out of the closet, picked up the bat, and looked around. *What's wrong with him?* I did find, at the very back of the closet, two laptop computers, both partially disassembled. I laid them on the bed and scrutinized them for parts that might have been taken from mine. One of the keyboards had a familiar stain on the letter *N*. Months ago I had accidentally squirted heroin from a needle onto my computer; a splotch had dried on the letter *N*. Now here was the stain. I scratched it with my fingernail, tasted it. Bitter, but not heroin bitter. Would heroin maintain its bitterness for months on the letter *N*?

Then again, wouldn't the dirt under my fingernails be about as bitter as what I just tasted?

"I wish you'd calm down," Stacie said. "Nobody's here. I've had those computers in that closet for over a year. Please, you're scaring me. You need to get some sleep."

"I'm tired," I said. "Hungry, too."

"Go to sleep," Stacie said. "Leave the bat and go to bed in Megan's room. Nobody's gonna hurt you here."

Luke was talking with Lori on the couch in the living room. Passing him, I said I was going to take a quick nap, maybe an hour, and I'd drive him home soon. He told me to relax; he was about to smoke a bowl of speed and he'd wake me when he needed to go.

In the morning I woke up in Megan's room. Luke was gone. He'd taken my car keys, told the girls he was going to pick up some food, and never returned.

Stacie said she would drive me to Luke's house but first I should eat something, and over breakfast I realized that Stacie and Lori had been telling the truth the night before: Danny and Maki really were back in prison, and Stacie was not selling my computer. She couldn't be, Lori explained, because only a few days after stealing it, Danny had dropped the computer and cracked the screen.

"So what about the hard drive?" I asked, thinking of my poems. "Do you know where that is?"

"Jimmy, they're fuckin' tweakers," said Lori. "They could have taken it anywhere, and now that they're in prison somebody's using it for parts. It's gone. You know it."

Later that morning Stacie drove me to Luke's neighborhood, and we found my car in a lot behind the sober-living, separated from it by a long, overgrown backyard, a wire fence, and needle grass. The car was unlocked, but the keys weren't there. I tore open the speaker, where my quarter-ounce had been stashed. The dope was gone.

After Stacie left, I sat in the car for about ten minutes, blowing the horn in frustration, getting ready to walk around the block and knock on Luke's door. But then one of his roommates showed up at the fence, called me over, and handed me the keys.

"Luke asked me to give these to you," he said.

"Where the fuck is he?"

He put his hands in the air and walked away and said, "Man, that's got nothing to do with me."

I drove around the block. I rang the doorbell at least twenty times, knocking, cursing, "I know you're up there." It was a loud doorbell, and I tapped out ferociously insistent little rhythms that echoed venomously up the stairs, saying, *That's right—fuck you—I'm not gonna stop.* After minutes of knocking, ringing, he still didn't come down, so I walked around to his window and shouted up to him, called him a cocksucker for starters, then a coward and a bitch, told him to come downstairs and face me like a man. Then I went back to jabbing away at the doorbell until the sober-living manager came to the door. A gay guy named Harry, one of my old GSL counselors, said, "Jimmy, what are you doing? It's Sunday morning. I can't have this here."

"I have to talk to Luke," I said. "Sorry, I don't mean to start trouble here, Harry, but I have to talk to Luke."

He shook his head, said, "Just wait," and then walked up the stairs.

A few minutes later Luke came to the door. He opened it halfway and groggily muttered something about this not being cool. He squinted and rubbed his eyes, poorly pretending that he'd just woken up. The ploy was so bad it was ridiculous, and yet I completely understood the impulse, when cornered and guilty, to squint and act groggy. If he was sleepy, not yet thinking properly, then it felt as though he couldn't really be held accountable—for not answering the door, for taking my car, for anything, really. And even though I didn't buy the act for a second, I did, almost involuntarily, lower my voice. It just seemed wrong to shout at somebody who hadn't woken up properly. I put a foot on the threshold, indicating I meant to come in, and whispered, "'Not cool'? What the fuck do you mean, 'not cool'? Where the fuck have you been? Where's my fuckin' dope?"

We went up to his room, and he sat on the bed with his head in his hands and told me a story about getting pulled over and tossing the dope out the window, about returning to the spot and searching for hours and hours, about I'm-sorry-I-felt-so-bad-but-you-have-to-understand-I'm-on-parole-dude.

I told him he was full of shit.

"What do you mean?" he said, feigning anger.

I asked him why the cop didn't arrest him for being high on speed. He said that the cop couldn't tell. I asked him where the ticket was for driving an uninsured vehicle. He said the cop didn't check for insurance. I said, "A cop pulls a parolee over at two in the morning and doesn't check for insurance?" I asked him where the dope was. He said he threw it out the window.

"So it's not here," I said. "Then you don't mind if I look around."

At first I made a show of it, turning over pillows and opening nearby drawers for a cursory scan. But when he just sat there with his head in his hands, I decided to push it, to see how far he'd let me go, to see how bad he felt. I checked under both beds and thoroughly searched his dresser drawers. I even unfolded his shirts. The further he let me go, the more painful it became. Luke wasn't just some tweaker who'd gotten over on me; we'd known each other at GSL, before meth and borrowed money, when there was only talking, and rolling each other cigarettes, and covering for each other when we slept too late. He'd given me advice about girls. He'd taught me how to lift weights. And now here he was, holding his head in his hands while I rifled through his room for the drugs he'd stolen from me.

When I went inside the huge walk-in closet, he began to object, saying that most of the stuff in there wasn't his. This was true, I could tell, but by then I wanted to get a rise out of him, so I started on his roommate's bags.

"Dude," he said, "get out of there. It's not even mine."

"So this is where the dope is?"

"Dude, shut up. I don't have your dope. Stop going through that dude's bag. He's not gonna let you go through his shit like I am, and you don't want to start anything with him. He's a convict; he's no joke."

"Fuck him."

Luke got up and stood in the closet doorway.

"Get away from the bag."

"Fuck you."

"Dude, if you don't get away from the bag, I'm gonna make you get away from the bag."

"Oh, yeah?" I said, looking up at him, and by now I was fighting back tears.

He shook his head and sat back down on the bed.

"Just admit to me that there was no cop," I said. "Give me that much, at least."

"There was no cop," he said quietly.

I walked out of the closet. I sat on the other bed and leaned back, putting my forearm across my eyes. I tried to cry but couldn't. I'd already fought the tears back and now they wouldn't come.

Luke amended his story to he *thought* he'd seen a cop. He'd sketched out, and now he was sorry; he would help me get the money back. He said he knew a girl running a successful scam stealing clothing from her job at Nordstrom in the Tyler Mall, and he could definitely convince her to . . . but by then I wasn't listening. I sat there nodding my head, saying, "That'd be cool." Then I had to go.

I hadn't been to my room in several weeks, and I was more than a month behind in rent, so when I finally returned to the house in Norco, I was expecting my landlady to kick me out. I went with a tweaker named Richard. We planned to move all my stuff into my new room at his girlfriend's house, a room that Richard had convinced his girlfriend to rent me for only a hundred dollars a month. With promise of a cheaper room where I didn't have to worry about being caught on hidden camera, I couldn't have cared less about being kicked out by my landlady. That is, until I came inside and my landlady told me that she'd called the cops to make sure I didn't steal anything while I was leaving.

I ran back out to the car to give Richard a heads-up, to tell him
that the cops would be there soon and that he should stash whatever
he had. I told him I would understand if he wanted to take off through
the field. He just laughed, though. He said that this was Norco and
that, having seen my landlady, he was pretty sure we'd be okay. Not
understanding, I raced back inside and started gathering all the paraphernalia in the room. I folded spoons and needles into Wendy's soiled
panties, then threw all the clothes, hers and mine, into her old suit-
cases. There were also her purses, jewelry, and CD player, as well as
my boom box and CDs scattered behind the nightstand; so it took
several trips, and soon the cop was there, talking with my landlady in
the hall.

Passing them, I pretended to be furious, rolling my eyes and scoff-
ing at the accusations she was making. The cop didn't stop me, so on
the next trip I was more confident. Carrying a trash bag and the CD
player, I stopped in front of them and stared at my landlady, bug-eyed
with rage and incredulity. "Are you kidding me?" I shouted as she complained to the officer that I'd gone through all her drawers and that
my friend had woken her up at five in the morning. Then I stormed
out to the car. On the next trip I began to do this again, but as soon
as I stopped in the hallway, the cop put his hand up and nodded as if
to say, *Don't worry; I understand. I know what's going on here.* I didn't
know what to make of it.

I went into my room and gathered the rest of my stuff and then
headed back down the hallway. The cop wasn't there anymore; he was
talking to Richard by the car. I walked past him and tried to squeeze
the last bundle of clothes (including Wendy's panties wrapped around

syringes) next to Wendy's suitcase, but it was no good—the trunk wouldn't close. Panicking, I tried to rearrange everything without looking too flustered or nervous, but then I overheard Richard and the cop talking. They seemed calm, even friendly. I stopped and listened and knew that I could relax when I heard the cop say, "Yeah, it's gotten to the point that *we're* the minority."

Driving away, I felt pretty cocky. I'd gotten away with not paying rent for the past month, and now I had a cheaper room and, it was beginning to seem, a new partner in Richard. But that arrangement fell apart within a couple of days: The girlfriend, a bank teller, began to understand that Richard was trying to rob her bank account. They got into a fight, and she had him arrested for domestic abuse.

The next day my parents called and told me that they knew I was getting high. Before kicking me out, my landlady had called them and recited her list of my strange behavior. At first I denied it, but after quickly reassessing I figured it was time for damage control and I admitted to *slipping*.

They asked me where I was living, and I told them at a house on Main Street in downtown Riverside belonging to friends of Wendy: Paul and John Ruden. This was a lie with a grain of truth. Wendy had introduced me to Paul and John before she went back to prison; since then whenever I was in their neighborhood I stopped by to say what's up and smoke a joint, and every once in a while I slept on their couch. Paul was a plumber in his fifties who'd cleaned up his act about ten years earlier, discharging his parole and becoming a law-abiding citizen (except for a joint or two when he got home from work). John was Paul's son. He was in his twenties and he shot heroin, though he worked for, rather than stole, his dope money—he wasn't a street thug. This was the only house I knew where you weren't supposed to shoot up and where you might get kicked out for forging stolen checks on the coffee table, the only house where I had a chance of getting phone messages from my parents.

I told my parents that I was struggling to stay clean, but that I was stable and that Paul and John's house was safe. I also asked them for some money to pay Paul a little rent; and, to my surprise, they agreed to send a few hundred dollars under the condition that they could reach me at the number I provided and that I promised to not get high. It turned out that all they wanted, at that point, was to keep me safe and in one place: A week earlier Joe had been released from the Southwest Detention Center in Murrieta, and with one son fresh out of jail and the other slipping, my parents had decided it was time to take a trip to California.

They would arrive in about three weeks, but until then I would hardly talk to them. In fact, the first week after they sent the money, I didn't return their calls at all. I shot drugs and stayed in motel rooms, and most of the days were a drugged-out blur.

Congratulations, baby—it's a good thing you called! You've been selected to talk live, one-on-one with a hot and horny girl who will fulfill your every fantasy, all at the premium price of two-ninety-nine per minute. These sexy babes are just waiting to get you off. They'll lick and suck and—oh—wanna find out more? Then press one to pay with your check-ing account. Simply enter the number located at the bottom of your check. No operators, no hassles. So press one now, or enter your Visa,

Master Card, American Express, or Discover card number, followed by
the pound sign. . . .

A few prompts and age verifications later and the phone sex line
informs me that my credit card will be charged an additional dollar
ninety-nine per minute for the premium service I've selected of talking
live, one-on-one, with a sexy babe who is looking to get me off. Then,
after falsely describing ourselves, Elena and I spend hours chatting and
talking aimlessly. Because I'm tweaking and incredibly lonely (and
because I'm using somebody else's credit-card number), the conversation can go for fifteen minutes without touching on anything more
erotic or even flirtatious than my asking Elena where she is and if she
thinks we might actually meet. When she tells me that it's possible
but that first she wants to get to know me a little better, I pretend to
become angry and, in my most sardonic voice, go on a rant explaining
to her that I know her job is to keep me on the phone for as long as
she can while my credit card gets billed and that I plan to keep talking
with her either way, so she might as well not bullshit me. Then she
tells me I'm really smart. She asks me how I got so smart and I tell her
my parents are both therapists and I have a talent for reading people.
Then the conversation takes a few more turns, and ten minutes later
the phone sex line disconnects us. I take a shot of meth, call back, and
come on the carpet before the recording is finished.

I put my boxers on and look around the room at my mess, at my
dope and needles on the tan table, at the scraps of paper scribbled with
credit-card and checking-account numbers. The Playboy channel is
muted. During these rare minutes before I'm horny again I feel smart
to wonder whether the faces and exaggerated grinding movements are

more or less ridiculous without the music. A chair is leaning against the drapes, holding them shut. Here at the Memory Motel if you don't use a chair (or a stapler), the drapes part slightly at the top and then people can look into my room, and I'm sure that everybody wants to look into my room. Beside the TV is a case of the meal-replacement drink Ensure. I bought it from the store a few hours ago, figuring that if I can get all the necessary vitamins and nutrients from these drinks I might as well save some money and stop buying food.

A noise from outside. I get up and check the peephole and a figure darts behind a bush on the Magnolia Avenue median. Slowly I step back from the peephole and duck. I don't know how long I've been awake. Then I crawl back to the door, line up below the peephole, and creep as close as I can to it without casting a shadow for somebody on the other side of the door to see. Aside from Elena I haven't talked to anybody in days. I take a deep breath and pop up. The figure is so fast, though, that by the time my vision settles, he's already in motion. And then it's like trying to keep track of a grasshopper jumping through the air: There's a streak, and then all I know is that he's landed behind that bush.

I take a cigarette from the table, loosen the filter, and light it with a few aggressive pulls that I can't even fully inhale. Then I burn a hole in the drapes. Pretty clever, but my stalker must have seen the flaming cherry of the cigarette, because even though I'm peeking through a tiny hole in a curtain on the second floor of a building about two hundred yards away, he anticipates me and jumps behind the bush as quickly as before. I smell the burning drapes, the stink of sizzling synthetic fibers; and I realize that I'm burning cigarette holes in my motel room, trying to catch a glimpse of what every tweaker in Riverside laughs about when they're not sketching: the bushmen. I have to get outside.

It's morning. On the balcony, about ten doors down, two Hispanic cleaning ladies are pushing a cart toward my room. One older, one younger, forties and twenties and pretty enough, they check all the rooms at the Memory Motel on Magnolia Avenue, check to see if the people staying at the Memory Motel want cleaning, dusting, older, younger, mistress, hooker. Really? They're whispering to each other, giggling.

"Hey," I say, and smile.

"You want now?" says the younger one.

"Umm . . . yeah, sure. Now."

"*Quiere ahora*," one says to the other.

The foreign language feels illicit, confirming . . . yes, really.

"*Sí*," she says.

"*Sí*," I repeat, bugging my eyes.

They laugh and wheel the cart into my room.

Standing in my boxers and undershirt, I watch them clean my room. They're doing a halfhearted job. This seems hopeful. I smile at the older one, thinking I have to arrange the deal with her. She smiles back and fluffs a pillow, turns away and goes for the vacuum cleaner. I rub myself a few inches below my waistline—nothing lewd, but a definite hint. The ladies finish cleaning and step out the door.

"Close it?" says the older one.

"Will you come back?"

"Sure. Later."

"Oh. Okay."

I'm hungry. The Ensure is not cutting it. I put my pants on and walk down the steps to the parking lot, headed for Taco Bell. The motel's morning manager—an Indian with rich, black hair parted on the side—is walking toward me wearing a striped polo shirt and brown khakis. He has a potbelly and bright cheeks that swell under his eyes as if he were smiling. He recognizes me.

"You," he says, definitely not smiling. "You get out of here."

"What?"

"You hear me," he says quietly. "You get out of here."

"What are you talking about? I fuckin' paid. I got till noon."

"No," he says, "you go now or I call the police."

Then he turns and starts walking toward his office.

"What? For what? What did I do?" I'm right on his heels. "What the fuck are you talking about? Go ahead—call the cops. I didn't do anything. You want me to leave, how about you give me my fifty dollars? How about that? Oh, what? You're just gonna walk away from me now? Ya know what, fuck you, you hajji cocksucker! You're gonna walk away and call the cops, you fucking bitch?"

The manager plods toward his office, not responding or even looking back.

I stop following him and stand for a minute, fuming, trying to figure out what to do. I scream at him, calling him a motherfucker, before running to my room to pack. I chug an Ensure and leave the case. I throw my clothes in a shopping bag, run to my car, unscrew the speaker face, and stash my dope. Then the sketching gets worse.

Turning onto Magnolia, I see every other car in the parking lot pull out and start following me. FBI, CIA—I don't know who they are, but they're following me. Turning randomly merely to lose them, I get on the 91 freeway and don't get off until somewhere past Colton, where I find myself driving on roads I've never seen before, back roads, winding roads, two-lane highways, driving and turning, driving and driving. I drive so long the scenery changes and I stop sketching. Now I'm in the desert somewhere between Chino and Rubidoux, with the window down and dust coming in the car and Pink Floyd's "Us and Them" playing on the stereo. I pass an abandoned house with broken windows, broken boards. Then one that's not abandoned, followed by a store, and soon a whole town has accumulated. I'm in Mira Loma.

I park and go into a diner that reminds me of a saloon. I take a seat at the counter. The waitress is in her late thirties, a redhead with large breasts, maybe a prostitute.

"What should I get?" I say to her.

"I don't know, hon. What do you like?"

"I like quesadillas."

"Quesadillas it is then. Chicken?"

"Sure."

While I wait for the food, the waitress asks me how I got here, am I okay? I tell her the story of how I came to Riverside, starting with selling drugs in New Jersey. I'm on drugs now, I tell her; I just got kicked out of my motel room. She tells me I should stop with that stuff, and I say, "I know, I know . . . ," trailing off and looking at the counter. "I was just at a rehab." The food comes. In between bites I tell the waitress about GSL, about Luke and Brady, about Wendy and how she went to prison. Suddenly I get excited because I think the waitress might know Wendy. But no, she doesn't. She's sorry but she doesn't. At the end of the counter, a man in a cowboy hat is listening. Whenever our eyes meet, he smiles kindly. Occasionally he and the lady glance at each other, and I catch one of these glances, and I remember that I'm in Mira Loma and that this diner might really be a whorehouse, the waitress a prostitute, and the man at the counter her pimp. The food isn't very good. This seems hopeful.

"I forgot where I was," I say, meaning simply for the waitress to remind me, but once the words leave my mouth, I realize they sound absurdly desperate.

"Eat up, hon," she says, and I know she's not a prostitute.

When she brings the check, she asks me if have money in a tone that says, *It's okay if you don't*. But I do have money, hundreds of dollars, and I pay and leave a tip and ask for directions to Riverside. The man tells me to continue on Mission Boulevard and pass through Rubidoux. I thank them and get back in my car.

By the time I reach Rubidoux, I'm passing out every fifteen minutes, waking when my car bumps against the curb. I rent a room at a motel on the edge of town and sleep for two days; I only get up to order pizza and pay at the front desk. Then, having eaten and rested, I take a shot and drive to Patti's house, where I sit on the couches with Patti and Garrett, and I pet the dogs, and we all laugh about the bushmen.

PART 2: FAMILY

CHAPTER 10.
BIG MANNY FROM FONTANA

About two weeks before my parents were scheduled to visit, a girl named Marla called my cell phone looking for meth. She said that I knew her, that she'd come to Stacie's some weeks earlier with Big Manny and I'd sold her a fat bag. I didn't know who she was or what she was talking about, but I did know Big Manny—the Hispanic convict and tough guy who used to ride around with Danny White, seemingly as a bodyguard. Aside from Maki there wasn't a name Marla could have dropped that would have made me feel less secure. *Don't worry, you don't know me, but I know one of the scariest people you've ever met, so let's meet for a drug deal.*

On the other hand, a mysterious meeting can be pretty seductive.

I told her to meet me at eleven a.m. at the McDonald's on University Avenue, and then I felt very clever to show up at ten forty-five and wait in the parking lot to see if she came alone. Which she did, I'm sure, though I didn't see her pull up. After a few minutes of keeping watch, I forgot what I was supposed to be doing and spaced out, studying the floor of my car. Marla had to tap on my window.

"I thought that was you," she said. "Hi. So, do you just wanna like . . . do this here?"

"No, no, not at all," I said. "Let's go get something to eat."

"To eat?"

"Yeah, c'mon—I'll buy you lunch."

In all my favorite movies the gangsters made their deals over food. There was rarely an opportunity for this with tweakers, of course, but now I was in the parking lot of a restaurant, sort of, having an illicit meeting with a woman I still couldn't remember, and there was simply no way, no matter how crazy a look she gave me when I said "lunch," that I was going to pass up the opportunity to sit across from her in a booth and try to feel her out.

"Can't we just do it here?" she said.

"Right in the open? No way. C'mon. I'm hungry, anyway."

I led her to a booth inside and asked what she wanted. She said she wasn't hungry, but I insisted, saying it would look funny if only one of us was eating, so, c'mon, what do you want? She said chicken nuggets. That was no good, though, because I planned to order from the breakfast menu. She said it was past eleven.

"Yeah, like five minutes past eleven. They'll make me a McMuffin, trust me, but if it does come to an argument I can't really insist they serve me from *both* menus. That would be a little much. So if I can only get one, what do you want for breakfast?"

She said she'd have a McMuffin too, but that it really didn't matter because she wasn't going to eat it anyway. This irritated me, and when I got the McMuffins, no nuggets, I decided to give her a little less dope for her money. Then I sat across from her and started to eat.

"You do remember me, right?" she said.

"No, not really, but that's okay. That's why we're having lunch."
I smiled.

"You really don't remember me? You sold me a twenty in Stacie's bathroom. It was fat, too; that's why I called you. I was with Manny. He gave me your number."

"Vaguely . . . I'm not sure. But don't feel bad—I do a lot of drugs. And all the bags I sell are fat. Speaking of Manny, though, does he know you're here?"

"What do you mean?"

"Well, you said you were with him. I don't want to be—"

"Oh, we're not together. It's not like that. He's not my man."

"Either way," I said, "you're sayin' I met you with him."

"What? Do you want me to call him?"

"Yeah, actually, that'd be great."

Her offer hadn't been serious, but I was. Tweakers in Riverside, I'd learned, could get a little crazy when it came to their women, and I was pretty sure that selling dope without permission to somebody's girl (no matter what she said) was considered an even greater disrespect than insinuating that the girl had lied about hitting the neck of a pipe.

"Fine," she said. "If you really want, I'll call him."

"Please," I said, smiling.

She looked at me to make sure I was serious, then shook her head, dialed Manny, and told him, "I'm sitting across from—remember that guy Jimmy from Jersey? You gave me his number. Yeah, well, he wants to talk to you. I don't know—ask him."

She handed me the phone.

"Hey, Manny," I said. "It's Jimmy from New Jersey. I don't know if you remember me from Stacie's."

"Yeah," he said warily.

"I'm sitting here with a girl named Marla. She said you knew her."

"Yeah, I know her."

"Well, she's tryin' to cop something, if you know what I mean, and I just wanted to check with you to see if that was cool. I mean, I don't know what your relationship is, but I just thought I'd check with you first before I gave her anything—to make sure it's cool and whatnot."

"Oh," he said. There was a pause. "Yeah, sure. If she wants something, you can give it to her. That's your business, but I appreciate you calling and asking me."

"No problem," I said. "It's only right."

"Thank you. Is she there? Can I talk with her for a second? And thanks again."

Marla laughed when I gave her the phone. She said, "Yeah, sure, whatever," and hung up. Then we threw away the food, and after selling her a generous twenty, I told her I'd always take care of her with fat bags and I was sorry for all the bullshit. She acted grateful but never called me again.

I would have beaten myself up over it—over acting so unprofessional as to lose a customer by being cute about a McMuffin—if it weren't for the way things worked out with Manny. It turned out that not only was Manny really big on respect, but he'd been trying to win Marla over for months by showing her how much pull he had. And even though that never worked out—Marla was either unimpressed or simply couldn't see past Manny's two hundred and eighty pounds, pug nose, and whiskery goatee—I still impressed him by making a show of getting his permission to sell her the dope.

This all became clear a few minutes after I walked into Stacie's bedroom to find Manny sprawled across the bed in jeans and string T-shirt, smoking a bowl. Almost immediately he thanked me for calling him the other day, but he said it surprised him, honestly it did, because he hadn't thought I knew so much about respect. I told him I'd learned all about respect back home in Dirty Jersey. I'd learned how to show it and how to spot who deserves it. Manny nodded thanks and squinted at me, rubbed his chin, and hit the pipe.

He had massive biceps, and the word "Fontana" was printed across his chest in thick block lettering—a conspicuous tattoo that, as he would later explain to me, he'd gotten in prison to show everybody that he was representing his hometown.

After squinting a little more, sizing me up, Manny nodded: He'd come to a serious decision. He was going to make me an offer. First, though, he had to make sure we understood each other. He had to explain a few things to me, starting with the fact that I wasn't back home anymore. I wasn't in New Jersey, or Dirty Jersey, or whatever the fuck I wanted to call it. Now, he didn't mean any disrespect by that; he just wanted me to know that shit was different out here in Riverside, and though it was good I'd learned a thing or two back home, like respect, it was pretty clear that I didn't know as much as I should. Again, he didn't mean any disrespect by that. It was just that if we were gonna be working together, he needed to be able to tell me the truth.

"Of course—," I began to say, but he put his hand up to stop me. He hadn't told me the truth yet.

"The truth is, your name is getting around. It pops up in conversations with people I know, and these people, you have to understand, these people are like, 'Who the fuck is this kid?' Do you understand what I'm saying?"

I thought I did.

"That's good, Jimmy," he said, then paused, struck by a thought. "Ya know what?" he continued. "We should get this out of the way right now. Do you prefer Jim or Jimmy? 'Cause I wanna know what I'm gonna be calling you."

About a week or so later Manny would tell me that when he was in Tehachapi Prison he wrapped his hands in towels and beat a child molester into a coma, threw him against the bars, stomped on his head, made the floor shiny with a thin coat of blood by tossing and dragging the near-limp body around the cell so many times.

"Jim, Jimmy," I said. "Doesn't matter."

"I'll call you Jimmy," he said, "'cause I had a cousin named Jimmy, and I'm sure as hell not callin' you Dirty Jersey."

He told me about the arrangement he'd had with Danny White. Manny and Danny had known each other for almost ten years—they'd been in Tehachapi together—but over the past couple years, while Manny calmed down and fell out of the life by getting a union job in construction, Danny kept running around and getting high until it got to the point that that was all he cared about. Forgot about his friends. Forgot about respect. Forgot where he came from. Danny had even started shooting up, but Manny might as well stop right there before getting into what actually happened with Danny, because he knew I shot up and so he figured we might as well get that out of the way too.

"Now you probably guessed I don't like that shooting-up shit," he said, "but I'm gonna make an exception with you, and here's why. You've been on that shit since I've known you, and you've always been okay. I mean, you get high, but I've never seen you act all crazy and shit, and you always have money. I guess 'cause you started with that when you were young, you got used to it. See, Danny never did that shit, so he wasn't used to it, and it screwed him all up."

"Makes sense to me," I said.

Manny nodded, seemingly happy with the way this was going.

"Now, the thing with Danny was: My union had to let go of some people at work, and since I was the last to join, I got put out on my ass. Now, they're good people, they'll call me back eventually, but when it first happened I needed cash, and so even though I know Danny's all fucked up, I also know he comes up every once in a while, and so I give him a call. I make him the same offer I'm makin' you right now. I said, 'Danny, I'll watch your back, I'll make sure nothing happens to you while you do whatever the fuck you're doing, but when it's all over, when we part ways, I need to walk away with something: cash, or meth to sell. Something.' That's what I said to him, and it was cool for a while. We got into some shit; he was always okay; but then when we do get ready to part ways, he's like, 'What about *all* the dope I kicked you while we were riding together?' and I'm like, 'Nah, nah, nah, partner: First of all, wasn't never all that much, and second of all, you knew what the deal was.' And then he starts duckin' me like a fuckin' little punk. But that's okay, though, because Danny doesn't know: Even though he's locked up, I can get him on the inside just as easily as I can get him out here. You see, I got dirt on Danny: I know he cooperated with the police during a burglary investigation—he ratted on a skinhead—and there's a police report floating around somewhere that says he fuckin' cooperated. And if I can get my hands on that report, I got a contact in the penal system who can get it to the right people in Tehachapi—my wife's cousin. She'll definitely do it for me. I did her a favor one time, and even though my wife and me aren't together right now, she likes me more than my wife, anyway. Sometimes she even tells me stuff my wife says about me, 'cause she wants us—"

He stopped. Somehow he'd gone from making me an offer, to scaring and impressing me with how he planned to have Danny White stabbed in prison, to describing how his wife's cousin was trying to save his marriage. There was an awkward pause as Manny realized that he'd been going on and on and that he'd forgotten his point, that he'd been tweaking and I knew it. I wanted to smile at him and for him to smile back at me. I wanted smiles of recognition and acknowledgment, of *Yeah, I was tweaking* and *I know just what that's like*, because then, having actually understood each other, if only for a moment, we could have spoken plainly for a time. We'd have told the truth, or seen eye-to-eye, or whatever else he wanted to call it. But Manny didn't give the impression that he could be smiled at. Instead, he took another hit of the pipe and said that he was telling me all of this for a reason. Then, without sharing the reason, he returned to the offer and finally asked if I was interested.

• • •

Manny had two rules for our new partnership. The first was that I not lie to him. The second was that when I was talking about him I should never say, "Oh, he's just a piece of shit." He said that there were plenty of things that we could laugh and joke about—we could break each other's balls and whatnot—but that saying he was just a piece of shit was not a joke. I agreed.

Nothing happened during the first couple of days. We drove from Patti's to Chuck's to Stacie's, business as usual, and Manny got to smoke a lot of free speed, and I got to show off my new partner. Patti's was the only house where Manny's presence didn't make any difference. There, Manny was my new friend, not my muscle. This was mostly because everybody liked me at Patti's, but also because if I had needed muscle Manny wouldn't have been enough: Garrett wasn't scared of anybody, there was a rifle in the living room, and Patti knew plenty of scary people herself. Manny recognized this. He'd actually heard of both mother and son and said I was lucky that they liked me. Everywhere else, though, there was a distinct change in attitude toward me. Stacie was nicer, and there was less tension with the new junkies I was meeting at Chuck's. With Manny as my partner, I went from being another junkie pushing bags and pulling scams to a dealer with a means of enforcement.

Status boost aside, I also liked hanging out with him and we got along well. I wanted somebody tougher than I was to show me the ropes and watch my back. He wanted somebody to look up to him, listen to his stories, and share in the knowledge he'd gained over the years.

He was living in La Sierra at his cousin's apartment. The first time he told me to pick him up there, I pulled into the parking lot and honked, and when he opened the door he stood there for a whole minute, contemplating; then he waved me inside. He offered me an iced tea, which I felt obliged to accept. He told me to take a seat on the couch. He had such a grave and formal air that I thought somebody might have told him I'd called him a piece of shit. But then he sat on a chair across from me and said, "Jimmy, I want you to know something: I never show *anybody* where I live."

There were other gestures of friendship that were even more awkward. Once, in Rubidoux, after trading meth for heroin at Chuck's, we stopped on Mission Avenue for burritos. We could hardly eat them, though, we were laughing so hard, laughing at the characters at Chuck's, at one in particular, a tall, thin man named Pierre who always wore dress shirts and pants, often a full suit. He lived in the trailer near Chuck's mobile home, and he was at Chuck's almost every time we came over—morning, afternoon, evening—standing in the living room and drinking coffee and acting a bit snooty, actually. Manny and I would say, "What's up, man," and he'd say, "Hi," and snort a little, not really looking at us. He wouldn't look at us the whole time we were there. He wasn't interested, it seemed, in most of what went on at Chuck's, though he was there every day, in the living room, drinking his coffee and wearing his suit. *Who was this Pierre? And what was up with the suit? The name, too—Pierre—skinny bitch, drinking his coffee. Do you think he brings it from his trailer? I mean, really, why the fuck would Chuck have coffee? But, more important, why is he there? That's what I want to know!* Pepsi came up through my nose, and Manny nearly choked on a jalapeño. I covered my face and he banged on the table. When the fit passed, I paid the check, and Manny said for me to go ahead and he'd meet me in the car; he had to take care of something. I sat in the driver's seat, wondering why he'd been so cryptic about taking a shit, until he got in the car and told me to open my hand. I hesitated. He said he wouldn't ask me again, so I put my hand out, and he gave me a tiny soldier figurine, the kind that comes in a plastic bubble that pops open, transparent on one side. He'd bought it from a dispenser at the front of the store. He said, "Don't ever tell me I never gave you anything."

It went like that, friendly gestures as we pushed dope and made the normal rounds, until one day when I was running low on meth I called Patti and she was dry. She said I could come over and she'd smoke a bowl with me, or even give me a few shards for a shot, but she wouldn't have any quarters or halves to sell until Tuesday. I didn't know what day it was. Not Tuesday, I gathered.

The only other person who'd ever said he could get me meth at prices comparable to Patti's was a white supremacist in his mid-twenties named Mitch. He lived in Norco with his Dad, Brian, a fat truck driver with a lazy eye who once stayed up too long on meth, fell asleep while driving, and crashed his truck on the 91 freeway. Wendy had brought me to their house months ago, when we were first looking at rooms for me to rent. We smoked a bowl with Mitch, and almost before we'd even sat down he was showing us a shotgun that he'd just bought from a friend. It was a bolt-action sawed-off, single barrel with a pistol grip—a rare arrangement, Mitch assured me as he laid it across his lap. He kept it there while we smoked, feeling very cool, until his dad came home and told him to put the damn gun away.

Driving away, I said, "Wendy, what's up with Mitch and that fucking gun?"

"Oh, he's just a kid dying to get his stripes," she said. "He'd never use it. My boyfriend, Leroy, actually beat him up once 'cause they were gonna get in a fight with some Mexicans and Mitch ran."

"He ran?" I said. "What a punk. But I have to admit, it was a cool gun."

"It was pretty fucking cool, wasn't it?" She laughed.

"And what about the dad, Brian?"

"Brian's a fucking dirty old man," she said. "I mean, he's okay. You can trust him. For some reason he just looks like a dirty old man to me, with that beard and gut. Kinda sleazy. But it's not like he's ever done anything. They're both actually cool, especially when they get to know you; Mitch will chill out and shit."

When I was living in Norco, Brian and Mitch were just around the corner, so even after Wendy went back to prison, I used to stop by and get high with them. Since Brian didn't want to encourage his son to sell meth, he often bought from me, and, as Wendy had said, I could trust him. It got to the point where I felt confident fronting him as much as an eight ball. And Mitch did chill out. We smoked a lot of pot together, and he stopped showing off the shotgun. I still didn't like him—he was a loudmouth and he threw tantrums whenever Brian got on his case about getting a job—but he did have good pot, and we laughed sometimes, and the couch was comfortable. I was actually beginning to enjoy being able to stop by whenever I wanted, until one day, when I was smoking speed with Brian in the living room, the front door flew open and Mitch threw his girlfriend face-first onto the dirty wood-plank floor.

She whimpered. Blood spilled from her nose, down her mouth, and onto her shirt. Mitch grabbed her by the hair and pulled her across the floor. She tried to push herself up with her hands, to regain her footing, but Mitch changed directions and swung her hard into the kitchen counter. He kicked her and she bawled. She clenched her fists and held them to her face, cowering.

"Mitch, what the hell are you doing?" Brian shouted, and jumped off the couch, seemingly to put a stop to it, maybe even smack Mitch a few times. But then Mitch started shouting back, shouting about the girl and something she'd done, shouting as if he knew he had a winning argument. He cursed and stomped on the floor, turned and spat on her, a frothy spray that she wiped across her face, smearing it into the tears and blood. She looked at me pleadingly, then burst into a fresh round of sobbing. Mitch was still raving, practically froth-ing at the mouth about something he had caught her doing, though I couldn't follow any of it. I didn't know what was going on; I just wanted Brian to put a stop to it. I assumed he would, too, until I realized that his shouts of "Stop beatin' her!" had turned to: "Shut the fuck up, bitch! Stay still! I said fuckin' stay still or we'll have to get the handcuffs again!"

"Let me drive her home," I said. "Brian, come on, let me just get her the fuck out of here so you don't have to deal with this shit."

Strands of her hair were matted across her face.

"No, Jimmy," said Brian. "I think it's time for you to go home."

On my way out the door I heard him tell Mitch to get the handcuffs.

I hardly went to the house after that—only when Brian called me for speed, offering me twenty extra dollars to deliver it. Then, a few weeks before meeting Manny, I ran into Mitch and his girlfriend at a Mexican restaurant. He bragged to me about his new connection— quarters for two hundred—and his girlfriend smiled and put her head on his shoulder. She didn't even seem embarrassed around me.

So when Patti ran dry, I called Mitch and told him I was stopping by with my new partner. I didn't tell him the partner was Hispanic, two hundred and eighty pounds, and big on respect.

"I can't believe you got me out in Norco," Manny said as we pulled off the 15 freeway, turning onto Sixth Street. We made a quick left onto a winding, hilly road, bounded by grass and straw. Dirt was every-where. In between the fenced backyards to our right were a few small ranches: chickens and horses, mounds of hay, and watering holes. "I hate Norco. Fuckin' hick town."

Brian's house was just before a fork in the road, so when we came to the stop sign, it was directly to our left. It was one story, with unpainted wood. The windows were blocked out and Mitch's truck, a small green Chevy pickup with a piece of string to secure its bed, was parked on the front lawn. We pulled over next to it and went inside.

Mitch looked away when he shook Manny's hand, mumbled when he said what's up. He invited us to sit on the couch and then positioned himself so he looked at me and not at Manny.

"So what's up with that quarter," I said, trying to blow past the tension into business. But Mitch ignored me. Before he did any busi-ness he had to prove that he was perfectly relaxed, not scared of

Manny at all. He sparked a bowl of speed and then offered it to me.

"No thanks," I said, "I'm only shooting these days, in my neck and shit. It's a good rush."

Mitch laughed. It was a phony laugh that grated. He was stalling, trying to decide whether or not to actually snub Manny. After a brief silence, he offered him the bowl.

"No," said Manny flatly.

"I guess I'm taking this to the head, then." Mitch laughed.

"Go for it, man," I said. "And while you do that, let's talk about this quarter. How are we gonna do this?"

Mitch's connection was just across Norco. We could give him the money and wait here, or we could follow him. But we lost the first option when Brian came home, saw Manny with his bulk and prison tattoos, and asked us to leave. Unlike his son, Brian didn't have any illusions about being a tough guy; he was a trucker who wanted to do a little speed and keep his house safe. As we all filed out, he told me I knew better than to bring a person he didn't know to the house. He told Manny it was nothing personal, he just had rules. He didn't waste words on Mitch.

Outside, I gave Mitch the two hundred dollars, and Manny and I followed his tiny green pickup. Manny drove. He told me that he used to steal cars and he knew how to tail people. Nevertheless, it didn't take long for Mitch to lose us on those narrow roads. He sped up and disappeared at the bends. Twice we caught up to him, waving and honking for him to slow down. The third time we came to a four-way stop and he was gone.

We drove by the house, called Mitch's cell phone, searched for the pickup. At first Manny and I were terse with each other, though not unfriendly. Business tones: "What do you think, left?" There was self-conscious talk of staking out main intersections. We were embarrassed. We each thought it was our own fault, I for bringing Manny on an amateur mission, bringing him when I knew it would do no good, and he for doing his job poorly, for letting a little punk from Norco, of all places, get over on us.

We parked by a traffic light near Hamner Avenue. This being Norco, nearly every other car was a pickup. Within an hour we must have seen nearly every make, model, and color of every Chevy, Dodge, and Ford in existence, and I must have asked Manny thirty times, "Are you sure that's not it?" By then we'd realized that neither of us was angry or disappointed with the other. We kept watch and played with the radio, talking calmly as if nothing had happened, though Manny was repeatedly baffled by my guesses of which trucks might be Mitch's.

I explained to him that I was color-blind, that that's why I kept thinking the brown and orange trucks might be green and belong to Mitch. He told me that I could never steal cars, at least not for the people he knew, because they wanted a specific model, year, and color, and if I brought them a brown car when they'd asked for green, "Man, you don't even wanna know." Then he asked me what it was like being color-blind, and I told him that the ocean is purple and the grass is orange, but a green isn't always orange nor a blue always purple, that shade often defines color, so a dark green is brown and a bright one orange, but that this isn't even always the case, and that if I really understood it and had a system to figure out which color was which then I wouldn't be asking him if every car was Mitch's. We laughed. The sun had set and the hunt was over.

After driving by the house one last time, we rented a two-bed motel room on Hamner Avenue. I called Mitch's cell phone again, left a message, told him where we were and that I expected to hear from him. Then I called the house and Brian picked up. He said he hadn't seen Mitch.

"Did that boy pull anything?" he said. "Is he trying to take somebody off?"

"Yeah, man. I fuckin' gave him two hundred bucks for a quarter and then he lost us on the road."

"Oh, man. Didn't I tell you not to mess with him, Jimmy? Well, I'll make him call you as soon as I see him. I will do that."

"Thanks, Brian."

We ordered pizza and buffalo wings, paced, and smoked cigarettes. After eating, I took a shot in the bathroom and sat next to the toilet for a few minutes, breathing slowly and deliberately in order to keep the wings down. I came out of the bathroom buzzing, happy even, despite the two hundred dollars. I was high, with a friend and a pizza. But Manny wasn't as quick to forget about Mitch. He said I should call him again, and I did, and this time he picked up the phone.

"What's up, dude?" I said.

"I don't know, man," he said. "You tell me. You've been callin' my cell phone."

"I'm sayin', you fuckin' took off, dude. You lost us. I'm askin' you what's up."

There was a pause. Then Mitch started to yell. Manny raised his eyebrows.

211

"Look," said Mitch, "I ain't tryin' to do nobody dirty, but I ain't nobody's fucking nigger. I'm running around here, all over the place, and I'm not gonna be a nigger, dude—"

"Dude, what the fuck are you talking about? What did we say? Nobody's tryin' to make a nigger out of you. You're gettin' your cut—"

Manny shook his head and signaled for the phone.

"Look, dude," he said. "I don't know you, but you've got my issue, and I want it."

I could hear Mitch start up again, but Manny cut him off, shouting, "Hey, hey, hey! All that higher-power shit you're talkin' right now, I don't give a fuck about it. I want my fucking issue. I don't know who you think I am, but your dad seems to have a pretty good idea."

Mitch hung up. Manny clenched his jaw, growled, and held the phone in the air as if it were a grip strengthener. Then he took a deep breath and sat on a chair.

"There's something I probably should have told you earlier," I said. "He owns a shotgun."

"Yes, you should have told me that earlier," said Manny. "But I knew they had a gun in that house. Doesn't make much difference, anyway."

He handed me my cell phone, staring at the floor. When he didn't speak or move for a while, I said, "I'm gonna get some fresh air."

Manny nodded, and I went outside and smoked a cigarette in the parking lot. The motel manager, a thin man with a bad haircut and a faint accent, Turkish maybe, was telling a bum he had to leave the property. The bum wore fatigues and a shirt I could tell was filthy even though it was black. He seemed a little slow, drawling through his bum's beard, "Yeah, yeah, I'm going, I'm going."

"You say this," the manager said, "that you are going; you keep saying this, but you are obviously not going. *Going* is that way—out of the property. You are walking closer to the rooms."

"I'm going . . . I'm going. . . ."

"No, you aren't! And now I'm calling the police!"

The manager walked to his office and stopped.

"I'm calling right now," he said.

The bum had already changed directions. Without saying anything, he shuffled past the manager, around the office, out of sight. The manager looked at me and shook his head, smiling. I smiled back. I finished my cigarette and on my way back to the room I started chuckling, thinking about describing the little scene to Manny. When I walked in, though, Manny was on the motel phone speaking Spanish. He hung up and looked at me.

"Do you know how to operate an AK-47?"

"No, not really. Why?"

"Because it would work best if you could use that gun. Look—I just got off the phone with my homeboy. I haven't had to call him for something like this in like two years. He's in Mira Loma now, but he was actually heading up to La Sierra anyway; and now he's gonna come up here—tomorrow—with my thing and the AK, and he'll probably have a shotgun. Now, we pull up at that stop sign, and the house is right there on the right—almost like it wants to be shot up. He'll be driving, I'll be in the front seat, and you'll be in the back. I'll get out first and fire in the windows with my forty-five; then he'll come around the front of the car with the shotgun in case anybody comes running out, while you spray with the AK. It's really not that hard. An AK-47 doesn't have that much kick. It'll drift to the right, so all you really have to do is with your left hand hold it down, like this, and start at the far right side of the house. The gun will almost work by itself."

Manny seemed so assured as he described the plan, so focused on the details of the shooting, that I felt there was no way we could be caught, and I began to wonder whether shootings like this were actually more common than I'd ever imagined, the same way there were more meth and heroin users than I had imagined. Maybe people I knew had done shootings—no big deal. Maybe it seemed so scary and horrifying to me now only because I'd never done one before, and once I had overcome the taboo, the shooting would be no more awful than sticking a needle in my arm.

"All right," I said. "Okay. There'll be time for that, I guess, for you to show me how to work the gun. I mean, we'll do what we need to. But don't you maybe wanna call his dad again before we shoot the house up? I mean, he didn't sound like he was down with the whole thing, and maybe if he gets the idea, he'll pay the two hundred before he gets his family killed."

"That's not a bad idea," Manny said. "You wanna dial the number for me? Please."

I dialed and handed him the phone.

"Hello, sir," Manny began. "Yeah, we met earlier today, at your house. Uh-huh, yeah. Well, first I wanted to apologize for involving you in this at all. If I had known that that was your house and it was your son I would be dealing with, I never would have gone. I mean, he's a kid, and it's not right for him to be bringing that sort of thing to your home. Again, had I known, I wouldn't have gone. But now we have a situation. Your son has my issue, and I need it. Now I don't want to involve you any more than you—"

I could hear Brian talking, though I couldn't make out the words.

"I appreciate that, sir," said Manny. "And again, I'm sorry. Thank you."

He hung up the phone.

"He's gonna pay it," he said to me. We sat in silence for a few minutes. Then Manny said, "That was a good idea."

The next day we drove to the house and pulled over by the stop sign, and Brian came outside and handed me two hundred-dollar bills.

"Now I don't want to see you round here anymore," he said.

"Fair enough," I said.

CHAPTER 11. THE VISIT

The morning my parents arrived in Ontario, California, I woke up early and drove to meet them at their hotel, the Guest House International Inn and Suites. I felt incredibly responsible waking up early and finding the hotel. I thought of myself as having somehow earned my independence, as though I had become a man over the past months and now my parents and I could enjoy seeing each other without all the bother of my being their child.

Pulling into the hotel parking lot, I saw them unloading their bags and I parked next to their rental car. For some reason I thought they would be hugely impressed that I was arriving early, so the first thing I said was, "See, look—I'm doing all right. I'm getting up early."

After we hugged, they stood back and took me in, smiling determinedly.

"Oh my God," said my mom. "You're so thin."

I took it as a compliment and beamed.

"Still strong, though," said my dad, laughing and roughly handing me a bag. He grabbed me with one of his strong hands around the back of my neck, firmly and lovingly, and pulled me in a few inches from his face.

"How are you doing, man?" he asked.

"Great!" I said, hugging him again.

My cheek grazed against his neat goatee, and with my free hand I grabbed the back of his thick neck. At sixty-four, he was still strong—five foot six, with a compact build and a firm paunch—though he seemed older than I remembered. The close-cropped hair that fringed his shiny bald head was now almost totally white.

"I may need you to give me a jump when we get out of here," I said.

"Why?"

"It's been acting up—the starter. Sometimes I need to jump it to get it started."

"Well, we'll have to get that fixed while I'm here," said my dad.

"Look at your backseat," said my mom. "It's a nightmare."

The hotel was a dozen stories high, with rooms encircling a large amoeba-shaped pool and a plant-filled lounge and restaurant. Our seventh-floor suite had a front hall, kitchen, bathroom, and two bedrooms. It was by far the most luxurious room I'd been in since coming to California.

"This is a smoking room, isn't it?" I said.

"No smoking!" cried my mom.

"But mom, what the fuck? I smoke wherever I go. You expect me to change that for you. Why would I? What have you done for me lately?"

She figured out that I was joking, but it took her longer than I expected. In the past she would have known I was joking almost before I spoke, and it felt strange to have the connection severed—strange rather than painful, because I was high. I'd become so numb that even as I lamented what drugs had done to my relationship with my mother, I didn't feel guilty or even responsible. I had no idea that I had taken something invaluable from her. I thought we'd just drifted apart.

We ordered room service and over breakfast discussed our plans for the weekend. Joe, my parents told me, was living in Murrieta at an apartment belonging to the now-ex-girlfriend of his former cell-mate (apparently, while Joe was in jail, his cellmate had given him his girlfriend's address and phone number, asking Joe to check up on her when he got out, and Joe had ended up becoming her boyfriend and moving in). Today we would drive down and see how he was doing, maybe buy him some clothes. Tomorrow we would get my car fixed and visit Wendy at the CRC correctional facility.

I hadn't yet visited Wendy, because I'd been too high and scared and paranoid to walk into a prison; but with my mommy and daddy there to make everything okay, I was insistent that we go. Also, I wanted them to meet her. In spite of how tough and adult I thought I'd become, this was still my first significant stretch of life away from home, and I still had an adolescent urge to show that life to my parents. In fact I'd been telling them about Wendy since GSL, tell-ing them all about her, talking her up, almost as if I'd known that I would be asking them to do something absurd for her, like visit a prison.

My parents agreed to go, though not because I'd convinced them that Wendy was a great friend and influence. Rather, they were desper-ate, and they knew that she was important to me. They hoped that by proving once again that they loved me, and that they took me seriously, and that they were willing to do anything for me, maybe I would listen to them and go back to GSL.

"Do you know how far Murrieta is from here?" my mom asked me.

"About forty-five minutes," I said. "So Joe got out of jail and now he's living with some girl in an apartment down there? Only Joe. He's so fucked up."

As we were finishing breakfast, I got up to use the bathroom, and my mom tried to lift the sleeve of the baggy button-down I was wearing to hide my track marks. I pulled away from her. She looked sad but not surprised. I did not get high in the bathroom.

Murrieta is in the southernmost part of Riverside County, about an hour from Ontario on the 215 freeway. It was strange being driven by Mom and Dad. Over the past months of reckless junkiehood I hadn't driven in a single car whose check-engine light was off, and now I was in the leather-upholstered backseat of a Lincoln, riding one lane left of the shoulder at a mere sixty miles an hour, with no music because my dad had to *concentrate on the road*. We didn't talk much, either: My mom hadn't slept well, and now she was nursing a headache.

We picked Joe up at an apartment complex across the street from a combination Blockbuster and Pizza Hut, a hybrid my family would once have commented on wryly and in unison, but only I noticed it. Joe had gained weight since the last time I'd seen him, at the Mission Avenue shopping complex.

"What up, Jimbo?" he said after hugging my parents.

He tried playfully to wrestle me standing, but I was still bigger than he was.

Weeks out of jail, Joe had almost nothing to wear—just a few T-shirts and pairs of shorts he'd found in his girlfriend Sarah's apartment (probably her ex-boyfriend's)—so we spent the day driving to the many minimalls and shopping plazas in Murrieta, buying Joe everything from underpants to a windbreaker. He told my parents that he had a job as a waiter and that he planned to attend a massage-therapy school in Murrieta. It would have sounded plausible if not for Joe's history, and my parents didn't ask too many questions. I imagine that they hoped that it was true and decided not to play detective. He was twenty-three years old, and waiting tables was legal; they would be supportive parents, but they had another son to save.

My dad ran into stores with Joe while my mom waited in the car with me, and I sensed that they didn't want Joe and me alone together. Toward the end of the day, though, when my dad looked as though one more store would make him vomit, I asked him to pull over at a CD store so that I could run in and check out the Pink Floyd; then once I was already out of the car, I heard my brother slam his door. "Hold up, Jimbo, I'm coming!" When he approached me in the store, the mood was instantly conspiratorial.

"So, are you stayin' clean?" he said.

"Fuck, no."

"Hell, yeah," he said, laughing. "Fuck that shit, you know what I'm saying. Yeah, Jimbo."

"Will you keep it the fuck down?" I said, though I was smiling too. "Yeah, I'm moving a few things around Riverside."

"Dude, you gotta come out here, man. Look around, there's bitches out here—there ain't no bitches in Riverside, except bag whores—and it's not all grimy out here. You don't have to worry about nobody tryin' to stick you out here, no skinheads or southsiders—none of that dumb shit. And yo, you said you're movin' shit, like *movin'* shit. I'm sayin', you can hustle down here. What are you gettin' like a teenth for?"

"I sell 'em for eighty . . . and I like bag whores."

"You *sell* 'em for eighty. Dude, I can get you like a buck-forty, buck-twenty easy out here."

"Really? You can move it fast?"

"Hell, yeah. You come down—at those prices—set up in my girl's apartment—that shit will move. Is it any good? You got any on you?"

"No, I don't have any on me. We're with Mom and Dad. Asshole."

We both laughed.

"I'm working with a partner," I said.

"So? Fuck him."

"No, not fuck him. Dude's serious. Manny—Big Manny from Fontana."

"All right, well, then bring him down too."

"We gotta get back to the car. Here, I'll give you my cell phone number."

"You said you like bag whores. That's mad funny."

After we dropped Joe off at his apartment, we drove back to the hotel, and I waited for my parents to fall asleep so that I could do a shot of heroin in the bathroom. I hadn't brought any meth with me to the hotel, because while I was quite used to being on heroin around people, even I couldn't imagine sketching and parents mixing benignly.

• • •

The next morning my dad gave me a jump and then followed me to a garage in Norco, where he bought me a tune-up, battery, and starter. While waiting for the car we ate a late breakfast at the Cowgirl Café II. The girl who served us was in her twenties and pregnant, and appeared to be stumped when my mom asked for her eggs scrambled loose. When she left with our order, I laughed and bugged my eyes. My dad said, "Poor girl."

The food came quickly. Moved by the atmosphere of carvings in the table and animal horns on the walls, I put hot sauce on my eggs and then regretted it. We sat in the corner, in a tall, brown booth; the seat backs were so hard and bulbous that it took effort not to lean forward over the table. My mom wore a beret to protect her head from a draft, my dad had a black valise at his side, and as the conversation began, I wondered what the three of us must have looked like huddled so intensely in the corner.

"So, what are you gonna do, Jim?" my dad asked. "You're not going to school. You're living on a couch. I mean, do you even have a plan? You know you have a court date in September. This is what now, May? That's four months. What are you gonna do until then?"

"I don't mind living on a couch."

"You don't mind? Well, that's good you don't mind. But how long—"

"You want me to go back to GSL."

"Yes, we do," my mom said. "We think you need it."

"Okay. Okay. Well . . . I'm not ready to go back yet. I mean, I think I will—yeah, I will—but I'm not ready yet."

"What do you mean, not ready? To me that sounds like you just don't want to go. Seriously, Jim, are you just gonna wake up one day and be ready?" my mom asked.

"No, I'm not just gonna wake up. I just—I mean—I'm living on my own for the first time in my life. You send me money, and you help, and I appreciate it, but for the most part I'm on my own. And I didn't say I didn't mind living on a couch to be a smart-ass or something; I said it to illustrate how my life is different out here, and I don't need all that fancy shit. The house. My bed. The fancy dinners. I have friends here, real friends. I mean, I'm driving on the freeway with the window down and the music playing, and I know where I'm going, and I'm happy for the first time in my life. I know it's not gonna last forever, but this is something special. I don't know. Does that make any sense to you?"

"Yes, that makes *some* sense," my dad said, "but is it worth—not to sound too dramatic—but, really, throwing your life away? We don't know what kind of dangerous stuff you're doing out here, what kind of shit you're involved in. You're running around here doing God-knows-what, and how are Mom and I supposed to sleep? And you know what? If you were doing something *of value* that was dangerous and kept me up at night, if it was something you *needed* to do for yourself, that would be fine. Fuck my sleep. But *this*—this is crazy. When you talk about sleeping on couches, you're talking about a kind of initiation, a rebellion—you're out on your own, you're driving around—and I do respect that. Of all people, I respect that. But there are other ways. I mean, Jim, you've done it, man; you've gone way past the point. I want to respect what you're feeling, but what more can you possibly get out of sleeping on John's couch, or whatever the fuck his name is?"

"And I have to add, Jim," said my mom, "that haven't we proved by now that we respect you and how important your friends are? We're about to visit a goddamn prison, for Christ's sake. Now, you've told us all about Wendy—we like Wendy—but do you really think we'd be visiting a prison if not for you, 'cause we understand about your friends? I don't think I've ever heard of such a thing. What parents—what greater length could we possibly go?"

"No, no, of course," I said, "and I didn't mean to say you haven't. You've been great, really. Thank you. But as to how much more I can get—how can I know until I've gotten it? It's been a relatively short time out here, and, look, I've lost all this weight; I know a little something about cars from my friends who are mechanics. I'm living. It's unsheltered, and it just . . . it just doesn't feel like it's time yet. It's a feeling thing. I mean, at Paul and John's house, we all chip in and make the house work, and the sink doesn't drain—there's no pipe system. It just empties out into a bucket in the cabinet under the sink, and you have to remember to dump it outside before it spills over. Of course you forget and it does spill over, and then you've got a fucking mess—but I don't mind doing it. I love it, because it's real."

"Well, if it's a feeling thing, then what if you feel like this for another ten years? I want to support you, man, but when you talk—"

"It won't. I'm not talking about ten years—"

"But if it's a feeling thing, then how can you know? How—"

"Can you tell us when? Do you know?" my mom asked.

"No, honestly."

"Well, Jim, I'm sorry; I want to respect your feelings, but how are

Mom and I supposed to live with that? We go home and hope you feel differently some time before your court date, and meanwhile you're doing God-knows-what. What parent could possibly accept that? Is it fuck us? Is that it?"

"No, it's not fuck you—and I am coming back for the court date, regardless—but . . . I don't know. Fuck. I just don't know."

"Well, what are we talking about here, a couple of weeks?"

"A little longer than that."

"Jesus Christ. And in between now and whenever—longer than a couple of weeks—are you gonna be getting high?"

"I'm not sure."

"That means yes," said my mom.

"No, Mom, that doesn't fucking mean yes; that means I'm not sure. It means that what I'm talking about isn't about getting high. The way I'm living now, this feeling, isn't about drugs. Haven't you been listening?"

"Well then, can you promise that you won't get high?"

"No, I can't promise that if someone's smoking a joint I'm not gonna hit it."

"That's not what I'm—"

"Look, I'm happy for the first time in my life, and I'll cut this short, in part because I know I have to and also for you. But in between now and then, I don't want to limit my experience."

"And what if we don't give you the money for rent?"

"Then I'll come up with it. Don't worry about that—I'll get it. I have no trouble finding a place to stay, maybe not at Paul and John's—"

"Look, let's not do this," said my dad. "Let's . . . shit, man, come on. Let's at least nail it down. Let's come up with a date. Can you do that for us? I think you owe us that."

I breathed loudly through my nose and nodded my head.

"June," I said.

"June?"

"Yeah, June."

"What's going to be different in June?"

"Fuck, I don't know. Maybe nothing, but I'll go in June. I'll do that. You wanted a date—for you—I'll commit to that."

"The first?"

"No, not the first. *In* June."

"Well, the first week then. Come on, Jim, give us that."

"The first week. Okay. Okay."

"So by the seventh of June, at the very latest, you'll be in GSL."

"By the seventh of June, at the latest, I'll be in GSL."

Bumping along a dirt road lined with barbed wire, we passed one parking lot and administrative building after another, going, it felt, deeper and deeper. Since GSL I'd heard people talk with pride about prison and being a convict in a way that sounded almost nostalgic, conjuring images (in my mind, at least) of impregnable stone walls with enormous steel watch towers surrounding a field that was swarming with angry muscle-bound men, all of them either lifting weights, playing cards, or looking for a fight. But, of course, as my parents and I drove through CRC toward the visiting area, that's not what I saw at all. The place was simply dull, somewhere you would get bored quickly and want to leave. There were many yards, all small and muddy and separated from one another by tall chain-link fences. Men stood dejectedly, talking in small groups; others walked the perimeter.

It was twelve thirty when we reached the parking lot of the visiting area. Wendy had told me to make sure we left our cell phones in the car, and we did so carefully, feeling that it must be very important. Then we looked at each other.

What else should we know?

We walked up a concrete ramp and into a small room, half of which was bare with only a wooden bench and a water fountain. We were the only visitors. In front of us, on the other side of the room, were a metal detector and a desk with bulletproof glass to the ceiling. Behind the desk was a tall guard with a black beard. Cordially, he asked to see our identification.

"You know you're early," he said. "Visit's not until one, and then it usually takes 'em an extra fifteen minutes to get ready."

"We didn't know how long it would take for us to be let in," explained my dad.

"It should only take a minute. We just have to run your names through the computer, but you're welcome to take a seat."

The bench was hard.

"I'm just thinking," my dad said to us quietly. "What if they run Jimmy's name through that computer and it comes back that he has all these charges in New Jersey? Phil has worked out a court date, but I don't know if that means your name is clean. Who knows what's in that computer?"

I was thinking the same thing.

"I don't know," I said, clenching my jaw.

My mom put a hand on my back and asked me if I was okay. I told her yeah, I thought so, and then another guard walked through a door behind the desk and said something to the tall one.

"You've got to be kidding," he responded. He then turned and pointed to my parents. "You guys are fine, but we can't let him in."

"Why, what's the problem?" I said.

"You should know," he said curtly, then turned back to the other guard.

I didn't know anything about my legal situation in New Jersey. I didn't know what my lawyer had arranged with the courts, or whether I had any open warrants; and if I did have warrants, I didn't know whether the prison guards could arrest me. But I wasn't thinking about warrants or New Jersey anyway. I had an overwhelming fear of *being caught*.

My dad gave my arm a squeeze, then walked up to the men behind the desk, and they all huddled together. I don't know what he said to the guards, or what the guards were supposed to have done, but months later I would discover that at the time I was on the most-wanted list of Mercer County, New Jersey, yet for some reason the guards let me go. Maybe all the details of my criminal status didn't pop up on their screen, or maybe my dad was just that convincing, or desperate-looking. Either way, somehow he made it all go away. I heard him thank the guard, and then my dad walked back over to my mom and me.

"Okay, Jimmy needs to get out of here," he said. "Do you still want us to visit Wendy?"

"Yes," I said. "Please."

"It's you she wants to see."

"She wants to meet you, too," I said. "She wants to see somebody. Fuck. I don't know. Please."

"All right, we'll see her," said my dad. "Now I guess—okay, I'll drive you to your car. Honey, you have a headache. Are you better off coming or staying here?"

"I'll stay," said my mom. "It's okay. I'm okay. It's warm. You guys just go."

We drove back to the garage, and along the way, as I began to breathe again, relaxing from the scare, something else welled up in me and I tried to keep from crying.

"That was close, you motherfucker," said my dad once the prison was out of sight. He slapped my thigh, trying to be playful, as though this were all a big adventure. "Those guys were ready to arrest you if I didn't talk to them. I think they felt sorry for me! 'So what did you do this weekend, Dr. Salant? Oh, I visited a prison in California and talked the guards out of arresting my son.'"

I smiled, but that made it harder to keep from crying.

At the garage, while my dad paid the mechanic, I sat in my car and wrote Wendy a note. It started as an ABAB rhyme with no meter about Riverside, and the crazy girls I was sleeping with, and how I wished she were here. But by the end, crying openly, I dropped the attempt at verse and wrote plainly about pain, about shooting drugs to swallow it up, and about how sometimes I wanted to die—all things she would understand.

I gave the note to my dad to give to Wendy, trusting that he wouldn't read it. He told me to go to the hotel and that he and my mom would meet me there after the visit. After he left, I broke down again, crying and banging on the steering wheel. When I saw the mechanics looking at me, I stared back fiercely, tears streaming, and then started the car and pulled recklessly onto Hamner Avenue. I weaved in and out of traffic, honking and cursing and turning randomly. I sped along roads scumbled by dirt and sand until I stopped crying. Then I pulled into the parking lot of a restaurant, took my heroin out of the trunk, and did a shot. I had to stick myself several times, searching for a vein, and when I finally got it, I eased back into my seat and watched the blood bead on my forearm.

It was one thirty; my parents were talking with Wendy. I wondered whether they'd remembered to bring one-dollar bills for the candy machines. Wendy had asked me to bring the bills the last time I spoke to her from Stacie's.

"Please," she'd said, "because we can hardly get that stuff here."

"Yeah, sure—I already told you—no problem."

"But what you haven't told me, Jim-Jim, is when you're gonna get clean. You haven't told me that."

"Yeah, I have. I said when you get out."

"Yeah, but from where? When I get out of CRC or when I get out of rehab? 'Cause I told you I'm going to Whiteside Manor for sixty days after I get out of here. I don't even have to do that, Jim-Jim, but I wanna stay clean. I'm serious. And you're my best friend. I feel responsible for you. I can't have you slammin' dope when I'm outta here. I don't want you slammin' dope now, but I can't stop you from here."

"When you get out of Whiteside, I'll be clean."

"Jim-Jim, that's like July! No, Jimmy, you clean up before that, so you can visit me at Whiteside."

"We'll see."

"We'll see?"

"Yeah, we'll see. I'll be there to visit you soon anyway, and you can yell at me in person—or, actually, don't, because my parents will be there."

"Maybe I will anyway."

"No you won't."

"No, I won't, but I should. I really fucking should, Jimmy."

That night my parents and I went out to dinner, and they made me reiterate my promise to be in GSL no later than June seventh. They said that Wendy, who was worried about me, had said she was happy that I'd given a date to check into GSL. She told my parents that she would hold me to my word.

The following morning my parents went to see Joe in Murrieta again and left me at the hotel. I noticed my dad's checkbook on the bedside table but left it alone. In the afternoon they returned and packed for their flight, and my dad gave me a present: a "money belt" with five hundred dollars for rent and food zippered inside the pocket. Before leaving for the airport they walked me over to the Best Western down the street and rented me a room. We hugged, and my mom made me promise to try not to get high. Once they were gone, I shot up and watched *Law and Order* until I passed out. In the morning I stashed my heroin in the money belt and drove back to Riverside.

CHAPTER 12. MY BROTHER JOE

As far back as I can remember, Joe always wanted to spend time with me. Even when he was sixteen and I was twelve, when he was drinking and fucking and I was still a stay-at-home fat boy, Joe would want me to tag along when he went with his friends to the mall or the movies. If I refused, he would call me a fat bitch and tell me I would never get any pussy. But if I went, he would transform into the older brother I'd always wanted, and for the few hours we were out he wouldn't bully or even forget about me. He would still tease me, but not nastily; there would be talk of girls and "when already," but no snickering or calling me a faggot. Even so, I almost never went. His wanting to spend time with me didn't make all the shit he put me through okay. Actually, it worked the other way: The bullying and nastiness became more painful, because, knowing that he could be a great brother, I couldn't just dismiss him when he grabbed me by the face and put his mouth to my ear and said, "Fat bitch."

As the years passed and I became bigger, badder, stronger, our relationship changed and eventually Joe wasn't able to bully me anymore. When I started selling drugs, my thug friends and I would laugh at him, at the way he dressed and his black ghetto accent, at the gangster rap lyrics he tried to write. Of course, we all wore baggy pants and backward baseball caps and began our sentences with, "Yo," but Joe was over the top, trying too hard, a clown who tried too many styles and who still used the word "phat." He'd become the younger brother. The only thing that never changed, in spite of the reversal, was that he still always wanted to spend time with me. So I wasn't surprised, a few days after my parents left me in the motel in Ontario, when Joe called my cell phone and invited me to come sell drugs in his girlfriend's apartment.

"Come on down," he said. "You can set up shop here. There are so many little punks runnin' around this apartment, my girl's friends, with money from their parents; they'll spend like a buck-fifty on a teenth. You can crash here—stay until you need to re-up. It'll be you and me back together."

"And you're sure it's cool with your girl, that me and Manny come stay there? I don't wanna drive down there and get jerked around."

"*Dude*—it's my girl. What do you think? Of course it's cool. But I don't see why you gotta bring this guy, Manny. It's not like you need muscle down here."

"He's my partner."

Manny asked me the same question I'd asked Joe—if I was sure we weren't going to be jerked around—and I told him that Joe was a bullshitter and I couldn't guarantee anything, but that I thought we should go anyway. Murrieta wasn't that far, and if Joe was telling the truth, we could make a lot of money. So we picked up a quarter ounce of meth, a bag of heroin, and a ten-pack of needles, then took the 91

West to the 15 South toward Murrieta, through a desert filled with billboards and corrugated warehouses. Manny drove with the radio on 96.7 KCAL, Trapt and the Red Hot Chili Peppers, and I stared out the window, daydreaming, as I had years ago on many car trips with my mom and my brother.

Several times a year my mom, my brother, and I would drive out to Amagansett, New York, to visit my grandmother. And on almost every trip we played our family's variation on the game Twenty Questions, called simply the Guessing Game since there was no limit on the number of questions. The game usually ended on my turn, and it usually ended badly.

I was about ten, Joe fourteen, and my mom asked me, "Is it an animal, mineral, or vegetable?"

"I don't think it's any of those things," I said.

"So then is it dead?"

"No."

"Well, is it a thing? Is it man-made?"

"I don't think so."

"It's another Jimmy-thing," said Joe accusingly.

Although Joe's contempt for Jimmy-things was extreme, he did have a point. Jimmy-things slowed the game and were technically against the rules. This had been decided after the time my mom and brother spent ten minutes or so asking questions and I wasn't able to answer any of them: I simply couldn't decide what gravity was made of, whether it was bigger than a car, or if we had any in our house. Over the years we had run into similar problems when I picked God, time, the law . . . so by now, although we'd never actually defined a

Jimmy-thing, my brother knew what one smelled like: And there was a good chance I was thinking of one if I couldn't confidently say if it was an animal, mineral, or vegetable.

"It's the letter *L*," I said, and even my mom laughed. She petted my head and told me to think of something else, which I did: a concrete thing. It was man-made and smaller than a car. Yes, we had it in our house. Yes, we all used it. No, it wasn't mechanical. It wasn't made of wood, metal, or paper. Actually, I wasn't sure what it was made of, but that was okay; you didn't have to know *everything* about it. No, we didn't keep any in the bedrooms. This was how the game was supposed to go—you weren't supposed to guess it right away. Frustrating at times, but mostly tickling for the guesser. *What could it be? Man-made, in the house, we all use it . . .* And I was happy because I'd thought of a good one, but then Joe accused me of choosing another Jimmy-thing. I hadn't, but Joe couldn't stand the smirk on my face, couldn't stand that *he* couldn't guess what *I* was thinking, and so even after my mom assured him that it couldn't be a Jimmy-thing, not if it was man-made and in our house, Joe wouldn't let up. Clearly the game could not go on until I revealed the answer. So I did, triumphantly: soap. Then Joe called me a faggot and my mom told him to leave me alone.

The game was over, the car quiet and tense. I stared out the window, hoping the mood would pass. But I wasn't too upset. I knew that even though my mom couldn't actually ask me if I was okay without sending Joe into a fit—*Why wouldn't he be okay? Because of me, right?*—she wanted to ask; she cared; she was with me. That made it okay.

In a couple of minutes, though, Joe took her away too. First, he wanted to play his Eazy-E tape again. "In a little while," my mom said; she was exhausted, and we'd just heard it. Then he wanted to stop at a McDonald's, but my mom didn't know when the next one was coming up, and besides, there was good food in the car, the stuff that *he'd* asked her to get for the trip. Ignoring the "besides," Joe said that we'd just passed one; couldn't we just turn around? No, we were on the highway; it could take half an hour to turn around twice and wait at the drive-thru. It wouldn't take that long. Yes, it would; I've been driving this road since I was a teenager, since before it was a highway, and I don't want to get stuck in rush-hour traffic just because you want to eat shit. It's not shit; it's better than what you keep in the house. The answer is No. Well, then can we at least listen to my tape again?

She tore open the center console and grabbed the tape. She fumbled with the holder for a few seconds, then shoved the tape into the player.

"Jesus, Mom, what's wrong with you?" said Joe.

"I already told you, Joe, I'm exhausted. I hardly got any sleep last night. I'm still recovering from a few nights ago when you and your friend woke me up at two in the morning."

"So you're gonna yell at me for that now?"

"No, I'm not *yelling*. You asked what's wrong with me. I told you. I'm tired."

"But I'm not asking you to do anything. I just wanna listen to my tape."

"So you're listening to your damn tape."

"Well, I don't want to listen to my damn tape when you're acting all fucking crazy."

I stared out the window, hating Joe, wishing my mom would come to her senses and make it stop, but at this point she was totally entangled. They had their hooks in each other, couldn't let go. They were still at it long after we'd exited the expressway. Every time there was a lull, every time it seemed the pettiness had been exhausted, one of them would say *the thing* that I knew would get the other going. Eventually my mom swerved off the road and put her foot on the gas. She screamed, "I'll drive this car right into a fucking telephone pole!"

"Whoa, Mom—stop!" Joe said, and tried to grab the wheel.

"You see what you do to me!" she said once we'd come to a stop.

We sat in silence for about a minute; then my mom apologized. Joe apologized and they hugged. My mom turned to me and asked if I was okay, petted my head, looked into my face. I was fine.

"I could take a little rest out here," said Manny once we reached Murrieta. "I couldn't live out here—I'd go crazy—but for this, for a short little rest, to get away from all that shit in Riverside, this is perfect."

"Is that Ivy Street?" I said. "I think I remember this. Joe said we have to make a left and take it down to Washington. Jesus Christ, look at this fucking town. You know what this reminds me of? Princeton, New Jersey—just 'cause of all the fags walking around. Look at the shopping centers and flowers and fucking fenced-in communities."

We passed a T-Mobile store on a knoll at the edge of a strip mall, sunlight glaring off its plate-glass window. The grass looked silky.

"Yeah, but trouble won't find us here," said Manny. "You're young. You run around Riverside a few more years and see if you're not happy to spend a weekend in a place like this."

"I wasn't sayin' I didn't wanna be here—"

"And a lot of the fenced-in communities are just apartment complexes. Your brother's probably staying in a place just like these. You'll like it a lot more when you're inside the gate."

I nodded.

We stopped at a traffic light, and two skinny teenagers, about my age, wearing baggy skater shorts, crossed the street in front of us. One was short with a backward baseball cap and shaggy hair curling behind his ears; the other was tall with a crew cut and a wallet chain. The tall one looked at us. We were staring at him, so he couldn't look away, and as his friend turned to see what was going on, Manny and I both shouted, "What the fuck are you looking at?"

The tall one turned to us and threw his arms up.

"What, motherfucker?" he said.

"We'll turn into this parking lot right now," I shouted. "Turn around. Meet us *right over there*."

They looked where I was pointing but didn't stop walking across the street. To save face the tall one called over his shoulder, "Come to Golden Ridge."

"Aww, you fuckin' punk," Manny shouted after him as the light turned green.

I turned around on the seat and kneeled, watching them as we left the intersection. The tall one was trying to make himself feel better by talking and gesturing to the short one, who kept glancing back over his shoulder.

"All right, c'mon, sit down," said Manny.

"That was funny," I said. "Did they say Golden Ridge?"

"Yup."

"Isn't that where my brother said he was staying?"

"Yup."

"Maybe we should have asked them for directions."

"Your brother said we'd see it from Washington."

"I know. I was kidding."

Golden Ridge was huge: lettered rows and canopied parking spaces. There were countless apartments, stacked two high, identical despite the decorative curtains and gardens with miniature windmills. We called Joe for the row and apartment number, then parked and walked up. He came to the door in sandals and baggy sweatpants and a sleeveless gray tank top. Manny and I were both wearing leather jackets, and I was reminded of the scene in *Pulp Fiction* where a full-suited John Travolta and Samuel L. Jackson blow away three kids lounging in a motel room. Joe tried to pick me up in a playful hug. He'd grown a thin goatee, an outline roughly the shape of a policeman's badge.

"What the fuck is that?" I said.

"This?" he said, stroking it. "It's phat, it's phat—that's what this is."

Manny then introduced himself as Big Manny from Fontana, and they shook while Joe bobbed his head energetically, saying, "All right, all right," as if accepting a challenge to a basketball game.

Standing behind him, in sweatpants and an Aéropostale T-shirt, was his girlfriend, nervous and waiting to say hello. She was strikingly pretty, with light-blue eyes, a hint of pink lipstick, and pale blond hair tied back in a ponytail.

"I'm Joe's brother," I said, giving Joe a little bump to get past him.

"Oh, I'm Sarah," she said, and awkwardly stepped forward to hug me. "Joe—well, I call him Angel—he's said so much about you."

"All good, I hope," I said with a cynical smile.

"Oh, of course," she said earnestly, missing the smile.

"My bad, my bad," said Joe, "I was just tryin' to say what's up to your boy. Manny, Jimbo, this is my little rabbit, here. Sarah, this is Manny."

"Nice to meet you," said Manny.

To express his enthusiasm for her, Joe gave Sarah a wet kiss on the forehead and ruffled her hair.

"All right, Angel," I said. "Calm down."

The apartment was clean, the carpet vacuumed. The furniture was mostly modern and new; I guessed Sarah had gone with her parents to IKEA. She invited us to sit on a tobacco-colored micro-suede couch, then offered us a drink. Beer? Water? Soda?

"No, thank you," said Manny. "But do you mind if we pack a bowl?"

"Please," she laughed.

While we smoked, I asked Joe about the kids he'd been talking about, the kids with all the money. He said for me to chill out, we'd just walked in the door; they'd be here.

"I know they'll be here, Joe, because you said they'd be here. I'm asking when?"

"Do you want me to start making calls? Is that it?"

"What are you getting all fucking defensive for?" I said. "I just asked when. You don't have to start making calls. I'm in no rush. Me and Manny are relaxing for a couple of days."

"Where are you staying in Murrieta?" asked Sarah.

"Where are we staying?" I repeated, looking at Joe. "Here, I thought."

"Baby," Joe said, leaning toward Sarah and trying to catch her eye. But whatever he was trying to communicate—something along the lines of *just go with me here*—seemed to irritate her as much as me. "Baby, you said they could stay. Remember?"

"Joe, that's not what I said—"

"Let's go talk in the bedroom, baby."

She got up, shaking her head, and went into the bedroom. Joe followed, but before shutting the door, he gave me a look that was so typical of Joe I could only laugh: wide-eyed bafflement followed by nodding assurance, as in, *I can't believe she's acting like this—but don't you worry, I'll take care of it.*

"I know he's your brother," said Manny, "but he reminds me of exactly the kind of guy I would have gone out of my way to fuck with in prison."

"I told you. That's fuckin' Joe, man. You wanna smoke another bowl?"

"Nah. If she makes it a big thing, let's just get outta here; tell your brother to call us when he lines up some sales."

"Well, then *I'll* tell them," we overheard Sarah say from the bedroom.

"No, no, baby. It's my brother. It's cool . . ."

Clearly, Joe wasn't going to convince her. She'd agreed to let Joe's little brother visit, not to have two thugs turn her apartment into a twenty-four-hour meth shop. Joe came out of the bedroom with his face decidedly on *I can't believe she's acting like this.*

"What the fuck, Joe?" I said.

"I don't know man. She's buggin' out."

"She looked pretty fucking calm to me. She just don't want us here. You didn't tell her shit about us coming down. You just assume shit's gonna work out, and meanwhile, you waste my fucking time."

"Dude, no! C'mon, man! I told her. You're my brother—I wouldn't do that. She said it was cool, and now she's buggin' out. But it's cool, though. You come back tomorrow and I'll have kids lined up with mad dough."

"Now we have to get a motel room tonight—"

"You'll make that up. You don't even have to give me anything. Just come here, chill, let her smoke a bowl, and you'll make mad dough."

"Oh, what, you're not gonna hit the bowls I pack? Just her?"

"Not if you don't want me to."

"Fuck you, Joe. We're leaving; we'll come back tomorrow. I'm just gonna take a shot in the bathroom."

"Shhh," he said, bugging his eyes and pointing animatedly to the bedroom. This was also typical of Joe: He expected not only that I lie to his girlfriend about my drug habits but also that I appreciate the urgency of the lie, that I cringe and whisper, "Oh, I'm so sorry—are you sure it's okay I do it here at all?" Which of course made me want to leave the needle on the kitchen table and then piss in the sink. "Dude, she doesn't like needles. She's scared of 'em and shit."

"I'm not askin' her to use 'em, Joe."

"Dude, c'mon—just try to keep it down."

"Why don't you keep her distracted while I grab one of her spoons?"

I got a spoon from the kitchen and went into the bathroom and broke open the ten-pack of needles, took one and drew twenty units of water from the tap, then dropped a chunk of tar heroin into the spoon, sprayed it with the water, cooked it, and shot it. My bag of heroin, sitting on the counter, was torn. I began to wrap it with the excess plastic from the needle pack, but thought better and instead dumped it all into the spoon. I drew seventy units of water into the needle I'd just used—these were big needles, a full cc rather than a half—then sprayed it into the spoon, cooked up all of it, and drew it back into the needle: almost a hundred units of thick tar, enough for about four shots. I opened the door a few inches and called for Joe, told him I had to talk to him.

"Check this out," I said once the door was closed. "I'm leaving you with my needles. I got a ten-pack here, and we're gonna be back tomorrow, so there's no point driving around Murrieta with all this shit. I'm also leaving you with my heroin—here, all in this needle. The bag was ripped, so I figured I'd just cook it all and then drop twenty, thirty units in a spoon whenever I wanna shoot up. But then I realized, how the fuck am I gonna carry this needle with the plunger stickin' all the way out of it, so I'm leaving this with you too, right here in the pack."

"Cool, cool," said Joe. "You know what I'm gonna do? I'm gonna put it right here under the sink—she'll never look there—so when you come back you know where it is."

"Whatever you think, just so long as it's here when I get back."

"Of course. You can leave the meth here, too."

"No, I think we'll hold on to that."

As Manny and I left, Sarah apologized, saying she hadn't known that we were both coming but we were welcome to come back and hang out tomorrow. It was okay, we said. Poor communication. And we would be back tomorrow.

Manny and I had dinner at an Applebee's, and I apologized to him for all the nonsense and, likely, wasted time. He was agreeable, though. He said, "I told you I wanted a little rest, man. I really don't care. The only thing is, your brother—your fuckin' brother, man—he's something else. I mean, he's your brother, so I'll treat him with respect. I know my brother can sometimes be a fuckhead, and I still wouldn't want anybody disrespecting him. You seem to be able to handle him, but tomorrow—we go back there, and there are no sales . . . that's pretty disrespectful. I mean, I'm gonna try to keep from saying anything to him, because he's your brother, but if it looks fucked up, I don't know how long we should stay. Cut your losses, you know what I'm saying?"

"You're right," I said. "And I appreciate you respecting my brother, but, honestly, if you feel the need to say something to him, go right ahead. I know you won't lose control or anything, and sometimes he needs to be told to shut the fuck up."

We got a room at a Motel 6, where I got some much-needed sleep. In the morning, after breakfast, we went back to Sarah's to find three of her friends lounging on her couch with their feet up on the coffee table. They looked like high-school stoners, giggling and whatnot. One had taken his shoes off but left his watch cap on. Joe introduced us, and the one with the watch cap asked me what was on my arm, and I told him, "Dirty Jersey—that's where I'm from," which he and his friends thought was the coolest thing in the world. They said it was mad tight, yo, and offered to let us hit their meth pipe. I declined. Manny said sure, thank you. Then we both sat at the table in the kitchen and asked each other what we thought, whether it was even worth asking these kids, who obviously had speed, if they wanted more. How long should we hang around for this bullshit?

"Talk to your brother," Manny said. "Tell him to ask the kids for us and to make some calls, but if we haven't moved anything in a couple hours, let's just go."

Sarah came out of the bedroom and offered us drinks again.

"I'll take a drink," said one of her friends.

"Not you. You can get your own damn drink."

"Goddamn," one of them said playfully.

Sarah forced herself to smile a little so as not to hurt his feelings, then paced the room with her mouth half open as if trying to remember something she was supposed to do. She emptied an overflowing ashtray and called her friends assholes for not doing it themselves. The one in the watch cap said that she was one feisty bitch today, and she forced herself to smile again. She was high, and there were too many people in her apartment.

Manny packed a bowl and didn't offer any to Sarah's friends.

I watched Joe work the room. First he sat on the coffee table across from the friends and said, "Yo, dog, let me hit that. Good lookin' out." One of them told a joke, and Joe slapped hands with him, laughing harder than anybody else. Then, with a wrinkled brow, he walked over to Sarah, took her face in his hands, and looked at her, seemingly astonished that she wasn't having as good a time as he was. *Baby, what's wrong? I'm here for you.* He fawned and hovered until she told him everything was okay; then he kissed her on the forehead and told her he loved her. Finally he took a seat next to Manny and me. His attitude then became that we—Manny, he, and I—were in this together; he was conning everybody else in the room by being nice to them so that we could sell our speed. He nudged me, sneered furtively at the friends.

"You got my shit, Joe?"

"Of course. It's right under the sink like we said."

The pack of needles was still there, but the one with the heroin was gone. After double-checking, scrounging around under the sink, I walked out of the bathroom with the needles in my hand. I called to Joe, "Where's my shit?"

Manny raised his eyebrows.

"What?" Joe said, walking toward me with his most shocked and innocent face.

"You know what, motherfucker," I said. "My heroin. Where is it?"

"What are those?" Sarah said, pointing to my hand.

"They're needles," I said. "Hypodermic fucking needles. The kind you shoot drugs with. Now, excuse me, I need to talk to my brother."

Everybody was looking at me.

"Do you think we could at least do this in the bedroom?" Sarah said.

Manny nodded at me. He said, "Go ahead, but just try to control yourself. I understand, believe me, but let's try not to let things get too out of hand in a place like this."

I looked over at the friends and snorted, then went into the bedroom. Sarah and Joe followed, and Sarah closed the door.

She said, "Okay, so what's the problem now?"

I smiled at her, a twisted smile: She was trying to get down to business, to handle the situation without getting scared, and I was telling her I thought it was cute.

"The problem," I said slowly, "is that I left a needle full of heroin with my brother, and now it's gone. It needs to be found."

"Are you gonna be sick?" Joe said. "Is that it? Is that why you're bugging out?"

"None of your fucking business if I'm gonna be sick. Fuck you! You steal my dope and then wanna act all fuckin' concerned, like you're worried and shit?"

"I am worried. Jim, you're my brother."

"Joe, I'm tellin' you—all you need to worry about is finding my shot. Now get the fuck out there and get it. I don't give a fuck where you get it from or what you did with it—just bring it back here."

He stammered, then said okay and walked out. Sarah asked me to please remember that there were other people in the apartment.

"You mean you think one of your friends might have taken it?" I said.

"What? No—I mean, there's no way. Seriously, I *know* they wouldn't. What I meant is—it's just—you have to understand, you're not the only person with problems here."

"Oh, I knew what you meant. But what you don't seem to understand is that everybody's little problems here—they don't matter until mine is solved. Got that?"

She looked stunned.

"Now, are you sure your friends wouldn't have taken it?" I continued. "You think I should search 'em? Or do you think it was Joe?"

She began to plead, saying she *knew* her friends wouldn't do that—they didn't even use heroin. She didn't know about Joe; she didn't think—she hoped—he didn't . . . but then she realized I wasn't even listening. I was shaking my head, sneering, looking past her at the posters on her walls, at her bed in the corner, a double with pink sheets and a mountain of pillows. She walked over and sat on it and stared at the floor. On the side of her nightstand there was a smear from a sticker she'd scraped off.

I opened the walk-in closet across from the bed, went in, and browsed through it as if shopping in a department store, rubbing fabric between my thumb and forefinger. I wasn't sure why I'd gone into the closet. The initial thought had to do with searching for my dope, but I hadn't really thought it was in there, and once I was inside, I knew I wasn't really going to search. But now Sarah was watching me, and she didn't know what I was doing, and I liked that. So I took my time. I recognized a few of the shirts as the ones my parents had bought for Joe during their visit.

Joe came back into the room and asked me what I was doing in the closet.

"You got my shit?" I said.

"Dude, I have no idea what possibly could have happened, but I looked everywhere. It's not here. It's not in the apartment."

I laughed, shook my head, and took my knife out of my pocket and held it at my side, unopened, in my fist, so he might see it, he might not. I stepped out of the closet.

"Are you gonna make me search these fucking kids out there?" I said.

"They didn't take it," said Joe.

"How can you know that?"

"Are you gonna be that sick, Jim?" he said. "Is that it? Have you been doing it for that long?"

"Are you fuckin' with me?" I shouted.

I snapped the knife open and stepped toward him.

"Jim, I'm your brother," he said.

"If you weren't my fuckin' brother, there would be no talk! And you know this! You know what I'm fuckin' doin' out there, and you steal my fuckin' dope?"

Manny opened the door and popped his head in and told me to try to keep it down. Then he saw the knife and shook his head at me.

"What do you want me to do?" Joe asked.

"I'll tell you what I want you to do, Joe. I want you to look for it. I know you said it's not here—and only you can know that—but I still want you to look for it. I want you to get down on your knees and crawl around the carpet like the lying dope fiend you are. You wanna steal my shit and act like a dope fiend, then keep fucking acting. Go fucking look for it. I don't care where. Ask those kids out there if they saw it."

"The kids left," said Manny. "They didn't wanna buy any dope, either."

Joe walked out with his head bowed, and I closed the door

after him, leaving Manny and me in the room with Sarah, who was still sitting on the bed and staring at the floor. Manny nodded toward her.

"I know," I said. "It's so fucked. Came here to sell some meth, and now I got my brother out there pretending to look for heroin that he stole—probably doesn't even remember what the fuck he did with it—while I'm in here flippin' out. Part of me really wants to cut that cocksucker."

"Believe me, I understand—"

"And sorry to you, man. I mean, really. I got you down here on some straight-up bullshit."

"Don't worry about it," he said, laughing. "Let's just make sure nothing too crazy happens here. And for now . . ." He nodded at Sarah again. "She didn't have anything to do with this."

"I know. You're right. Fuck." I turned to Sarah. "Look, I'm sorry. I know I've been goin' crazy in your house and you didn't do anything. I mean, you don't deserve this. I am sorry. It's just—my fuckin' brother! I don't know how you hooked up with him—"

"No, no," she said. "I understand. I mean, he lost your shit and that's not cool. It's just—I don't usually deal with this sort of thing. I mean, none of my friends do heroin. Needles aren't usually allowed in my apartment. And when Angel said his little brother was coming to visit, I was like, cool. I thought you'd hang out. And now you get here and he starts telling me to call my friends and make them buy speed from you—"

"And you know what he told me? That if I came down here, I'd be able to move as much speed as I could bring. That's what I do. I don't really *hang out*. But that's Joe. That's my brother. I half expected to get jerked around, but what I didn't expect is for him to steal my fucking dope."

"Excuse me," Manny broke in, "but I can't help asking: How did a pretty girl like yourself end up with such a—no offense—fuckhead?"

We all laughed, Sarah nervously. I sat on the bed next to her and asked her how she met Joe. Why did she let him into her apartment? Why did she keep putting up with his shit? She said she knew it was crazy, but for some reason she cared about him—though, after this, she wasn't sure if she wanted him living with her anymore.

"Let us know," I said. "We'll get him out of here."

I didn't ask if she wanted us to leave.

"Do you wanna smoke a bowl?" I offered.

"You know what?" she said. "Yes, please. That would be perfect right now."

Just as Sarah was sparking the bowl, Joe opened the door. I told him we were talking, waved my hand for him to leave. He stared for a moment before shutting the door. When the bowl was finished, we came out of the bedroom, and Joe was gone.

"Fuck it," I said. "That shot is long gone."

Manny sparked another bowl, and I asked Sarah—since we were here anyway—if she knew anybody looking for meth. She said probably not, but she could make some calls if we really wanted. "Don't worry about it," Manny said, "we've put you through enough shit today."

"And if my brother comes back after we leave, don't feel bad about not letting him in, if that's what you wanna do. I know I haven't exactly made a good impression, but I am his brother, and if you ask me, you don't want him here."

After taking a shot of speed in the bathroom, I said good-bye to Sarah, and Manny and I walked to the car. But before we reached it, we heard a yelp. Then a "Ha ha!" followed by a "Wheeeee!" My brother was coming up the lane toward us, skipping and hopping and swinging his hips, like a sketching Charlie Chaplin. Wildly he swatted the air and tried to pinch it, as if going for a fly. Then he came to an abrupt stop, cautiously eyeing a spot on the ground about ten feet to his left, a distance that he covered with a few monkeyish hops, landing in a crouch with his butt sticking out and his face next to his knees. Warily he sniffed the pavement, twice, pausing as if to consider the smell. Then, still in his crouch, he reached his right arm far over his head with his forefinger extended before turning the finger downward and slowly, dramatically, lowering it toward the spot he had just sniffed. When his finger reached the pavement, he suddenly leaped into the air, shouting, "Whee-hee!" I'd never seen anybody act so strangely in my life, and at first I thought he was faking it to save his pride (better crazy than punked by your little brother), but then I remembered the missing heroin. Alone it couldn't explain Joe's behavior, but combined with all the meth he'd been smoking . . . maybe. Soon he was skipping toward us again, this time emitting buzzing noises like a kid imitating a bee.

"What the fuck is wrong with you?" I said.

"Yo, Jimbo," he said, stopping and then taking a few ridiculously high and slow strides as if he were on the moon—or Special K. "You don't even know. I left here, I was buggin' out, I walked to the church down the street, and the pastor said I had magical powers. Mmmmmmmmagical powers! Ya-ha!"

He was now pinching the air again, trying to catch imaginary flies. He seemed to see one right next to my ear, and he came very close to smacking me in the head.

"What the fuck?" I growled, stepping forward aggressively.

Joe jumped backward, landing in a squat and smacking his hands on the pavement. Then he sprang up and shouted, "Wheee! Magical powers! You don't even understand. I have these energies. Crazy fucking energies! And I can control them. Watch this."

With his mouth in an O, he formed an imaginary ball with both hands, shifted it in front of his face, tossed it in the air, and caught it.

"You better calm the fuck down, homeboy!" yelled Manny.

Just then a police car cruised down the main Golden Ridge drive. It approached row G and slowed, but then kept driving.

"Fuck," said Manny. "Let's go back inside for a minute."

We all walked back to the apartment, Joe skipping and buzzing. Manny told him to knock it off, and Joe said, "I can't help myself," before letting out another yelp. When Sarah came to the door, we told her about the cop and asked to wait inside for fifteen minutes or so to make sure he was gone. We promised to keep Joe under control.

"What's wrong with him?" she said.

"What's wrong with *me*?" he said. "Nothing—I have mmmagical powers!"

"We found him outside acting like this," I said.

As we filed in, I watched Joe carefully. I wanted to see if he would try to catch Sarah's eye, to let her know that he was acting. He didn't.

Instead, he snatched at flies in front of her face, stood on one foot, and conjured another ball of energy. Then, once we were all inside, Manny told me to lock the door, and Joe became hysterical. He jumped on the couch and cried, "Are you guys gonna harm me?"

"Jesus fucking Christ," I said. "No, we're not gonna hurt you."

"That's only 'cause you're his fucking brother!" Manny shouted. He'd had enough. "But if you don't shut the fuck up now and sit down, I'll duct-tape you right to that fucking couch."

After that, Joe was pretty quiet, though he never totally stopped buzzing or yelping. He sat balled up in the corner of the couch with his feet on the cushion, while I, sitting in a chair across from him, watched with disgust. After about ten minutes Manny said it was probably safe now, we should go, and I pointed to my brother.

"I don't think we should leave him here. Look at him. Who knows what he'll do? I don't think it's safe."

"Safe?" Joe said. "What do you mean? I'm fine!"

"Look at you—you're not fuckin' fine! You're goin' fuckin' crazy!"

"What, this?" he said. "Jimbo, I'm fine—no—I can stop whenever I want."

He put his feet on the carpet and sat up straight, stopped jittering, and tried to look me in the eye. But he couldn't stop. He lifted one foot, buzzed again, said, "No, no, really"—then let out a yelp. Maybe he was really losing it, or maybe he simply couldn't, at this point, admit to faking it, even if it meant getting thrown out on the street. Probably a bit of both.

I gave him eleven dollars and told him he had to leave. When he started to object, Manny shouted at him, saying he was lucky I was giving him anything at all; he should thank his brother and be happy. I told him not to come back, that I was giving Sarah my cell phone number and she would call us if he did. Saying this, I turned to her, and she nodded; she would. I held the door open for Joe, closed it after him. Before leaving, Manny and I waited about ten minutes to make sure he didn't come right back. About a week later my parents told me that Joe was in jail.

CHAPTER 13. FEET OF CLAY

Days after our trip to Murrieta, Manny and I were at a motel on Magnolia Avenue with a woman we'd met for the first time only an hour earlier, while trading meth for heroin at Chuck's. She had sauntered into Chuck's TV room wearing tight jeans and a low-cut green blouse that showed off her large, freckled breasts, and upon seeing all the drugs on the table she'd sat down between Manny and me and asked, "So, where's the party?" Her name was Ann. She was in her forties and nearly six feet tall, and she had a large beauty mark on the right side of her chin. Thin to the point of gauntness, with dark, tough skin and wrinkles that exploded around her eyes when she smiled, she had visible veins running up her neck and a deep hollow between her collarbones that made her look like a lizard. When we got to the motel room, I threw the meth and the heroin on a desk next to the bathroom door, meaning to do a shot, but then I realized that I'd forgotten my needles in the car. When I came back, the meth was no longer there. Manny was grinning. He shrugged and then nodded toward Ann, who was standing with her hands on her hips and her breasts thrust forward dramatically. Smiling, with a whorish pretense of coyness, she looked first at me, then pointedly at the bag of meth stuck in her cleavage.

"Can I have my meth?" I asked. "I kinda wanna do a shot."

"Sure," she said. "You just gotta take it."

I walked over and fished out the meth, and Ann kissed me on the neck. Then, proud that I hadn't hesitated, I told her to wait while I did a shot of meth and heroin in the bathroom. Meth (which makes you horny) and heroin (which keeps you from coming) combine to make the perfectly balanced sex drug, and as soon as the rush hit me, I knew I'd gotten it right.

When I came out of the bathroom, Manny was already positioning himself behind Ann on the bed, and Ann was calling me over. It felt like a dare, to put my dick in a woman's mouth while another guy was fucking her. I'd never had a threesome before and had never particularly wanted to (at least not with an extra guy), but doing it wasn't nearly as scary or embarrassing as walking away from the dare. Also, I was high and horny—a factor that should never be underestimated.

Standing at the foot of the bed, I watched Ann and played with her hair, until, a few minutes into it, Manny started grunting violently, making a show of grabbing at his hip.

"You all right, baby?" said Ann, kneeling.

"Yeah," said Manny. "My hip. I'm gonna sit for a second. Go ahead."

Pulling up his boxers, he stumbled to and slumped in a chair in a far, unlit corner of the room. Ann smiled, then kissed me and said, "Come here."

I stomped at my bunched khakis while she fumbled in the pockets of her jeans on the floor for a condom. I'd never used one before, and after a minute or so I pushed myself off of her and said, "C'mon, I hate this fucking thing." She glanced at my needles on the desk.

"Are you clean?" she asked.

"Sure," I said. "I think so."

I followed her eyes to the needles and shrugged my shoulders.

"Oh, fuck it," she said, reaching over and taking off the condom.

I was uncomfortably aware of Manny brooding in the corner, and after a while I became so distracted that I lost my hard-on.

"I'm gonna take a break," I said.

"You go right ahead, honey," said Ann, scratching my back.

At the foot of the bed I found my boxers and almost fell over putting them on. Then I sat in one of the chairs, put my feet up on another, and smoked a cigarette. Manny walked to the bed, and Ann passed him, warmly sliding a hand across his chest, on her way to the bathroom. I gave him a cigarette. He accepted and lit it, then sat on the edge of the bed, smoking and gazing pensively at the television, the distorted reflection on the black screen. He looked at me and nodded.

"You know," he said, "I saw you from over there, and I gotta give you credit. I mean, you were fucking—ya know—you were doing your thing. Yeah, you were . . ."

He trailed off, finishing his sentence by nodding with a frown of masculine approval.

"Thanks," I mumbled awkwardly.

I could tell that he was hiding his embarrassment, trying to play it cool with careless compliments, but it wasn't possible, not for Manny, with his tough-guy pride. To make him feel better, I almost explained that my extended endurance was due to the drugs and that without them I probably wasn't any better than he was. But I thought better of it and instead did my best to ignore him. We sat in silence: He brooded with a head full of crystal meth, while I spaced out. High, watching wisps of smoke rise from our cigarettes, I was only vaguely aware of a dangerous shift in mood.

After Ann came out of the bathroom, she and Manny sat on the far side of the bed and smoked a bowl, laughing and talking heartily, a tweaking conversation, a who-knows-who-in-Riverside. At some point they began to whisper, occasionally sneaking glances at me. I was too high to make anything of it, but they were talking crime in Riverside—the sort of conversation that almost always turns to suspicious characters and possible undercover cops. Ann hardly knew me, and Manny, still smarting, had been up for days.

I went into the bathroom to do a shot, and when I came out, Manny was gone. Ann said that he had told her to tell me that he had to go take care of something, and that he'd borrowed the car.

"Cool," I said, rubbing her thigh. "Do you think he'll be back soon?"

"No," she said. "Why do you ask . . . ?"

We were loud. I sucked on her breast until milk came out; then, cradling her head, I bit her shoulder. Later, when she came, I kissed her open mouth and she kissed me back—tenderly as her orgasm passed—and then what had been pure drug-fucking became, minute by minute, kiss by kiss, something more intimate.

During the intervals we got high and smoked cigarettes, dampening the cigarette paper with our sweaty hands. Toward morning we were both lying on the bed, me leaning against the headboard and her staring at the ceiling with her head by my hip. We talked warmly as I ran my fingers through her hair and lazily massaged her shoulder. At one point she asked me an odd question. Or, it wasn't the question itself that was odd but the tone, as though she'd thought she had known the answer and now was reconsidering.

"So . . . who are you?" she asked. "How did you end up in Riverside?"

I told her. I told her the whole story about selling drugs and getting arrested in New Jersey, fleeing to California and checking into GSL, meeting Wendy and Luke and trying to stay clean; about the sober-living on Franklin Avenue, then Patti's house, Stacie's house, Chuck's house; about Wendy's going to prison, and how I'd sent her a package; about Danny White, Maki, and Brady and the day I picked him up on his bike—the whole thing up to the present, being partnered with Manny. I even told her briefly about my parents' visit.

"Yeah, that was a trip," I concluded.

She was silent for a minute. A ray of sunlight from the window, where the curtains couldn't quite close, cut diagonally across the bed and a few feet up the dresser on the long wall. It was morning. Where was Manny with my car?

"So, you know Brady, too," Ann said thoughtfully.

"Yeah, he was in GSL at the same time I was. Aside from Wendy and Luke, he was like my best friend in there. You know those black boots he's always wearing—I gave those to him for Christmas. Why? How do you know him?"

260

"Jimmy, I've been friends with Brady for over ten years," she said, sitting up slowly. "Manny still hasn't called?"

"No. Actually I'm a little worried about him. I mean, he borrows the car a lot, but he's never disappeared for the whole night without calling before."

"He's never done that before," she repeated.

Then she turned to me. She looked scared.

"Jimmy, I think I know why you haven't heard from Manny. I think we should get you out of here." She stood and looked around. "Where's your cell phone?"

"What? What are you talking about?"

"Jimmy, just trust me. You have to trust me. Where's your cell phone?"

"Over there, on the table. What's going on?"

Having reached some decision, she ran across the room to my cell phone, flipped it open, and dialed carefully with her thumbs, shifting her weight from foot to foot and mouthing, *C'mon . . . c'mon. . . .* Just then the motel phone rang. It was the harsh, true ring of an old-fashioned motel phone, and with Ann freaking out it made me jump. *Ring! Ring!*—I remembered Manny huddled with Ann hours earlier, suspiciously glancing at me over his shoulder—*Ring! Ring!*

"Hello."

"Is this Jimmy from New Jersey?" said a deep voice with a thick Mexican accent. It wasn't Manny.

"Yes," I said, chest pounding.

"I'm calling for Big Manny from Fontana. He asked me to call you. He's doing something for us right now, and he wanted me to let

261

you know that your car is fine. He wants you to stay where you are, and he'll be back in a few hours. Something happened. It wasn't his fault. Good-bye."

Although certainly not Manny's, the voice sounded vaguely familiar.

"Who was it?" said Ann.

"I'm not sure," I said. "Somebody calling for Manny. They told me to stay here; he'd be back in a few hours."

"Yeah, that's what he wants you to think. That's perfect. Jimmy, you can't stay here. We're getting out of here. Get your shit together."

"What the fuck are you talking about? Why would I get out of here?" I asked, though I had already put on my pants and was looking for one of my boots. It was beginning to dawn on me: Manny's embarrassment, the hush-hush tweaking conversation earlier . . .

"Look, you just have to trust me. He fuckin' sketched out."

"About what?"

"About *you*! Look, I don't fucking know you. I was sketching about you too until we talked. You're from out of town, you know all these people. He got high and sketched out about you."

I'd never seen Manny sketch before, so I didn't know what he was capable of. He could have been at his brother's apartment, hiding under his bed because he thought that I was coming for him along with the rest of the undercover cops, or he could have been on his way back to the motel with an AK-47. But then again, it occurred to me, Ann might be sketching right now.

"Jesus fucking Christ," I said.

I found my boot and started to put it on.

There was a loud knock at the door. Ann checked the peephole and opened the door, and for a second I thought she'd opened it for Manny and betrayed me. But it was Brady who came bursting in!

"Jimmy, get your shoes on!" he shouted. "We gotta get you outta here!"

"What's going on?"

"Some guys are coming here to kick your ass—that's what's going on! You are fucked up, Jimmy, but I still love you, brother."

There was no second-guessing now. Brady, clearly on a good run, had thrown himself into the scene with such dramatic urgency that in another second I was out the door, down the stairs, and in the backseat of a gray coupe he must have borrowed or bought since I last saw him. Soon we were flying down Magnolia Avenue, and Brady was still shouting—"Ann, what the hell happened?"—and Ann was shouting back—"Manny sketched out about Jimmy! We were partying, and he sketched out and left with Jimmy's car!"

"What the fuck, Jimmy? I thought Manny was your friend!" Brady shouted, meaning that I should have listened to him and everybody else about not trusting people in Riverside, that I shouldn't have been so cocky.

I was perched in the center of the backseat, leaning forward between Ann and Brady, and though I was scared about Manny and my car, for once I wasn't sketching. And so I couldn't help wondering why, after we'd all left the motel room, we were still shouting and driving twenty miles over the speed limit. My cell phone rang.

"It's Manny," I said.

Ann grabbed the phone off my lap and answered it.

"Hello. No, it's Ann. Where's Jimmy's car? He's not here. You can't talk to him. He needs his car. Goddamn it, Manny! Where are you? Where's his car?"

She flipped the phone closed and gave it back to me.

"He hung up," she said. "He said he's not talkin' to me. He wants you to call him. I wouldn't."

I didn't understand why she'd answered the phone in the first place, but I didn't say anything. Ann and Brady were so fervent about saving me that I felt as though I couldn't question or object to anything for fear of hurting their feelings. At the same time, though, I worried about Manny: If they were wrong, how would he react to what Ann had said on the phone? And Brady was still driving like a madman.

"Where the hell are we going?" he shouted.

"Let's go to Taco Bell," I said.

"What?"

"Let's go fucking get something to eat. We don't know where we're going. We need to think. Let's eat and think. We'll be safe in a restaurant. And I'm fucking hungry."

"Fuckin' Jimmy, man," said Brady, smiling and shaking his head. "You buying?"

We ended up at the Del Taco on La Sierra Avenue and shared two Macho Nachos, sitting in plastic chairs on the cement patio. Brady, in shorts and a string T-shirt, lounged with his feet up and head back, dangling strings of cheese into his mouth, grinning when he got it all in. On the left side of his forehead there was an ugly scar running from his eyebrow to his hairline. As we ate, Ann caught Brady up on what had happened, reiterating that she was sure Manny had sketched out and was now trying to set me up. At the same time, though, now that

I had had a chance to relax and think, I was beginning to suspect that Ann and Brady were the ones who had sketched out, and that now they might be more of a hindrance than a help in recovering my car. But I wasn't sure.

"I gotta call Manny," I said.

"Don't do it," said Ann.

"How else am I gonna get my car?"

"Well, just don't tell him where you are."

"Okay."

I dialed Manny and he picked up on the first ring.

"Why is that bitch answering your phone?" Manny asked. "Where are you?"

"Um . . . where are you?" I stammered.

"Oh, so *that's* how it is—"

"No, no, I mean—"

"What, you don't trust me?"

Ann was staring at me, shaking her head.

"Should I trust you?" I blurted out.

"Are you fucking—," he began angrily.

"No, sorry," I said. "That's not what I meant. I mean, let's meet somewhere."

"That's what I'm saying. *Where are you?*"

"Meet me at Patti's house."

"Is that where you are?"

"I'll be there in five minutes."

There was a pause.

"Call me when you get there."

"Okay."

I asked Brady if he would drop me off at Patti's, and he said that though he didn't think it was a good idea, I was my own man and he could only do so much to keep me out of trouble. Patti's was only a few blocks away, across the overpass, and along the way Ann implored me not to meet with Manny. Lying, I told her that now that I'd talked to him I was sure that it would be safe. She said she hoped I was right and gave me her phone number to call and tell her I was okay. They both hugged me good-bye.

I must have looked scared, standing on the front lawn after they drove away, because when Garrett came outside to see who had just pulled up, he actually asked me if I was all right. I told him I was fine, that I was just meeting a friend.

"Where's your car?" he said.

"My friend's got it. I'm about to call him."

Garrett shook his head.

"You're sure you don't need any help?"

I looked up to Garrett and was grateful for his offer, but I didn't know what help to ask for.

"No, I think I'm good," I said. "Thank you, though."

Garrett went inside, and I called Manny.

"You're there?" he said.

"Yeah, c'mon by."

"Oh, no—I'm not coming there. You walk to the end of the street, the way you'd go back to La Sierra, and I'll meet you there."

Walking down the street, I didn't feel my feet hit the pavement; I only felt the pressure in my shins as I took one step after another toward my Celica, which had just parked by the corner, about a hundred yards away. Manny didn't get out of the car, or even look at me when I reached the passenger door. I hesitated for a moment, then opened the door and got in. He still didn't look at me. He just started the car and drove with his right hand on the top of the steering wheel so that his shoulder hid his face below the nose. He drove back across the overpass, turned right on Magnolia, and a few minutes later pulled in to the Galleria at Tyler, the ritziest shopping district between Corona and downtown Riverside.

"You coming in?" he said.

We were parked in front of a Sprint store.

"I need to buy a new phone," he explained.

It was Saturday, I discovered, late morning, and the store was packed. There was a strong glare from the plate-glass wall. Manny put his name on a list, and we joined the other shoppers, shuffling from stand to stand, checking out the latest features on phones secured by plastic cords.

"They've all got fucking cameras," I said. "Who needs a camera on their phone?"

I'd never been so relieved to be inside a cell phone store—probably the last place Manny would have taken me if he had been planning something.

"I've got a homeboy who won't even let you in his house with a camera phone," Manny said.

"So . . . ," I said. "What happened last night?"

"I can't tell you everything," he began, and then went on to explain, in vague, clichéd language, how *his people* had called him and asked him to do them *a favor*, and that he'd spent the night staking out some building with an AK-47. I was, of course, relieved that he seemed to want to forget about the night before, that I wasn't in any danger; but at the same time I had this depressing suspicion that Manny was lying—and not in order to set me up or hide some serious business that I shouldn't know about, but simply to save face and protect his image. These were the kind of lies I told, about who I'd been back in Dirty Jersey. He went on and on, spewing hackneyed phrases, and the more he talked, the more I began to doubt other stories he'd told me, about prison and guns and stolen cars and his connections to organized crime. And then, when Manny said that he'd had one of his people call me at the motel, it hit me—it all just came together like the fast-cut sequence at the end of a movie with a twisty ending—and I was able to place the voice on the phone. It had been Manny's cousin, who worked a full-time job and in no way qualified as one of Manny's mysterious people. I can never actually know, but it's likely that Manny went to his cousin's house, fuming about his sexual humiliation, and ended up just staying there until morning with my car. Then he had his cousin call the motel pretending to be some sort of gangster, maybe to reclaim his image, or maybe just as an excuse for having disappeared with my car all night.

I played along and pretended to believe his story; then the sales-clerk called Manny's name and he bought a cell phone. But over the next couple of weeks, having seen his clay feet, I stopped answering Manny's calls, and we stopped being partners. Manny was a tough guy who could fight and had been to prison, but for some reason he still needed to fake it, and I could do that by myself.

PART 3: HITTING BOTTOM

CHAPTER 14. OVERDOSE

After my partnership with Manny ended, I spent a lot more time at Chuck's house in Rubidoux. Not with Brady, though. I didn't see him for weeks, and then one day I was shooting heroin in Chuck's bedroom when Junkie Jack turned to me and said, "You heard about Brady, right?" I had the needle in my arm.

"What about Brady?" I asked, pushing down on the plunger.

The rush was surprisingly strong, and I had to breathe slowly with my head between my knees to keep from throwing up. I ripped off my belt and tossed it to Junkie Jack on the bed. It was his turn. Next in line were Al and Becky, an emaciated couple I'd come to know over the past weeks. Al had a large nose, several missing teeth, and high cheekbones that looked like they were about to break through his skin. Becky had been pretty once—you could tell—but now she was just run-down, haggard; she gave blow jobs for twenty bucks.

"He's back in prison," Jack mumbled as he wrapped my belt around his arm.

For a second I didn't know what he was talking about. Then I remembered and said, "Aw, fuck. How long's he down for?"

271

"Long time," said Jack.

"For what?" I began to ask, but as Junkie Jack pressed down on the plunger, his whole body, starting with his head, slumped.

"Jack," said Becky. "Jack, are you all right?"

Junkie Jack, in a limp slouch, didn't respond at all. Becky reached down to shake him but jumped back when, suddenly, his whole body went rigid. His long legs, stiff as boards, cantilevered over the edge of the bed, and the tendons in his neck bulged grotesquely. Then, just as suddenly, he went limp again. His head lolled from side to side, and drool spilled out of his mouth.

"Jack!" cried Becky, leaning over and sliding the needle out of his arm. "Oh God, Al, he's fuckin' OD'ing! Jack, you stop that! You come back here!"

Al took his shirt off, a torn short-sleeve button-down, and threw it to the side. It rippled through the air and then landed in a corner, collapsing into a surprisingly small pile. I wondered why that was necessary.

"Get some water," Al said to me.

I wandered into the kitchen and opened drawers, cupboards, cabinets; I stared into them and dreamily contemplated the containers. Did he mean a cupful of water, or more like a pitcher? From the bedroom I heard a smack, followed by a groan, then a few shrill cries of, "Oh, come on, Jack!" My pants were loose around my waist, and I realized that at some point I would have to get my belt off Junkie Jack's arm. I stared at the counter for a while longer, then grabbed a dirty glass from the sink, filled it with water, and walked back into the bedroom.

"Don't do this to me now, brother," said Al, sweat dripping down his bony back. With both hands he gripped the collar of Jack's shirt and bent over him, bringing their faces only inches apart. Jack was still drooling. "I'm sorry to have to do this to you, brother," Al whispered in his ear, almost sensually, then, with an open hand, struck him in the face. Jack went rigid again. He bit down, clenching his jaw, and his eyes rolled up into his head. But this time the fit only lasted a few seconds before he went limp. Then Al turned to me. He took the water and, to my relief, handed me my belt.

"You stay right fuckin' here, Jack! You're not goin' anywhere!" Becky shouted.

Al took a step back and from the other side of the room threw the water all over Junkie Jack, sending him into another fit. Then Al rushed across the room, grabbed Jack by the shirt, and pounded on his chest.

"C'mon, brother!" Al shouted in Junkie Jack's face. Then he turned to me and said, "Close the door."

I did as he asked. I put my belt back on, walked out the door, and closed it. Then I walked to my car, and drove away, and got high somewhere, and didn't think about Junkie Jack until a few days later when I saw him again. He was alive and high, but not on heroin, having sworn not to do it anymore. The following week we split a gram.

Shooting meth at Chuck's, I watched my cell phone ring and ring, HOME flashing on its screen. It was June seventh, the date I was supposed to have checked back into GSL, and while my parents were hitting the redial button, I was working on a story that would convince them to send me money even after this last broken promise. I thought of not answering the phone, then calling a few days later and telling them I'd been kidnapped. But that would require too elaborate a story, and, besides, I needed the money now. So . . . not kidnapping, but something like it, something involving the sort of people Manny always used to talk about.

My dad called, and I picked up the phone and told him I was in trouble with some serious people and I would have to call him back. I was still going to GSL, I told him, but I had to handle something, and I would call him in a few hours, tomorrow at the latest. Then I hung up and did a shot of meth. I'd been up for several days and I was starting to sketch. A few hours later I did another shot, because I felt so guilty that I wanted to sketch, wanted to be fucked up, paranoid, and believing my own lies—not responsible for what I was about to do to my parents.

I spent the night walking from Rubidoux to Riverside and then sitting in a Denny's restaurant, drinking water. At about four a.m., I called my parents and told them that before Joe had gone back to jail, he had borrowed a thousand dollars from dangerous people. These people, I said, had somehow discovered that I was his brother, and now they were threatening to kill me if I didn't pay them. When my dad agreed to send the money, he said he was perfectly aware that he might be paying for a good story, but how could he take the chance?

With the thousand dollars I bought a half ounce of meth and an eight ball of heroin and set up shop at Chuck's. There was another guy selling meth there, named Cliff. We had a friendly competition, getting high together and sampling each other's wares, and it soon became clear that I had a better connection, while he had more customers. Once, when I was going to buy from Patti, he asked to put in with me, and then instead of splitting the dope, we made sales together and split the money. He was from New Mexico and had a thick southern accent. He liked to pull up next to cars at traffic lights and, pretending to be British, demand directions to streets that he knew didn't exist. He also liked to shoot an astonishing amount of dope, and by this time so did I. In fact we were shooting so much that even though we were selling for close to 100 percent profit, we were nearly broke within a couple of weeks.

Then the starter to my car broke, and Cliff had an idea. Instead of buying a new starter, I should just trade the car to a meth dealer he knew for an ounce; he had a car to drive us around, and we didn't have the money for a new starter anyway. I agreed. I traded my car for an ounce of meth, and we started dealing again, this time at Stacie's (where I brought all of Wendy's things I'd been storing in the trunk of my car). I also agreed to let Cliff hold our drugs and money. I was getting so fucked up that I didn't want even that responsibility. So long as he drove me around and broke me off enough meth and heroin to keep me high, I was happy.

In early July Wendy got out of prison. She called me and said she was coming over to Stacie's for her stuff and that I'd better be there. After she hung up, a guy sitting on Stacie's couch said, "I heard that bitch from here, man. You better listen." This was a guy I'd heard of but had never met before, a vicious debt collector named Bill from Mira Loma. He was built like Manny but not quite as tall or fat, more compact. Part Mexican, part Native American, he had short black hair and a wide, flat face. His eyes were black slits and there was a scar on his chin. Rumor had it he was a jujitsu master, without the self-control that went along with it.

"Yeah, she's no fuckin' joke," I said. "She told me to stay here, and that's what I'm gonna do."

"I hope so." Bill laughed. "I kinda want to see this."

When Wendy arrived, though, she didn't even say anything to me at first. She just walked in, nodded coldly, and then began inspecting the pile of her things in Stacie's TV room.

"Where's the rest of it, Jimmy?" she asked, with her back to me.

"That's everything," I said.

"What do you mean, that's everything? That's not everything. Tons of my shit is missing. Where's your car?"

"I sold it."

"Yeah, I heard," she said, turning to face me. "Are you sure you got everything out of the trunk?"

I wasn't. Over the months Wendy's stuff had gotten mixed up with all sorts of garbage, and I'd been high and in a rush while trying to sort it all out.

"A few things might still be in the trunk," I said.

"Well, then, where's the fucking car, Jimmy?"

"I don't know. I sold it to Cliff's friend. He could call her. Let me go get him."

"No, Jimmy," she said. "I don't want you to go get *Cliff*. I don't want you anywhere near Cliff or anybody like him. I just want to know when you're going back to GSL."

"Soon," I said.

"What's that mean?"

"Like a couple of weeks."

"Are you high right now?"

I laughed and looked at the floor.

"You know, I talked to your parents," she said.

"Yeah?"

"They told me how you lied to them, too. I'm not even gonna say it here, but that's fucked up."

I stared at the floor.

"You're sure you don't want me to find your things?" I asked.

"I don't care about my things, Jimmy. And *I'll* find 'em if I need 'em. All I wanna know is when you're going back to GSL."

"Soon," I said. "I just got a few things I gotta take care of."

"What kind of *things*—," she started angrily. "You know what? I'm not even doing this shit. Good luck with your things. I'm going to Whiteside Manor, 'cause I wanna stay healthy; call me when you're at GSL."

Wendy brought all her stuff outside in a few trips; then, on the last one, she stopped and gave me a hug. She said she loved me but that she couldn't be my friend if I kept doing drugs. Before leaving, she asked me one last time to please go to GSL.

"Goddamn," said Bill, once she was gone. "I'm sitting here, expecting fireworks and shit, and instead I get this heartbreaking scene. I think I'm gonna cry, man."

I tried to laugh.

"See, look, you're still *recovering*, trying to play it off," he said. "You're all broken up. You should have seen the look on your face when she asked if you were high! Nah, but I'm fuckin' with you. She cares about you, dude; it's cool. She's not your girl, is she?"

"No," I said, sitting on the other couch. "She's my best friend. I took care of her while she was down."

"You never fucked her?" Bill asked.

"No."

"Really? She's a big girl—she'd probably fuckin' break you. But either way, it's cool she cares about you. It tells me something about you, that you got people like that who care about you. And I like that, seein' as you're workin' with my boy Cliff now. And the prison thing, taking care of her, that's cool too."

Bill, resting his arms on the back of the couch, was wearing a gold-plated Citizen watch with a black face. It looked a lot like the Seiko watch I used to own, a watch my dad had given me years ago and that I'd lost only a few weeks earlier, putting it up as collateral at a motel and never returning.

"I really like that watch," I said.

"Yeah?" he said, immediately taking it off. "Me too."

He handed it to me.

"Go ahead; check it out."

This, I'd heard, was a prison thing. In prison when you say that you like something that belongs to somebody else, you're threatening to take it, and so now Bill was daring me to take it, putting it in my hand, saying go ahead and try it. Of course, I hadn't meant to threaten Bill at all—I was just being friendly—and as he pushed the watch into my hand, I tried to tell him just that by smiling and shaking my head. In response he looked at me quizzically, then waved his hand, telling me to relax. He sat back on the couch, looked at me again, and laughed—laughed at the idea that he would even think that I was threatening him—though I was sure that was what he'd been communicating by pushing the watch into my hand.

"You like it so much, I'll sell it to you," he said.

"How much?"

"Sixty bucks. And you know that's worth a hundred at least."

"You know what? I think I'm gonna take you up on that. Thank you. Let me go find Cliff—he's holding the money."

"No, don't even bother Cliff," he said. "Just pay me whenever. You hold on to that."

"Really?"

"Really."

The next day I was in Stacie's bathroom with a needle in my arm, watching the plunger go from the ninety-unit mark all the way to zero. I had just enough time to take the needle out and set it on the counter—carefully, like a drunk—before my head slumped. Drool accumulated on my heavy lower lip until it spilled over, a stream darkening my khakis, and I realized that I didn't care about wiping it up. I enjoyed not caring.

"Jimmy," said Cliff. "Jimmy . . . oh, what the fuck?"

I'd never been so high in my life and I wasn't scared at all. I didn't even know that I had overdosed until Cliff tapped and then pushed my head, knocking it off the hand that had been propping it. Sitting on the edge of the tub, I lurched forward but didn't fall. My head swung loosely, and drool dropped on the carpet.

Cliff yelled something, and then people started calling my name.

The difference between life and overdose was not nearly as drastic as I'd assumed. It was like watching a television show attentively and then, while it's still playing, receding into thought. There are lights and noises, and the characters are still talking, but none of it matters. When my head slumped, the world was still there; it just didn't have anything to do with me anymore.

Somebody splashed icy water on my face, and then a tall man named Moose bent down to my ear and said, "You stupid motherfucker—keep your eyes open."

"Maybe we should hit him with some speed," somebody said.

"Heart might explode," somebody else mumbled.

"Yeah, but he's on heroin. It might bring him out of it."

It was only then that I recognized that I wasn't in control. Until then, I had thought that I could come out of it at any time—that I was *choosing* not to wake up and tell everybody that I was okay. But when I tried to tell them that there'd been a ton of speed in the shot I'd taken and that another shot might kill me, I couldn't. It was a struggle to keep my eyes open.

Somebody threw more water on me, this time down my shirt and pants, and I started breathing again. I hadn't known that I'd stopped.

Everyone was buzzing around me frantically, and as I began to feel their panic, I also began to fight the urge to close my eyes and go to sleep. But then it occurred to me that for once I had everybody's attention, and if I came out of my stupor I would lose it. I didn't want to die, but I wanted this to go on, so I let myself slide a little closer to the brink.

"Jimmy!" said Stacie.

I hadn't known she was in the room.

There was another splash of cold water. I blinked, breathed, faded away . . .

And that's how it went until I woke and found myself sitting on the couch in the living room. Cliff told me that I'd been out for hours and that he and Moose had walked me to the couch. Every once in a while somebody had checked my breathing and forced me to open my eyes.

CHAPTER 15. GRAPES

Cliff often stayed on Mission Avenue with Molly, in the same two-room apartment that Brady and I had stopped at on our way to the hospital. It was virtually empty except for a couch facing a TV on a milk crate, and a filthy mattress in the corner. The house itself—the former sober-living that had been abandoned to the junkies for cheap rent—had shattered windows, broken floorboards, and wood rotting all over.

About a week after my overdose, on a sunny California morning, Cliff and I were hanging out at Molly's, and then all of a sudden he was gone. His car wasn't in the driveway. Molly said that he'd probably run out to sell some speed, but by late afternoon Cliff still hadn't returned. Then Bill stopped by and asked me for the sixty dollars I owed him.

"I don't—," I began.

"What the fuck do you mean, you don't have it?" he demanded. "It's been over a week." When I started to explain that Cliff had all my dope and money, Bill cut me off, saying he didn't want to hear it; this was between me and him. "I can't deal with this shit right now," he said. "I been up for like four days; I'm gonna pass out. We'll deal with this when I get up. Just don't go anywhere."

Then he walked over to the mattress in the corner and collapsed.

I had also been up for four days, but I couldn't sleep now. I took a shot of speed and started calling Cliff every fifteen minutes: "Dude, where are you? I've been calling you since morning—where'd you go last night? I'm still stuck at the house on Mission, and I got Bill's watch, and I need to pay him for it. Call me back?" Junkie Jack came into the apartment, but he just shrugged when I asked if he'd seen Cliff.

About an hour later Bill got up, went into the bathroom, and drank some water from the tap. Bleary-eyed, he looked at me as if trying to remember something.

"You got it?" he asked.

"You know what, Bill?" I said. "I can't find Cliff, so I think I'm just gonna give you the watch—"

"I don't want the watch back," he snapped, before collapsing on the mattress again and immediately falling asleep, with his belly hanging out and his head resting on his right bicep.

It was getting dark, and I was sitting in the corner, listening to Bill snore. Junkie Jack was sitting on the chair in front of the TV, mumbling to a junkie with broad shoulders and a ratty beard called Texas, who slept on a small couch in the hall downstairs. Molly, in tattered gym shorts and a gray T-shirt, was on the couch watching TV with her mouth open.

This place, this section of Riverside, these junkies—this was "the East Side." *You think it's rough where you been? Well, this is the East Side. This here's the bad place. This is where it really goes down.* Of course, the junkies across town by Magnolia and La Sierra said the same thing about "the West Side." *This is where it really goes down.* Colton,

Fontana, Rubidoux—the same thing. But I'd never been stuck in any of those other places with no car, no money, not even a change of clothes; so *this is where it really goes down* had never meant anything to me. It had always sounded like vague bullshit: This is where *what* goes down? Now it was perfectly clear, and the East Side was a scary place. I sat on the carpet and watched the greasy junkies come in and out and make their deals, and I realized that *this is where kids get stabbed for owing money to people like Bill.*

I got up and went down the stairs to the front porch and started talking to a woman in her early twenties with red hair and large breasts, freckles and full lips. She had a way of rolling her eyes without actually rolling her eyes, without making even that much effort. I asked her for a cigarette and she didn't look at me. I asked what her name was and she sighed, leaning against the banister, stoned. Every day she hung out on this porch until her pimp drove her to one of the motels on University; he waited, brought her back here, then gave her some dope and money. She lived in a shack in the backyard.

"Do you know who I am?" I said to her.

This made her laugh.

"Who are you?' she said. "Some big shot?"

"That's right," I said.

"If you're such a big shot, why ain't you got no cigarettes?"

"My partner's got 'em," I said.

"Yeah, okay," she snickered, turning back to the banister.

I walked from the porch to the sidewalk, laughing. Why had I just talked to her? To amuse myself. And that's why I was laughing now, because she was funny; she thought she was hot shit. Why had I told her that I was a big shot? Because I *was* a big shot: I bought ounces of speed while she sold her ass for a twenty bag, and when Cliff came back I'd show her more meth than she'd ever seen in her life. Dumb whore.

But when would Cliff come back? Would he come back at all? Had he fucked me, left me on the East Side with nothing but a needle and a few chunks of meth and tar? I called him on my cell phone and listened to the hollow ring while watching cars drive by. I smiled at a woman in a blue sedan. Brief eye contact, but she quickly looked away. My arms were tracked from the forearm to the upper bicep, and I was wearing a string T-shirt and khaki cargo shorts. *Does she I think I'm one of these street junkies, like the whore on the porch? No way—I'm talking on a cell phone.* Actually, I was listening to nothing; I remembered hearing Cliff's voice and the beep some time ago. It was probably too late to start a message. Hanging up, I looked down the street for the sedan. It must have turned a corner.

The sun had just set, the night was grayish-blue, and to my left Mission Avenue was empty. I could have walked downtown; I could have left Bill in that house and not come back. But then there would be no chance of getting my share of the drugs and money from Cliff. I wouldn't be able to hunt for him in places where Bill might be hunting for me. Also, there was still the possibility that Cliff wasn't avoiding me at all, that he'd merely fallen asleep somewhere with no intention of screwing me over. If that were so, I would be throwing away the partnership for no reason, my share along with it: We wouldn't be able to sell drugs together anymore, not with Bill after me, and then Cliff would have to choose between keeping everything to himself or meeting me on some corner and giving me half. Which would cut the re-up in half, which would mean he'd have to buy drugs at a steeper price. I couldn't even blame him for not doing that: Why should he lose money because I got into trouble?

Not that I was thinking clearly, staring down Mission Avenue. I was scared with nowhere to go. All I knew was that unless the woman in the blue sedan turned around and brought me to her house for sex, I should get back inside before Bill started to wonder where I was.

When I walked into the apartment, Bill was waking up, sitting on the mattress and rubbing his eyes and eating a packet of peanuts. I was afraid at first, when I saw him, but then suddenly I became angry with myself: *Here I am, a criminal for four years now, from when I was selling drugs in New Jersey, and I'm flippin' out because I can't come up with sixty dollars?*

"Ya know what? Fuck that," I said, before Bill had even looked at me. "Sixty dollars—what the fuck is sixty dollars? Like I can't get sixty dollars!"

Bill sat for another moment, seemingly confused. Then, still chewing, he stood, stepped forward, and got in my face. There were moist flecks of peanut at the corners of his mouth.

"So what the fuck are you saying?" he said. "You got some sort of problem?"

Molly and Texas and Junkie Jack and everybody else were watching, eating it up.

"I'm saying," I said, "that I'm gonna go get your money. Right now. I'm gonna do a shot, then I'm gonna go out there and come up with your money."

Amused, he stepped back, shrugged, and looked at me as if to say, *What are you waiting for?* He sat back on the mattress and went back to eating his peanuts.

I finished off my meth and heroin with an enormous shot—energy for the night ahead—and told Bill I'd be back before morning. I told the whore I'd be back too. Then I walked. I walked west on Mission and made a left on Commerce, then a right on University, and continued west under the 91 freeway overpass, where University dips into a valley whose slopes are covered with wood chips and dead shrubs. Leaning against one of the shrubs was a toppled shopping cart. I walked past the Pizza Hut on Lime, entering downtown. The shoe store and the café looked dark and lonesome. At Market I made a left and walked all the way to Fourteenth, where two guys in their twenties, white and black, the white one in a backward baseball cap, were laughing outside a corner store that was still open. An older man, in his forties, came out of the store. Tall, bearded, and wearing a long-sleeve T-shirt, he said, "You think it's funny, huh?" Then the younger guys laughed harder. They turned and moved quickly down the street, skipping and grabbing each other by the shoulder, looking back at the tall man, who'd taken off after them. He rushed a few paces, stumbling a little before easing into his stride. He made a noise from deep in his throat that could have been laughter or rage. Head down, he was only a few yards behind, but then they turned a corner and he followed before I could tell if it was serious. I still smiled, though, alone in the street, as if I'd known what was happening.

Thirsty, I went into the store. Behind the counter a bald Indian with heavy wrinkles under his eyes told me he was closing up, two minutes. There were two coolers in the back, one filled with juice and soda and water, the other with dairy. I fished around in my pockets: not even a quarter. I picked up a small bottle of water and asked the Indian how much it cost. He said, "Seventy-five cents. I'm closing." I walked around the tall shelf in the middle of the shop—ramen noodles, cans of black beans—and I thought about what would happen if I snapped my knife open and rushed the Indian and demanded the money in the register. I peeked at him through the shelf, but he was staring right at me, so I walked out of the store and made a right on Fourteenth.

I walked and walked, turning frequently, and eventually I was somewhere I'd just been. I laughed, put my head down, and kept walking. Laughing didn't make me feel any better. I'd been laughing and smiling all night, at shop windows I found creepy, at the longer streets, the ones with more shadows and fewer lights. Each time it made me feel a little lonelier. The joke was utterly my own.

It was late, well past midnight. On a corner at the edge of downtown, I came across three bums. Two were sitting on the ground in a way that made it seem comfortable. The other was standing, hunched over and leaning against a wall. They didn't talk at all or even face each other; they'd positioned themselves like strangers at an outdoor concert who've ended up on the same bit of grass.

To the one who was standing, I said, "Hey, you know where I can come up with sixty dollars around here?"

He wore a striped windbreaker—green and what was once white—and even with his hood up I could see lines of dirt on his forehead.

"You want what now?" he said, his voice thick with phlegm.

"Sixty dollars," I said, gripping the knife in my pocket. "Do you know where I can come up with sixty dollars?"

Shifting in his windbreaker, he looked at me and then at the sidewalk.

"Sixty dollars," he said. "No . . ."

He paused as if he might be forgetting something. Then he shook his head.

"No. Sorry."

I told him thanks anyway and started off briskly down the street. I walked, it seemed, for miles, my boots thudding numbly against the pavement. Coming up a hill I realized (this came with another laugh) that I hadn't slept in, what, five days now?—and that I wasn't tired because I'd been pumping myself with thick shots of meth and heroin, that these chemicals were the only reason I hadn't passed out already. At the top of the hill was a twenty-four-hour drive-thru restaurant. I sat at a picnic table next to the parking lot and watched cars drive up, listening to the people order food and hoping for a single woman to drive by so I could convince her to bring me to her house for sex.

"Jimmy? Is that you?"

A short man had gotten out of his car and was walking toward me across the parking lot. His face was flattish and his cheeks seemed wider than his head.

"Jimmy from Jersey, is that you, man?"

"Hey," I said.

"It's Rick," he said, stopping about ten yards from me. "Rick from GSL."

"Oh," I said. "Hey." I thought I remembered him, but I wasn't sure.

"What are you doin' out here?" he said.

"Nothing, man. I'm all right. I'm walking."

"You need a ride somewhere," he said, "I'll give you a ride. I can't take you in—I wish I could, but I already got screwed over like that. You remember Mitch? Mitch C.? Yeah, man, I took him in and he screwed me. But if you need a ride, I'll take you somewhere."

"Nah, dude, I'm good."

"You're sure."

"Yeah, I'm fine, really. Thank you—I appreciate it, but I'm fine."

"Okay. Well, I guess it was good to see you. I hope you get it together."

"Thanks. It was good to see you, too."

Rick got in his car, and I walked over to the drive-thru lane and waved to him as he drove away. Late as it was, the drive-thru had a long line. I stood next to the giant menu, waiting for somebody else to talk to—a single woman. Soon enough one actually came: a brunette in a sweatshirt, the last car in line. She wasn't pretty, so I figured I had a shot. She stumbled over her order, said she wanted one thing, then another, then back to the first thing and I'm so sorry, but what does that come with again? The voice from the menu became testy, repeating the order deadpan and then waiting. She made a geez-I'm-sorry face, and I laughed. She ordered the number two, and I said, "Good choice."

"I hope so," she said. "I was running out of time here."

"Yeah, like, hurry up, miss," I said jokingly. "There aren't even any cars behind you. And like you're supposed to know the menu or some shit?"

She laughed a little, and the voice told her to go to the next window.

"What are you doing out here?" she asked.

"Actually, I'm looking for a ride."

"Oh."

"Don't worry, I understand if you don't want to let me in your car."

"Yeah . . . ," she said. "Probably not safe."

"Actually, it is safe. But I know there's no way you can know that."

"Still . . ."

"Don't worry about it. I understand."

"Well . . . bye."

"Nice to meet you."

I sighed wistfully as she drove to the next window. *So close.* Then she was gone and the drive-thru was empty and I started to worry that the guy taking the orders had heard me talking to the girl, making fun of him, and would now call the police. Or, even if he hadn't heard me, what if another employee had seen me standing by the menu and thought I'd been harassing the people driving through? I knew I should go, I really should . . . but I didn't want to. There was a bench here, and another girl might come soon. Maybe I should go up to the menu and talk into the microphone, ask if anybody minded my being here. No, that would be stupid. Chances were they hadn't seen me or simply didn't care—I would be needlessly drawing attention. Then it hit me, the obvious thing to do. Feeling very clever, I walked back across the parking lot and began gathering all the trash on the patio. They wouldn't call the cops on me for cleaning their eating area. They might even thank me. At first I kept an eye out for approaching cars, because I didn't want my single woman to see me picking up trash; but then I got into it, I developed a system. I put the ketchup packets inside the burger wrappers, then the wrappers inside the brown bags—everything into the trash. I imagined the people inside watching me, stopping work to watch, in awe of my efficiency and meticulousness. I heard them talking, marveling at my method of spotting ketchup packets in the gravel beyond the patio, at the way I stepped back and tilted my head—*Oh, he's good*—to such an angle that I could see the silver of the packet shimmering in the light from the window. And the few times I mistook leaves for wrappers, bending over and coming up with nothing—they understood. Even Jordan doesn't make every shot.

An hour or so later the garbage was gone and I needed to piss. I figured that since I'd cleaned up the patio, the people inside should let me use their bathroom—they owed me that much, at least—so I walked over to the nearest window and started banging on it, peering into the room. It was the room adjacent to the one from which they hand out the food. Inside, a fat woman called to somebody, and I stopped and waited patiently, and soon she called again. Then a skinny man with glasses came into the room, followed by a skinnier teenager who hung back, smirking self-consciously. The fat woman stood off to the side, wide-eyed and indignant. They all wore visors and red shirts that were too big.

"Yes?" said the man in the glasses. "Can I help you?"

"Is there any way I can come in to use your bathroom?" The window was thick, so I had to shout.

"No," he said, shaking his head and shrugging. "I'm sorry—no."

"Well, how about the ones out back? I thought I saw some outdoor ones—what are they called? I saw some around back. And also maybe some water?"

"What?"

"Never mind," I said. "Fuck it. Don't worry about it."

I walked away, furious. At the edge of the parking lot I paused and looked around; I thought of pissing right there but got scared and ended up waiting until I reached an alley at the end of the block. The sky was already turning gray, and I decided to head downtown. By the time I reached the Maxi Foods on University it was early morning, and I had nothing for Bill. I crossed the street and paced in the parking lot of the Riverside Inn. I imagined knocking on one of the doors and robbing the lodgers at knifepoint. But I knew I wouldn't do it. I felt weak. I was tired and hungry and thirsty and *is that dope on the ground?* I walked over and stooped, but I'd lost track of it, whatever it was, probably not dope but who can be sure? Hands on my knees, I scanned the ground for a time, a long time; I thought I saw money, but no. I mistook a pebble for a piece of tar. Then I wrenched myself away from the ground and laughed.

There was a shopping center across the street and the stores were opening: a check-cashing place, a doughnut store, a bodega, a Chinese restaurant—I was so hungry. I saw the bus depot, adjacent to the motel, and I went over to one of the benches and sat with my head in my hands. Standing to my left were two men in suits, drinking coffee, on their way to work. A bum was sleeping several benches over, with a tattered blue sweatshirt for a pillow. This was July, Southern California. The sun was already blazing and the tar by the curb was soft and glistening.

I'd been up for five days now.

On the ground a few feet in front of me was a piece of paper that looked like a receipt. The words "Western Union" were printed at the top. Near the bottom was a number, a dollar amount: two thousand. There were other numbers printed across the center, likely belonging to the credit card with which the money had been sent. *No fucking way. Too good to be true.* But there it was, right in front of me: WESTERN UNION, $2000.00, a long number with a space after each fourth digit. All I had to do was call Western Union, give them the name on the receipt and the credit card number, and then wire myself two hundred . . . five hundred . . . a thousand dollars! I could pay Bill and buy an ounce of meth, an eight ball of heroin, a hooker, a motel room . . . *Too good to be true.* I got up and stepped toward the receipt. I looked down: WESTERN UNION. It looked almost as if it had been planted there. . . . Had it? I stepped back, looked around; and just as I did, one of the suited men on his way to work—*seemingly* on his way to work—turned away from me and checked his watch. *Of course.* I was being set up.

I laughed and sat back down on the bench. From across the street I heard a radio crackle and then the words *He knows.* A man rushed out of the bodega in the shopping center, hustling toward his position in the contingency plan. *Damn straight, I know.* I stared at the man in the suit who'd checked his watch. I stared until he looked at me, and then I smiled and nodded and he smiled and nodded back. We understood each other. He knew I wasn't stupid. *How are you gonna get out of this one, Jim?* I stood and looked at the receipt, then slowly walked around it, listening to the cops across the street: *Hold it, not yet . . .* They were in their new positions, watching, tense, ready to run down on me with their guns drawn. But they weren't going to catch me. I was too smart for them. I walked over to the curb and rubbed my boot in a soft splotch of tar. Then, before the tar dried, I walked over to the receipt and stepped on it, stole a quick glance to make sure it was stuck. Then I marched proudly away from the bus stop, while across the street the cops went berserk. They radioed back and forth, *What should we do? What should we do?* Behind me, the suited undercovers waved desperately at the bodega, trying to signal the operation commander for instructions. They threw their arms up in dismay. *We can't take him now, can we? Surely he'll get off—he could just plead ignorance. A man can't be held responsible for every piece of trash that gets stuck to his foot!* With an enormous grin I marched down the street, away from the bus stop and the shopping center, away from all the swarming cops. I'd gotten exactly what I wanted, and they had nothing on me! The operation commander, now several blocks behind me, came out of the bodega with a machine gun hanging from his shoulder. He took off his hat and shook his head. He actually smiled at how damn slick I was.

I marched all the way across town, grinning, with the receipt stuck to my boot. I passed the Pizza Hut and went under the 91 freeway overpass. Still there, leaning against a shrub, was the shopping cart I'd seen the night before, a token of the harsh, seedy world that I had just conquered. I was victorious! I marched back to Commerce and made a left, then a right on Mission. I marched all the way back to the porch where the whore had been.

She wasn't there now, but somebody else was, leaning against the railing and talking with a thin teenager in a baseball cap. I stopped in front of the porch to get a better look at him—I found it hard to believe that he thought I was that stupid. Cliff had come back. He'd shaved his head and grown a mustache in order to disguise himself from me. Laughing, I walked right up to him and said, "Hey—*Cliff.*"

"What?"

He was now speaking with a Cajun accent. As if that would fool me.

"Cliff," I repeated slowly, pointing my finger at his chest.

"Look, I don't know no Cliff, homey—"

"Whatever, Cliff. You owe me seven hundred dollars. And I'll be here tomorrow to collect that shit."

He looked to his friend, and they both seemed so bewildered that for a moment I doubted myself. But no: I was sure it was Cliff. I turned my back on them and went up the stairs and into Molly's apartment.

Molly was sleeping on the couch and Junkie Jack was still nodding in the chair. Across the room Bill and Texas were smoking a bowl. Texas saw me first.

"So, you get it?" he said.

Whether or not I had gotten Bill's money had nothing to do with Texas, of course, but this was how Bill worked: He so scared everybody that when one person got into trouble with him, everybody else positioned themselves next to Bill as his deputies. *Didn't you say you were gonna bring him that dope yesterday?* This way, not only was Bill saved a hassle, but also the person ended up hating the deputies more than Bill himself. At the moment, though, I didn't care who wanted to toady up to Bill or how. I had something good for him. I looked at Texas, then at Bill.

"I got something even better than sixty dollars," I said.

There were no chairs in the apartment, aside from the one Jack was in, so I brushed past Texas and went into the bathroom; then, leaving the door open, I sat on the toilet cross-legged with my right ankle resting on my left thigh. Bill and Texas were both staring at me. I showed them the tar and the receipt—I pointed to the bottom of my boot and said, "This here's worth a lot more than sixty dollars."

Then I tried to pull the receipt off my boot, but the tar had hardened so that the receipt was now embedded except for a few gray corners that I was careful not to pull and rip. Instead, I worked from the outside, pinching the tar at the very edge of the sole, trying to pull it up so I could work one of my fingers underneath.

Bill watched for a few minutes before chuckling and sitting back on the mattress and returning to his bowl.

"*That*," said Texas. "That there, what you're scraping off your boot, is worth more than sixty dollars."

"Yeah," I said emphatically. "You don't even know what this—"

"Well, it kinda looks like tar and fucking . . . garbage that got stuck to your boot."

I shook my head impatiently.

"You'll find out if you lemme fucking explain—"

"Please—"

"It's a Western Union receipt for two thousand dollars. You know how much money I can scam with this thing?"

"Then why's it stuck to your boot?"

"Because these guys were watching me. I couldn't just pick it up."

At this I heard Bill laugh loudly.

"So," said Texas, "you're saying you had to, like, fake these guys out by smearing it on your boot?"

"That's right," I said. "Now I need a fuckin' knife or some shit to get this thing off. Wait a minute, I got it."

I took my knife out of my pocket and began digging into the side of my boot sole. Bill laughed again. Texas walked away, saying, "Don't cut yourself," and the words echoed in my head as I began tweaking with the knife. *Don't cut yourself.* A few times, when I got frustrated, I jabbed at the sole and then quickly stopped myself for fear of damaging the receipt. I could hear people in the apartment talking about me. Everybody in the place, people from the street, scores of them—they'd come up to stand outside the bathroom and watch and point and whisper, whisper that I was going insane.

I put the knife back in my pocket and stared at the mess on the bottom of my boot, then at the apartment outside the bathroom. Junkie Jack had woken up; he was getting out of his chair. Texas was talking to Molly on the couch. I stepped out of the bathroom and sat on the floor, a few feet from Bill on the mattress.

"You get that receipt?" he said. "Or whatever it was?"

"No, man," I said.

"Was there a receipt?"

"I think so. But I'm fucked up. I'm sorry, man. I couldn't get the money."

"I know you're fucked up," he said. "Anybody who looks at you knows you're fucked up."

"You wanna just take the watch back and I'll still owe you the money, whenever I can get it?"

"The watch is yours. I don't want it back. But look, you don't need to be all scared right now, 'cause I know you wanna pay me, and I know you can't. And we both know that if I want the watch back, I'll take it back, and if I wanna take that knife away from you and stick it up your ass, I'll do that, too," he said, smiling. "But then I wouldn't get my money out of you, my little sixty dollars. So you just need to calm down, maybe get some sleep. Think of somebody who owes you money, and I'll go and collect that shit. But first you need to get your head straight."

"I'm not gonna be able to sleep," I said. "I'm out of heroin."

"Well, then you'll kick first," he said. "There's a toilet. Probably be good for you. Wait a minute, I gotta go talk to somebody."

Cliff—shaved head, mustache, and all—had come into the apartment with his teenage friend. Bill asked Molly to get off her couch so that Cliff and his friend could sit; he then sat across from them on a crate he pulled from the corner. I watched intently from across the room. It seemed Bill was angry with them. I heard him say, "'Cause none of that shit's gonna be happenin' while I'm here," and they both nodded, scared. I imagined Bill was telling Cliff that he shouldn't have disappeared with my share of the money, that he had to pay me so that I could pay Bill. This was hopeful. After a few minutes Bill left Cliff talking with his friend on the couch and walked back over to Texas and me. I nodded toward Cliff and snorted. I said, "Fuckin' joke. Like he's fooling somebody."

Bill smiled and began to nod in agreement, but then he stopped and looked at me.

"Who?" he said curiously.

"Fuckin' Cliff over there," I said. "Like he's fooling somebody with that shaved head."

Bill said, "Holy shit," and began to roar. He staggered a few steps in hysterics, then went over to the guy on the couch with the shaved head, grabbed him by the arm, and walked him across the room.

"Look at this guy," Bill said to me.

He brought him right up to me so that our faces were a foot apart.

"This is not Cliff."

"I don't even know no Cliff," the guy said in his Cajun accent. "My name's Mark."

I couldn't tell. I was a foot away, staring directly at him, and I couldn't tell if this was somebody I'd spent every day with for the past two weeks.

"This dude was saying I owed him money," the guy said to Bill.

"I thought you were someone else," I said. "I'm sorry."

His face was morphing in front of me: All the distinctive characteristics were somehow blurry—the wrinkles and blemishes, the lines that made up his nose, mouth, and eyes—and the pigment and tint of his skin kept shifting like a chameleon's. I looked at Bill. His face was doing the same thing.

I began to panic.

Eventually they all stopped laughing, and Mark and his friend left. Then, as soon as nobody was looking at me, I walked out of the apartment and down the stairs. When I hit the porch, I started running. I made a right on Mission and ran, gripping the knife in my pocket, too scared to look over my shoulder. At the end of Mission, a few blocks down, I ran out of breath and slowed to a fast walk. I passed two people: a pretty woman with dark hair, about my age, whom I'd seen in the apartment the day before; and a slight street kid on a bike, a Mexican in baggy shorts and a string T-shirt.

"Are you all right?" the woman asked.

I shook my head but didn't stop. They began walking next to me.

"Why don't you come with us?" the woman said. "Trust me—you don't wanna go back to that house."

I looked at her but kept walking, kept gripping the knife.

"What's wrong with him?" said the Mexican.

"He's scared," she said. "He thinks someone's gonna hurt him."

"Nobody's gonna hurt you, dude," he said to me. "Not if you're with me."

"He's not gonna stop," the girl said. "I told him he should come with us, but look at him; he's so fuckin' scared."

"Dude, nobody's gonna hurt you."

"He's not gonna stop. He's so scared, he doesn't know what's going on. God knows how long it's been since he's slept. He's all fucked up. He doesn't even know that we're friends. He's holding that knife in his pocket and he doesn't know who he can trust. He's going insane and he's ready to stab the first person he runs into. Stab, stab, stab, whoever, for no reason, because he's gone insane and he's going to kill. He's going to kill the first person he runs into; stab, stab, stab . . ."

At Third Street I slowed and looked around to find that the girl and the Mexican had stopped following me a few blocks back. Had they ever even been there? I was alone, hearing voices on a busy street, with no money and nowhere to go.

I called Cliff again, sure he wouldn't pick up.

He answered, saying, "Jesus, how many times did you call me?"

"What?" I said. "What do you mean? I didn't know where you were."

"I was sleeping. I went out to make a sale and I fell asleep. Jesus Christ, man. Relax. I'm coming back now."

"I'm not there anymore—I'm on Third Street, not too far from Kansas, you know. I had to leave. Now I'm in front of—I think it's a restaurant. It's like a brick wall with no windows and a bar-type door—"

"Just be outside. I'll drive down in twenty minutes."

"Call me when you get in the area. I want to get off the street. I'm gonna get some water."

I hung up and went into the restaurant. There was only one person inside, a man in a green shirt, and he told me he was closing, that they only served lunch.

"Only lunch?" I said.

The chairs were already flipped onto the tables.

"*Sí*, only lunch. Open again tonight, after nine."

"I'm waiting for my friend," I said. "Can I . . . can I please have some water?"

He brought me some water and let me sit down, and then he paused and looked at me and asked if I wanted food, some tacos maybe, but I'd have to eat them fast because he was closing, he was closed now.

"Please," I said. "Thank you. Thank you very much. My friend will be here soon."

"You like spicy?"

"Yes. Please. Thank you."

He disappeared behind the bar and I rested my head on the table. Then there were tacos in front of me, and the man was shaking my shoulder and asking if I was okay; when would my friend be here? I told him soon, very soon.

"You say you like spicy," he said, smiling and pointing at the tacos. Then he checked his watch and said, "But please, eat fast. It's fifteen minutes; I'm closing; I have to go."

The tacos burned all the way down to my stomach, but I was so hungry I didn't stop for water until they were gone. Then I downed the glass in one draft, water splashing on my shirt, and the man came over and asked me where my friend was. I said, "Please, five more minutes." He walked away and I let my head rest . . . then he was shaking my shoulder and I was pleading for more time, telling him that my friend was coming, more time, please, please. He nodded and walked away, looking sad, and then I put my head down, he was shaking my shoulder, and I was asking for more time, here soon, please, please . . . until I woke up in an alley with dirt in my hair. I had no idea where I was or how I'd gotten there; standing, looking around, I still didn't know. I began to panic, but then I noticed that my watch was still on my wrist and my phone was still in its clip, and I remembered the man in the restaurant and felt bad that I'd forced him to drag me out here.

Cliff did not answer his phone.

I walked out to Third Street and headed east toward my old sober-living. A few blocks before Franklin, three Mexicans were hanging out, sitting by the curb. One of them stared at me as I approached, a fat boy, no older than fourteen; he stared and the others saw him staring, his uncles, I suppose; and then they stared. When I reached them, I stopped and stood in front of the oldest. He was a thin man with yellowish skin and a scrappy beard.

"I'm hungry," I said. "And I'm lost."

"Oh, yeah," he said, looking up at me from the curb. Several of his teeth were missing. He waved his hand at me and pointed down Third Street, signaling for me to move on.

"I'm hungry and I'm lost," I repeated, arms slack at my sides.

Again, he pointed down Third Street, and when I still didn't move, he began angrily tying his boots, saying, "Okay, you don't want to move. . . ." The fat boy stared at me. The other man was already standing. I looked at him and he stepped to the side, and then the older man sprang forward and swung his arm over his head, a windmill punch. Stumbling backward, I blocked it, throwing my right forearm above my head. He threw the same punch three more times, hammering down on me frantically, as if he would break right through my forearm and smash my face. By the third blow I managed to regain my footing and push back with my arm. I took a swing at him. He blocked it and stepped back, and then we were all in the street, the other man to my right, the fat boy to my left. The fat boy had a rock the size of a baseball. I took out my knife, flipped it open, and lunged at the two men. They jumped back; the older man pulled out his own knife, while the other stepped further to my right. I backpedaled so as not to be flanked, but then the fat boy threw his rock, hitting the side of my face. I fell—hard because I wouldn't drop the knife. Pain swallowed my skull and I could smell the rock, taste it, as it bounced off my face back toward the fat boy. I scrambled to my feet, swinging wildly with my knife and then backpedaling desperately. The fat boy picked up the rock, threw it again. This time I put my left hand up to block it, and the rock broke the watch off my wrist and smashed into my ear. I fell again. The money belt my dad had given me snapped at the buckle and fell into the street. Scrambling, wheezing, running out of breath, I took a few more wild swings, then turned and sprinted a few paces. When I turned again they'd stopped chasing me. They were gathering up my watch, belt, and cell phone.

My face was throbbing, my elbow scraped; the sun was setting, and I had the chills. I walked down to Franklin and made a right; I sat on the curb in front of my old sober-living, the yellow house with the wheelchair ramp. All the lights were off and the driveway was empty. It seemed to have closed down.

Soon it would be dark; I was kicking, and with my cell phone gone I couldn't even call Cliff. I remembered César, the dope dealer whom Luke and I had talked to on the street a few times when we were living here. Maybe he would remember me. Maybe he would front me some dope. I looked around and spotted a man watching me—tall and burly, with a thick beard and mustache and curly black hair. I walked back to the corner and asked him if he knew César.

"Yes, I know César," he said in a thick Spanish accent.

He wore a dark, striped suit and a shirt with the top three buttons open, showing three gold chains and a cross. He was even taller than I'd thought from across the street, and he spoke with such confidence, so grandly, looking down at me and then gazing across the street, that I thought he was a politician or maybe a mob boss.

"Yes, I know him, but why would you look for him?" he said. "César's crazy. He's probably in jail. He does stupid things. Why? Why would you want to find somebody like him?"

I pointed to the sober-living and said, "I used to live in that house . . ."

"Ah, yes," he said, nodding.

"And I knew him," I continued. "You know what I mean? I knew him, and now I'm looking for some dope. I thought maybe he could front me something."

He stared at me for a moment, nodding and stroking his beard. Then he pointed at the sober-living.

"I am taking over that house," he said. "Soon it will be all new. There will be new staff, the best people. It is my project, and I will pour all the money into it necessary . . ."

He went on to explain his plans for the house. He called it a hospital and said it would have the best medicine. He said if I wanted he could get me the best medicine. He pointed all around, saying he'd known this neighborhood since he was a boy, but now it was falling apart. I didn't know what he was talking about. My nose was running, and on the ground by his foot I thought I saw a sack of heroin. I looked up and he wasn't talking anymore. He was looking at me as if he'd asked me a question.

"So can you front me a quarter?" I asked.

"A quarter of what?" he said.

"Heroin."

The man looked across the street and sighed.

"Now, my friend," he said, "I must walk away from you."

As he walked down the street, I felt ashamed, as if I'd been scolded, and I didn't think it was fair. I knew I'd said the wrong thing, but I hadn't meant to disappoint him—why couldn't he give me another chance? Soon, though, he was out of sight, and I remembered the dope on the ground, and when I didn't see it I dropped to my knees and examined chunks of dead crab apple for fifteen, thirty, forty-five minutes, until I realized what I was doing and laughed. I dusted myself off and walked to the old corner store, then to the Mexican restaurant behind it to ask the waitress if she knew César, and another stranger ended up buying me tacos. While I was eating them, I noticed that the tops of my cheeks were wet and thought I might be crying. But no: it was sweat from the hot sauce.

It was night when I left the restaurant. I walked back around the store and sat on the front step, watching cars pull up, people running in and out, and soon I got into another fight. I started it too, with a bunch of Mexicans in a minivan, for no reason other than I thought one of them was laughing at me. It didn't make any sense, getting up and pointing at him; there was nobody around to whom I wanted to prove anything. I wasn't even sure that he was laughing at me, and yet all of a sudden I was furious. I stood and pointed and grabbed my chest, mouthing the words, *I got your heart.*

Immediately he jumped out of the van, ready to fight. He came toward me, and I whipped my knife out, and then all the other Mexicans jumped out of the van. Altogether there were four of them, about my age, all with knives, and they spat at me and yelped, a sort of high-pitched battle cry. I took a swing at one of them, smiling and bugging my eyes to scare him by showing him that I wasn't scared, that I liked this shit. But he just smiled back and took a swipe at me. Then another one came from the side and I fell over trying to avoid him. Scurrying backward, I got kicked in the ribs, and soon I was all out of breath. I could do nothing but put my hands in the air and try to say sorry. They jeered and spat and I fell over again. One of them said, "Don't fuck with us, pussy!" and then they got back in the van and drove away.

My forearms were bleeding. I walked back and forth in the parking lot for an hour or so, getting colder and colder as I wondered where I would sleep. The Asian clerk came outside and asked me not to fight in his parking lot. I promised I wouldn't. Later a man on a bike with a goatee and a gold chain came around the store, from the bar, and threatened me, a soft threat, asking me what I was doing there.

"I need to make a phone call," I said.

He took out his cell phone and dialed the numbers 9-1-1, showed it to me.

"You wanna call?" he said.

I shook my head.

"I'm not sure if you should be here," he said, leaning on the bike. I wasn't sure if he was giving me advice or telling me I had to leave.

"I'm asking you," I said. "Is it okay for me to be here?"

"No," he said quietly.

"Okay . . . I'll go."

He shrugged and rode back around the store. I looked down Third

Street, east and west; I didn't even know of a park within walking distance. I was about to go back into the store to beg for quarters—though I didn't know whom to call—when somebody called to me, saying, "Jimmy from Jersey, is that you?" A couple had pulled into the parking lot in a white Honda Civic, a couple I'd sold dope to at a motel in Corona about two months earlier, when I was rolling with Manny.

"Yeah, it's me," I said. "Yeah . . . it's me."

"Jesus, are you all right?" the guy asked.

"I'm fine." I laughed. "It goes like this sometimes, you know."

"You need a ride or something?"

Getting in the car, I realized that I stank. They offered to take me wherever I needed to go, and drove me all the way to Patti's house in La Sierra. I sat in the backseat and stared at the floor, didn't talk at all, except here's the exit and thanks again. Thank you for the ride. They even gave me five dollars.

It was past midnight, and Patti came to the door ready to curse somebody out, dogs barking behind her. Then she saw me.

"Go lie on the couch and shut the fuck up," she said.

Gremlin kept barking at me, and Patti picked him up by the scruff of the neck. "Shut up. Come sit with mama."

"Patti," I said, "I think I left some clothes here a while ago, some shorts and my leather jacket. Well, I really need them now—I left all my clothes in the trunk of this guy's car."

"You goin' somewhere?" said Patti.

"No—but, when I do go . . . I need 'em."

"I can see you need your clothes," she said. "But right now it's two in the morning and I'm watching my favorite movie, so lie down on the couch and shut the fuck up."

Her favorite movie was *The Big Easy*, and Dennis Quaid was singing to Ellen Barkin, asking her why she didn't call him anymore. On the couch Champ rubbed against my shins and demanded petting. I tried to cry but couldn't. Inside and safe, I was now indulging in self-pity, in melodrama: *Here's this dog I knew from better times, snuggling up to me, and look at how fucked up I am.*

This is how I was feeling in the morning when Garrett passed through the living room on his way out to work on the truck. When he saw me huddled on the couch, he stopped, put his fists over his eyes, fake crying, and said, "Aww, look at the poor baby." The second he walked out the door, I got up and asked Patti for my clothes. I would leave; fucked up as I was, I would walk right past Garrett and go about my business. *Who's a fucking baby?* Patti found my jacket, a pair of jean shorts, and a clean string T-shirt. After changing in the bathroom and washing under my arms, I thanked her for last night and walked out, walked past Garrett and down the street, hoping he would notice.

"Dude, where you goin'?" he called after me.

It was a good question.

"I need to make a phone call," I said.

"What?" he said. "There's a phone inside."

"I know. I mean, I'm gonna call and then I'm gonna get picked up."

"Are you all right?" he asked.

"Yeah, I'll be fine," I said, smiling, then turned and walked down the block, elated. Not only had Garrett stopped work to ask where I was going and if I was all right; I'd gotten to shrug off his concern and walk away with bruises on my face, proving that he'd been wrong: I was no baby. This picked me up the way only attention from someone you look up to can. It picked me up and kept me up, down the block to a gas station, where I spent my five dollars on a burrito and milk. It kept me up until I ate the burrito and nearly vomited. Then I realized that I was kicking outdoors, having left the only house that would have me.

I walked to the shopping center across the street and used my change to call Cliff. He picked up and asked where I'd been, said he'd driven up and down Third Street, what the fuck? I told him about passing out in the alley and about the two fights. I asked him to pick me up in La Sierra, please, because I was about to start shitting and throwing up behind stores at this shopping center. He said he was coming. Forty-five minutes later I called again and he said that his car had broken down on Magnolia. From the background noise it sounded true. I told him I'd try to get a ride to him.

Then I called Manny. I hadn't spoken to him in about a month, and when I told him where I was and that I needed help, he said, "So now you wanna call. You don't answer my calls for weeks, and now you need help?" He said that since he was just down the road, at his brother's, he would come, but I better have something for him. I waited at the Ralph's supermarket until he pulled up in a car with his brother and his brother's two sons, who looked about ten. As soon as Manny got out, he asked me what I had for him, what was he going to get out of this ride? When I offered my leather jacket, Manny said he already had two, why would he want mine? He was furious.

He asked me if I remembered our arrangement, that he would be my partner and watch my back on the one condition that when we parted company, he walk away with something. What had he walked away with? I began to say I'd given him a lot of dope while we were running together, but he cut me off, saying I was just like Danny White. Then his brother shouted something from the car, something in Spanish, and though I didn't speak much Spanish, I got the gist of it. He wanted to beat me up.

"Con los niños?" I said. *"Dónde está tu cabeza?"*

Manny rushed me. He grabbed me by the collar and pushed me into the supermarket's plate-glass window, yelling, "Don't you fuckin' get smart with him!" Then he backed up, and I lost my footing and fell, and Manny looked around to see if anybody was watching. He said, "You're fucked up, partner," then walked back to the car.

I watched him drive away, then got up and checked my pockets to find that I didn't even have the change to call Cliff again. The chills were getting bad, so even though the sun was blazing, I kept my jacket on tight, the leather jacket my parents had sent me for Christmas, which was now several sizes too big, collapsing at the shoulders so that the sleeves hung empty for several inches. My hair was greasy and curling and sticking up in clumps; I tried uselessly to push it down, smooth it out. My shins were caked with dirt.

I'd been too sick to really sleep at Patti's, just a few sweaty dreams, so there was that, too: seven days, a personal record. Sitting on the bench, I stared at nothing with my mouth open and then remembered that I was in a public place, a shopping center; and there were people around, their voices surging as if in a stadium, and I looked up to see a little old lady go into the supermarket and a black woman order food at the Jack in the Box drive-thru. That was it—hush, the voices died.

"Excuse me," I said, getting up and approaching a man with a short-sleeve button-down shirt tucked into his jeans. "Excuse me, could you possibly spare a quarter for a phone call?"

He stopped but didn't look at me. He gave me a quarter and nodded, looking in the other direction. *Asshole.* Next, I tried to stop an older man in a Hawaiian shirt, but he ignored me, or couldn't hear me, I couldn't tell which. It didn't matter, though, because when I said, "Excuse me," and he kept walking, I suddenly felt too timid to say it again.

I didn't really want to make a phone call—I wanted to buy lemonade in the Chinese restaurant next to the packaging store: a dollar twenty-five. My mouth was parched and I wasn't even thinking about Cliff.

"Excuse me, do you think . . ."

A man in sunglasses and a white T-shirt gave me a dime without stopping. He shrugged, saying, "That's all I got."

"Excuse me, ma'am . . ."

Nothing. And she'd heard me—I'd come right up to her and she'd put her head down and kept walking. Even though I didn't consider myself a beggar—I was thirsty and after a rough couple of days didn't happen to have money—being snubbed made me feel like one. Being ignored and treated like less than a person was not only humiliating but also exhausting; my emotions flared and I wanted to call after the woman, call her a selfish cunt, but then immediately I felt drained and depressed, and I wanted to lie down. So each time it happened I waited on the bench for a while before asking again, and since most people ignored me, hours passed before I had a dollar.

The voices returned. *Don't ask him. Trust me, you don't wanna ask him.* A couple walked out of a store, talking, and their voices melded with those of the people eating on the patio of the Jack in the Box, some hundred yards behind me, and even after the couple had gotten into their car and I'd realized there was no way I could hear the people on the patio, the voices stayed, clamoring, speaking to me and to each other. One of them began talking about me as if I couldn't hear him, telling all the other voices what I was doing, moment by moment. *He's about to ask money of a man with a mustache . . . a man with ties to law enforcement.* I walked up to the man in the mustache—"Excuse . . ."—then doubled back and stared at the ground.

"Yo!" somebody yelled to me. It was Garrett in his truck. "Cops are lookin' for you!"

"What?" I said, stumbling as I got up.

"On the police scanner they said somebody in a leather jacket was hassling people as they were coming out of stores. Said you been trying to sell something around here."

I tried to open the truck door, but he pulled forward a few yards.

"You ain't gettin' in here, fool!" he said.

I looked at him helplessly.

"Walk," he said. "Just fucking walk. Take off your jacket and walk that way."

He pointed across La Sierra Avenue to the Metrolink train station. Then he drove away and I took off my jacket and walked as fast as I could, out of the shopping center and onto Indiana. *Now he's crossing La Sierra Avenue on the way to the Metrolink; he's been up for a week and he's going insane watching the sun rise.* At the station I passed through a huge parking lot and then sat on a concrete bench under a green canopy. There were pay phones and ticket machines and an American flag. *He's hearing voices—he knows he's hearing voices—but he can't make out the real ones from the ones in his head.* People were checking watches and schedules. I asked an Arab man in a baseball cap for a cigarette; he gave it to me, and I thanked him and walked away and then came back for a light, laughing, how silly of me, I'm sorry. I'm sorry to trouble you. *Maybe it's time to die.* I sat on the concrete bench, smoking and staring across the parking lot at a hilly field of tall grass and nettles, a field that was now swirling, morphing, swirling . . . the grass seemed painted. Even the horizon line blurred and shifted as the wind blew. *He's come to this place and the train is coming and he doesn't know what he's going to do.* Wispy white clouds disappeared as I stared at them, absorbed by a blue sky that throbbed and pulsed as if it were alive. *I am the voice of reason.*

A train pulled into the station, and then all around me there were friends meeting, shaking, then—come here—hugging; wives and husbands greeting, kissing; families huddled together. It didn't make any sense to me: the smiles, the laughter. They were happy and it seemed bizarre. *For he has fallen so low that his knees are beneath the earth, he cannot reach the grapes of the gods, and he can no longer understand the average man.*

I began to cry. After the people got into their cars and drove away, I walked over to the pay phone and called my parents collect. I told them I wanted to go back to GSL. I cried and cried.

CHAPTER 16. GOING BACK

My mom called GSL and within a couple of hours one of the counselors picked me up from the station and brought me to Grand Terrace, where I ate bowl after bowl of Lucky Charms. The nurse gave me the familiar cocktail of antibiotics, muscle relaxants, and benzodiazepines; and I was given a bed in the detox room, which was now where the women's dorm used to be. For a few days I drifted in and out, eating cereal and taking pills, dimly aware of the client assigned to watch me watching a movie.

I must have still been terrified, because later clients would tell me that I cursed at them while I was sleeping, telling them to get away from me when they put water on my nightstand or asked which movie I wanted to watch. I don't remember it, though. While dreaming and half awake I actually felt pretty cozy, comforting myself with a nostalgic fantasy of GSL as it had been when I was last there, a fantasy of Wendy and Luke and Mya, of laughing and lifting weights and falling in love. I half expected Luke to be there when I woke up, handing me a coffee and a cigarette.

But then I did wake up. The nurse was telling me she had to start tapering my pills, I didn't have any cigarettes or clothes, and, even

317

worse, I remembered what it meant that the women's dorm was now the detox room. The counselor had told me on the drive over: GSL wasn't coed anymore. There would be no flirting across the classroom, no massages during smoking breaks. The fantasy shattered, giving way to residual fear from my nights on the street. I was in yet another place where I didn't know anybody, including this client who was supposed to be watching me, a Mexican with a lightning bolt tattooed on his forearm, chuckling at a movie, *Anger Management*. When he saw that I was awake, he asked me if I would be getting up today.

"No," I said.

"Still sick, huh?"

"Yup."

"You must have been doing *a lot* of dope," he said, "to still be sick."

I thought he was implying that I wasn't sick, that I was faking it so I could stay in bed.

"What, are you calling me a fucking liar?" I said.

As I sat up, my head felt like a fishbowl, half full, rocking and splashing.

"Hey, dude," he said. "I'm just—"

"Because I will get up to kick your fuckin' ass."

He turned in his chair to look at me. He had a thick mustache and curly brown hair. He weighed more than two hundred and fifty pounds. The nurse called to a counselor in the hall, saying we were about to fight.

"Whatever, dude," the guy said, turning back to the TV. "Whatever."

A few hours later the head counselor came to my room and asked me if I really wanted to be here, because I could fight all I wanted on the street. I told him I did and I was sorry. When I got out of detox, I also apologized to the big guy, thanked him for not kicking my ass. He was cool, understanding—as were most of the other clients I'd been rude to while kicking. They gave me cigarettes and lent me clothes until my parents sent me a package. Soon I was a regular at cards as well as the lunchtime basketball game, though it wouldn't be long before I started breaking rules and picking fights again.

On the weekends Wendy called me from the Whiteside Manor women's rehab in downtown Riverside. She'd checked herself in as soon as she got out of prison, just as she'd planned; the program would help her find a job and a sober-living until she could afford her own place. She joked that now that I'd lost all of her stuff in the trunk of Cliff's car, we were even for her prison package and phone calls. She also told me many times that if I went back to drugs when I got out, she wouldn't be able to be my friend anymore.

My parents informed me I had a court date in late September, that our lawyer said it couldn't be postponed any longer. Distribution of cocaine and Ecstasy—a mandatory five-to-seven years unless we could cut a deal with the prosecutor to get me into a rehab/probationary program called Drug Court. Our lawyer thought we could, but until then I had to stay out of trouble. I had an open warrant for the distribution charges, and my lawyer had already told the prosecutor that I was currently in rehab; if I was picked up on the street for jaywalking the deal would be blown and I would be extradited to a New Jersey prison. So the plan was that I stay at GSL for the two months until my court date.

I called my parents almost every day. They analyzed my dreams and I read them the ridiculous poetry I'd started writing again, which of course they encouraged, since it was creative, life-positive. They spent hours on the phone with me, doing all they knew to get me to stick to the plan, to keep me safe and in one place until my court date. This included listening to me whine whenever I was forced to get up early on Sunday mornings for breaking a rule, whine that I didn't think I would make it for two months. My parents implored me to just hold on, to do whatever it took to swallow my pride and stay in the program; they would always be there, I could always call. But I kept getting into trouble and the staff started talking about kicking me out. I told my parents that GSL had changed; the best counselors had left, and the clients were now mostly guys who were there only because their parole stipulated a ninety-day program—they weren't serious about their recovery.

The truth, of course, was that I wasn't wholly dedicated to recovery. As much time as I spent writing a dream journal and bad poetry, I spent more talking shit about the year I'd spent on the streets of Riverside. I felt as if I'd accomplished something by going crazy and getting my ass kicked. In fact I had: I was tougher than I'd been a year ago. I'd been through some shit, and I wasn't scared to fight. This is what I'd wanted since I was fifteen, and now that I had it I was supposed to just give it up, to lead a straight life and walk away from fights. It was like losing weight and then being told to wear baggy clothes. To some degree everybody hides behind an image; even people with self-respect define themselves in order to feel secure. If I abandoned the Dirty Jersey–tough guy–junkie image, recognized it for the nonsense it was, what would I have left to define myself? At nineteen, what had I accomplished?

Not that I wasn't conflicted. I wasn't lying to myself and to my parents when I wrote poems and talked for thirty minutes about a dream and its psychological symbolism; I was grasping for another image, something vaguely intellectual, because tough as I thought I'd become, I was still scared to go back. And I loved my parents. I'd made a promise to Wendy. I didn't want to die.

Still, I couldn't acquire a new identity overnight, so I walked around GSL for a month sticking my chest out until I got into a minor scrap with one of my roommates and the staff kicked me out. It was actually the best thing they could have done for me—the only thing they could have done—since kicking me out was the only way they could demonstrate that I wasn't special, something I badly needed to learn, something begging for quarters and getting beaten up hadn't taught me. Actually, my trek across Riverside had worked the other way, taking on a grander and more epic tone with each retelling—a special adventure for a special guy. Grapes of the gods, I'd even heard a voice. But now I'd been kicked out, plain and simple, for the good of *others*.

My counselor dropped me off at a bus stop with two garbage bags full of the new clothes my parents had sent. I took the bus to downtown Riverside and from there walked to Paul and John's house on Main Street, the same house where I'd told my parents I was staying the month before they came to visit. When I got there, I learned that John was planning on kicking heroin. He was packing for rehab—GSL had just called to say a bed had become available. "What the fuck?" he said when he saw me. "Wendy said you were at GSL. I thought at least I was gonna know somebody up there, asshole." I told him I thought he got my bed, and since he wouldn't be using the one here for a while . . . "Yes, you can stay here, you fuckin' asshole. Just check with my dad." Paul said it was fine, but if I was gonna be staying a whole month, some rent would be nice, a couple hundred bucks if I could swing it.

When I called my parents, they were disappointed and scared, but not angry. There was no point in being angry. They had one goal: getting me home for the court date, now one month away. Fourth quarter, score tied, I'd just fumbled the ball—this wasn't the time to complain but to buckle down on defense. They didn't want to bring me home early, because I still had the open warrant—"safe and out of sight"—was what their lawyer had recommended, so they told me to stay at the house and to call every day. When I asked for five hundred dollars for rent and food, they sent me two hundred and fifty: two hundred to pay Paul half the rent up-front, fifty for food. They didn't want me having extra cash.

I gave Paul a hundred dollars (half up-front) and kept the other hundred and fifty for heroin. John left me his stash when he went to GSL, and I started using immediately. I hadn't planned to get high, but then it was right in front of me, and I figured I was going home in a month, so what did it matter if I got high a few times before then?

I still lied to Wendy, of course, though she was much harder to lie to than my parents. Determined to be a good friend and to get me back to New Jersey for my court date, she grilled me when she called from Whiteside Manor. What did you do today? Who'd you see? Why are you going to Maxi Foods for groceries when it's right by the bus stop where you know they sell dope and you could be going to the corner store on First and Mulberry, huh? A few days after I moved into John's room, Wendy stopped by on a day pass from rehab and gave me my clock radio/CD player, which had been in the trunk of Cliff's car.

She'd gone to the house on Mission, to Molly's apartment, trying to track down her stuff, and had found a bunch of her clothes and my radio lying in a corner. Molly had told her Cliff was in prison, that the car we'd been driving was a stolen car, and that he'd been arrested for it around the same time I'd checked into GSL.

"So you got *real* lucky, Jim-Jim," Wendy said.

"Yeah, real lucky," I said. "I just bought dope from Patti."

This was true. I'd felt guilty about being high even while talking to Wendy on the phone, but now that she was here, and now that I realized there was a decent chance of her finding out from Patti anyway, I simply had to confess. I flushed the dope down the toilet and said I was sorry, offering some excuse about being scared to go back to New Jersey. She told me to suck it up. This time, she said, because I'd told her, she would still be my friend, but she would also call Patti to see if I bought any more dope, and if I did she would not only never talk to me again; she would tell my parents. I believed her.

Unfortunately, though, I'd made a few of my own connections over the past year in Riverside, and when I ran out of John's heroin, I called Chuck in Rubidoux for more. He said no problem and then told me to wait; somebody wanted to talk to me.

"This Jimmy?"

"Yeah," I said.

"It's Bill."

"Oh, hey, what's up, man?"

"You tell me," he said.

"I was hoping to talk to you," I said, but then realized how lame it sounded. "I got your money. I'm real sorry about taking off on you—that's not my style—but you saw how fucked up I was. And since it's been so long, I'll just give you a hundred instead of sixty."

"Cool. That's fair," he said. "Now, you were in rehab, right? And you're already getting high?"

"Yeah, but just tar. I don't do too good with meth."

"You should stick to that," he said, "'cause you get fucked up."

"I will."

"How 'bout we make a deal? If you do meth again, I'm gonna hit you with a chest shot."

"Deal."

"All right," he said, laughing. "I'll be in that house on Mission for a couple more weeks. Come see me whenever."

"I'll probably be there tomorrow."

I called my parents and convinced them to wire me more money for food, and the next day I walked back to Molly's apartment, and I gave Bill the money.

"Good man," he said, shaking my hand.

This made me feel good—*a stand-up guy who honors his debts*—and so I didn't leave right away. I could have, though.

"You know, you left just before it got crazy here," Bill said. "People started getting stupid. Since you were gone, I already had to stick like three dudes."

"Yeah?" I said.

"Yeah."

Molly was watching TV on the couch. She had a sharp face with a curled upper lip and a receding forehead that made her look like a mouse; but she was pretty, or at least would have been, with a sleek neck and shoulder line, if it weren't obvious from across the room that her light brown hair was greasy—that she hadn't washed in days. She picked at her face, too, attacking blackheads the way only a tweaker can, clawing at them until they bled and then clawing some more. Her eyes were dark brown.

Junkie Jack was there, and he offered to run around the corner to his connect to pick up some meth and heroin. Before leaving, he left me with a little of each and I did a mixed shot in the bathroom.

"What were you doin' in there?" asked Bill as I came out.

I paused. He smiled.

"Okay," I said. "We made a deal. It's fair."

"Really?" he said. "I wasn't really gonna do it, but okay."

"No, man, it's cool," I said. "We made a deal."

I stood up straight and flexed my chest. I'd done push-ups throughout my month at GSL, and I felt strong—I thought I could take it standing. He hit me harder than I'd ever been hit in my life. I never even saw the punch. I dropped to one knee and fell to the side. Couldn't breathe. I staggered to my feet and then fell against the wall, clutching and hugging the bathroom doorjamb. Bill was having trouble breathing himself, he was laughing so hard.

"I caught you in the solar plexus," he laughed. "That's fucked up."

When I finally caught my breath, I shook Bill's hand, and he patted me on the back. "Thank you, brother," I said, in a jokingly formal tone. "A deal is a deal."

Molly, who I just realized was watching us, rolled her eyes. She had a reputation for being stupid, a reputation that I believed, and yet when it came to spotting an act of sucking up—joke or gesture, no matter how subtle—she was as sharp as anybody. She was equally good at sniffing out the twisted logic of a coward trying to save face while getting screwed, sniffing it out and snickering just loudly enough for the coward to turn crimson. Of course, she was a suck-up and coward herself. A petty opportunist, Molly had two cards—sex and the apartment—and she played them as often as she thought it would be to her advantage, meaning she allowed people like me to use her apartment in exchange for sharing dope with her, and she slept with people like Bill, who in exchange were supposed to make sure everybody else stayed in line and actually shared their dope. More often than not, though, the people like Bill didn't honor their part of the deal (but still demanded she honor hers), and then she just got bullied: She sat on the couch, watching TV and hoping one of the junkies would pass her a bowl.

"Molly," I said, "what happened to Cliff? When did he come back here? I heard he dropped a bunch of stuff off or something."

"He came back the day you ran out of here all crazy and shit," she said. "He threw a bunch of clothes and junk on the floor. I didn't even know whose they were, and then Wendy came by and said they were hers. Took all that shit."

"I know. She gave me my radio."

"Oh, that was yours? Wendy said it was hers, or I'd a just kept it."

"Yeah, right," I said.

We'd never liked each other, and I wanted to fuck her.

"Like I wouldn't," Molly said. "Wendy comes here to pick up your shit, and she yells at me, like I'm trying to keep that shit. It's fucked up: She says I'm trying to steal from her, and Cliff's in jail so he can't even explain. So you can get *your* radio."

"I didn't know she yelled at you. I didn't even know she was coming here."

"Yeah, right," she said.

Soon Junkie Jack came back to the apartment with more heroin and meth. I paid him for a chunk of each, then did another shot of meth in the bathroom and almost immediately started sketching (they say you start right where you leave off). I did another shot of heroin to come down, but then a few hours later I shot more meth—because even though the sketching was horrible, the rush felt really good.

I stayed at Molly's apartment for three ugly days.

Nights were paranoid. I peered out windows and whispered to the spies hiding in the trees, cut deals with them so they wouldn't tell the enemy where I was. Later there were snipers, infrared lasers all over my face. I sat down in the middle of the room in full lotus and recited one of the poems I'd written at GSL, said it over and over, trying to calm myself, fully aware that Molly and Junkie Jack were staring, listening, thinking that I was going insane, and I knew that I was, that there were no snipers outside, but I was still so scared that all I could do was repeat the poem, repeat the poem, repeat the poem until my hands stopped shaking. Then Jack and Molly and Bill—there were other junkies too, plenty of junkies during those three days—they started messing with me. Molly would say, "There's somebody outside who wants to talk to you," and then on my way out Bill would say, "He's got something for you—I want you to bring it to me." Outside, there would be nobody . . . except, maybe, yes, behind the shed, he had something for me: *Come into the shadows and get it.* I would run upstairs, saying I couldn't find him, and they would laugh and laugh.

Days were horny. Becky—the prostitute who'd been at Chuck's the time Junkie Jack overdosed—came to the apartment on the second day, working, and I gave her twenty bucks and some heroin for a blow job in the bathroom. I'd wanted sex, I'd even offered more money, but she'd said no, she couldn't. She was HIV positive. She was a heroin addict and prostitute who lived from shot to shot, john to john, and yet she had a line she wouldn't cross—a scruple that may have saved my life.

Of course, I didn't appreciate that at the time, and the next day, the third day, the last day I spent in that apartment, I accused Becky of taking a dime of dope that I'd accidentally left in the bathroom. She'd gone in after me and then it was gone, and I was sure I'd left it in the bathroom, wasn't I? Of course she denied it, saying all she had was the little bit of heroin I'd given her. See, look—she even turned out her pockets. And that's when I saw it, the heroin—in her hair—the dark brown heroin in her dark brown hair. She'd stuck it in a knot by her left ear.

"Oh, I can see it's not your *pockets*," I said, smiling.

"Well, then, please, where do I have it?" she said wearily.

"You know."

"Whatever."

A few minutes later, while she was watching TV, I snuck up behind her and ripped through a knot of her hair.

"Ow! What the fuck?"

"Sorry," I said, sitting down next to her. I pretended to watch TV until she stopped staring at me; then I reached over and gently lifted a lock . . .

"What the hell are you doing?"

"Nothing."

"Are you looking for dope in my hair?"

"Should I be?"

"Jesus Christ! I didn't steal your dope. Look, Junkie Jack is gonna be back in like two minutes with more dope, and I put in twenty—"

"So did I—"

"Exactly! We're gonna end up splitting a gram, so why would I steal your dope when I know we have to split what Jack comes back with?"

I reached for her hair again.

"Are you even listening to me?" she said.

Bill was sitting next to Molly on the couch, laughing hard. He thought it was so funny that he offered to buy me another blow job so I could search for my dope with reckless abandon. Becky wasn't interested, though.

"That's between me and him," she snapped.

"Don't take that fucking tone with me," Bill snapped back. "You'll do it if I say you'll do it."

Becky got up and walked out of the apartment.

"She took that shit," Bill said, once Becky had left. "I know her. She's acting all offended and shit now, but you know why she really went outside? So she can get to Junkie Jack first and convince him to give her more of the dope. That's how she works."

"Should I go out there?" I asked.

"Nah, Jack ain't gonna break nothing out on the street, and when he gets here, I'll make sure you get yours."

"Thanks," I said, wishing I'd just gotten up and followed Becky instead of asking if I should. Bill enjoyed making benevolent guarantees, but he rarely followed through, and of course I couldn't imply this by going outside now. Instead, I had to sit and pretend to be reassured, while imagining Becky intercepting Junkie Jack and convincing him to give her my dope.

Bill and Molly and I sat in silence, except for the TV, a midday court show. Molly, in shorts and a baggy T-shirt, was on the far side of the couch with her knees against her breasts, hugging herself. She was sitting at an odd angle, almost sideways, so that she had to look over her right shoulder to watch the TV. Bill sat on the other end of the couch with his head on his arm, his round face sagging, chin and cheeks and lower lip. But he didn't look babyish, as most chubby people do when their faces hang: He had that scar on his chin, and as he sat staring at the TV, his eyes sometimes fluttered and then flashed open, blank and menacing. His brawny chest heaved above his ugly belly.

The door burst open.

"They fuckin' got Jack!" Becky cried, running into the room, hysterical. "The fuckin' cops, they got Jack right out front!"

"Fuck!" said Bill, jumping to the window. "They fucking got him, those cocksuckers. Fuck! Goddamn it! Look at those motherfuckers—they're beating him! Are you fucking looking? Do you see?"

It took me a minute to register what was happening, and then another minute to realize that Bill was shouting at me. I got up and went over to the window.

"Are you fucking looking?"

Bill was peeking through the Venetian blinds so as not to be seen by the cops, so even when he grabbed my arm and pulled me to the window, I didn't get a good view. Just a passing glimpse: two cops swinging their nightsticks and Junkie Jack staggering and falling to his knees, his white hair wild.

"Goddamn! They're kicking him—they're fucking slamming his head against the curb! Look at that fucking blood! Do you see? Look at the fucking blood! Are you looking?"

"Yes," I mumbled.

"They're gonna come up here!" cried Becky.

We were on the second floor, but outside the narrow bathroom window there was a deck with stairs to the backyard. Becky ran to the bathroom, stood on the counter, and opened the window as wide as possible. Bill and I watched her—all one hundred and ten pounds of her—squirm and kick until she finally tumbled out headfirst onto the deck. Clunk, clunk, clunk, she ran down the stairs.

Bill turned back to the window and started shouting again, about the cocksuckers and the blood and they're kicking his fucking head, are you looking? Then he turned to me and said, "You know that dude's like my fucking brother, don't you?" I nodded dumbly. I was more scared of Bill than I was of the cops, and what was the correct answer to that question?

"Was it you he was getting the dope for?" he asked, gritting his teeth.

I didn't want to lie, because he already knew. I felt chills run through me, a tickle in my jaw.

"Some of it," I said.

"Well, then, you better hit me now, 'cause I'm gonna fucking stick you," he said, squaring himself in front of me.

"I could have lied," I stammered. "I'm telling you the truth."

"You better hit me now, 'cause I'm gonna fucking stick you."

I thought he was going to do it, that in another second he would tackle and stab me and leave me cut open on the floor. I was so scared I barely had control of my body. I was aware of my toes curling in my boots, of my arms going up, weightless. Molly was staring at us with her mouth open. I felt as if I might collapse. My hands began to drift behind my back.

"What, are you fucking going for something?" Bill growled.

I stuck my arms out again.

"No—nothing."

Bill stared at me, clenching his fists.

"He's like my fucking brother, you know that? And look what they're doing to him!" he shouted, turning back to the window. "Two more just pulled up. What the fuck? Those cocksuckers." He stepped away from the window. "All right—okay—this is what we're gonna do. There are four of them . . ." When he saw that my arms were still in the air, he waved at me—it was okay—but then, just when I'd started breathing . . .

"There are four of them. I got a .357 and a .38—are you going with me?"

I hesitated, dumbstruck. *This is how it happens.* I imagined following Bill down the stairs with the gun, stepping onto the front porch, and firing—they would fire back and kill me. Imagining it I realized that, scared as I was, I wouldn't be able to hit a house, let alone a person.

"There's four of them," Bill was saying. "We can take 'em. Are you with me?"

"Yes," I said, "I'll go. But I have to warn you, I don't shoot very well."

"What the fuck?" he said. "Do you even know how to use a gun?"

"Sort of," I said. "Depends what kind. A revolver . . ."

"What the fuck? You take off the safety, you point and shoot."

"Yeah . . . okay . . . I can do that. Yeah . . . I'll go . . ."

He walked back to the window.

"Forget it. There's too many of 'em now, anyway."

He turned to Molly.

"You can't let 'em in here."

"I'm on probation," Molly stammered. "I—I have to let them in."

"Fuck that!" Bill shouted, bounding across the room and picking up the big chair. "You ain't lettin' nobody in."

As he rammed the chair against the door, Bill yelled for me to grab the TV. I picked it up and brought it over, but Bill didn't give me any further instructions, so I stood holding it for a while and then set it on the chair, in the seat, as if that would make the slightest difference if the cops were knocking the door down. Bill, searching for more junk to pile against the door, picked up the mattress and then realized how flimsy it was. He threw it back on the floor, disgusted, enraged.

"You don't have shit in here," he yelled at Molly. "Well, fuck it. Nothing more we can do. We're all goin' to jail, so I know I want one last fuck. We're goin' to jail, so we might as well fuck. Okay?"

She nodded.

"And you're gonna hit my boy off too, 'cause we're all goin' to jail."

Bill called for me to come lie on the floor, and on my way I saw Molly getting up off the couch. I saw her face. It was pale from shock—that stupid look adrenaline pastes on you.

She got off the couch, and then she was standing, walking. We passed each other. We avoided touching and I saw her face. She was trying to smile a sexy smile for Bill, a coy, so-you-wanna-fuck-me smile.

I turned as I passed her so I could lie on my back, and she, directed by Bill, turned too, so she was standing over me, and I saw her face, the smile broken by a tug at the corner of her eye, a tearful quiver that she tried to hide from me, even as we moved, ordered and positioned like extras on a stage. She didn't want to show it to me, and I didn't want to see it. I didn't want to see it, see *her*, because I was guilty. Guilty of being horny, of still wanting to fuck her, of feeling—aside from the horror and shame and guilt and fear—just a little bit relieved because I didn't have a choice, now did I? I saw her lower lip tremble, and then her face disappeared as she bent down to unbutton my pants.

"You like sucking dick, don't you?" said Bill, standing behind her. "Mm-hmm."

He pulled her shorts down and then stumbled over my khakis as he tried to line up behind her. "In my way, here," he growled, tearing off my boots and pants.

He spanked her a few times, asking her how she liked it, how she liked his dick. "Oh, you can't talk, can you?" Then, after a few minutes, he stood and told us to get up; he was going to sit on the couch while she blew him and I fucked her. As she kneeled, he called her a dirty bitch. He was shouting. He asked her if she liked sucking his fat cock and she moaned yes, emphatically, only this time she wasn't lying. She was getting into it, getting wetter, and when Bill pulled her head up and told her to start jerking him off, she grabbed him, pumped a few times, and then lurched forward and put his dick back in her mouth as if crazed. She was getting wetter and she was sucking Bill's dick after he'd told her not to—she was doing it because *she wanted to*, and I told myself that made it okay. I hoped that made it okay, but I didn't want to fuck her anymore.

"I said jerk it, bitch!" he yelled, pulling her up by the hair again. "And you—fuck her in the ass. Don't go in too fast, but do it—fuck her in the ass."

Nodding at Bill, I became aware that my mouth was open and my teeth were numb, that I had that same pale, stupid look on my face. None of us had washed in days, and the smell was horrible, crotch sweat and now shit. I came almost immediately.

"Fuck her in the ass! Fuck her!" he shouted. "You didn't come already, did you?"

Scared and embarrassed, I lied. I shook my head and crouched behind her, made a few halfhearted fake thrusts, waiting for it to be over. Eventually it was.

"Cops are gone," said Bill, after he pulled his pants up and walked to the window. "I can't believe they got Jack. Look at all that blood on the sidewalk. And they got all your tar, too." He paused. "Fuck, I got a little if you wanna do a shot."

"Please," I said.

Bill walked into the other room, and after putting my pants and boots on, I joined him, while Molly stayed on the couch. Bill gave me about a dime of tar, and I cooked it up while he smoked a bowl of meth. He asked me if I could believe how much Molly stank and I told him I couldn't. I remembered how much I stank and that she'd just had her face in my crotch. I shot the heroin and felt a little better. It was the last shot of heroin I ever did. I told Bill I had to go, and he said, "All right, brother," and shook my hand. I didn't look at Molly on my way out.

On my way back to Main Street I crossed a main intersection, the light turned green, and a car honked at me. I gave the driver the finger, and he honked again. I kept walking. When I reached the sidewalk, the driver honked again and shouted, "Hey!"

"What the fuck!" I screamed, turning around and marching, nearly running at the guy. "You got a fucking problem?"

"Yeah, I got a problem," the guy said, laughing. "Why don't you get in?"

I knew him. He was a friend of Paul and John's, and after I apologized for cursing at him, he gave me a ride to their house. On the way I tried to make a joke of it, but every time I raised my voice to laugh I had to stop short for fearing of crying.

That was the end of my misadventures. I spent my last weeks in Riverside smoking pot and watching cartoons at Paul's house, waiting for my court date. A few times people stopped by with meth and I shot up, but I couldn't get anybody to bring any heroin, so I went through mild withdrawal. It was easier to go through the withdrawal than to go out among the junkies and buy more heroin. And that's all I cared about, what was easier. All the fight was gone from me. I was drifting. When my parents sent me money for a train ticket, I didn't have it in me to not get on the train. I didn't decide to turn my life around. I just stopped trying so hard to ruin it.

EPILOGUE: LUCK AND CIRCUMSTANCE

I've been clean since my return to New Jersey in September 2003. After four years of my lies and abuse, my parents put aside their pain, anger, and frustration and welcomed me back into their home without a word of judgment—as though my recovery was the only thing that mattered. I can only imagine how difficult this must have been. At the time, I couldn't fully appreciate what they were doing for me; I wasn't ready to face what I had put them through. But I did come to understand, for the first time ever as an adult, just how much they loved me. I came to appreciate the life that I had walked away from.

But I still didn't decide to turn my life around; I healed gradually. Once I had left Riverside and I wasn't wholly committed to being a junkie anymore, my parents pushed me a little farther, until I began to seriously consider giving up drugs altogether.

The courts pushed me even further. I pled guilty to charges of drug distribution in exchange for entry into the Mercer County Drug Court program, and I was given six months at an inpatient rehab called Turning Point, followed by four and a half years of probation. Before I could start the rehab, though, I had to spend a weekend in Mercer County Jail so that I would be fully aware of what would be in store for me if I failed to comply with any of the regulations the court imposed. It was a loud fifty-four-bunk cell with no hot water or even dividers between the toilets and showers. A year earlier the fear of jail alone probably wouldn't have kept me clean, but since I was already halfway committed to changing my life, three days there made an impact. Then I had six months to think about it.

The structure and philosophy of Turning Point were similar to those of GSL. We woke up early, did small chores, and met several times throughout the day for group sessions and AA meetings. I'm not a fan of AA—it's a religious program and I'm not religious—but that wasn't much of a problem for me. Within a few months the worst of the chemical urges had passed, and then with each passing day I became a little more committed to turning my life around. Whether or not I used AA to do it really didn't matter.

It was the other clients who were crucial. I happened to be at Turning Point at a time when most of the other guys there were more serious about cleaning up than about glorifying our old lifestyles. And they were all decidedly unimpressed with my tough-guy persona. "If you're so tough, why didn't you just do your time in prison?" They rolled their eyes at me until I stopped telling badass stories about who I'd been on the mean streets of Riverside and started making self-effacing jokes about how tough I used to want to be. Essentially this group of guys did for me what no parent or counselor could have ever done, something that clearly had to happen in order for me to get better: They convinced me that being tough wasn't cool.

By the end of my stay there, however, a whole new group of clients had arrived. Many of them seemed to think being tough and talking shit was cool; there were more confrontations, more broken rules. Since I was practically out the door, I was able to keep to myself, and the change didn't really affect me. But I can imagine how my life might be different today if I'd been sent to Turning Point at a different time with a different group of clients.

Once I was released, my parents supported me financially, buying me a car and renting me an apartment in East Windsor, since Drug Court stipulated that I had to live in Mercer County. Then I caught a few lucky breaks on my own. I stopped by my old high school to see the principal, and he offered me a job talking to the students about drugs; eventually I became the office manager of a company affiliated with the school. He gave me health benefits, a 401k, a business card. At my dad's gym a few of the trainers befriended me, offering tips and inviting me to work out with them.

Because of all this, I was able to gain a firmer footing on a new life with each passing day, and my progress was validated every few months in the courtroom of Drug Court as I was quickly allowed to advance from one probationary phase to the next. It was in that same courtroom, however, that I was reminded of how critical all my fortune and good luck was. Every week when I was required to report my progress to a judge, I would watch other drug addicts as they were sent back to jail for one reason or another. "Noncompliant" was how the judge would describe them. Then he would call my name and ask how I was doing. "Excellent, your Honor." My probation officer would confirm that I'd satisfied all my obligations—paycheck stubs, AA meetings, outpatient counseling—and I would be excused.

Wendy relapsed while I was in Turning Point. Within a few months she was arrested for possession of a fake ID, for which she served twenty-five months in prison. Upon her release she moved out of Riverside, to Hespia, California, in order to stay clean. To my knowledge she has been clean for more than two years, and we are still friends.

After about a year in prison my brother, Joe, became a born-again Christian. Immediately he started calling me, trying to establish a new relationship. He apologized for having been a bad influence and said we should put everything that had happened in California behind us. When he started attending a Christian college, he asked me to edit a few of his religious papers. They had titles like "The Historical Life of King Saul," "Jonah," and "The Tower of Babel." To me the topics and references might as well have been in Japanese, and what I did understand I didn't like. But that didn't matter. Aside from a few snarky comments, we stuck to grammar, syntax, and logic, working well together despite the cultural divide. And in a similar way we have over the years developed a warm and loving relationship. Joe has been clean for more than two and a half years, and he currently lives in Van Nuys, California.

My parents are happy. Against all odds, their desperate yet unflagging faith in me has paid off.